S. J. PERELMAN

Chicken Inspector No. 23

SIMON AND SCHUSTER · NEW YORK

PUBLISHED BY SIMON AND SCHUSTER
ROCKEFELLER CENTER, 630 FIFTH AVENUE
NEW YORK, NEW YORK 10020

SECOND PRINTING

LIBRARY OF CONGRESS CATALOG CARD NUMBER: 66–19431
DESIGNED BY EVE METZ
MANUFACTURED IN THE UNITED STATES OF AMERICA BY
AMERICAN BOOK–STRATFORD PRESS, NEW YORK, N.Y.

The majority of the pieces in this collection appeared originally in *The New Yorker*.

"The Great Stone Face" first appeared in *Holiday*.

"Samson Shorn, or The Slave of Love," and "Goodbye Broadway, Hello Mr. Square" first appeared in *The Saturday Evening Post*.

"Be a Television Writer" and "Walk the Plank, Pussycat—You're on Camera" first appeared in *TV Guide*.

"Palette and Tureen: Notes for a Life of Marc Grosgrain" first appeared in *Diplomat*.

"Misty Behind the Curtain" is based on material previously published in *The New Yorker* and *Venture*.

"Nobody Knows the Rubble I've Seen / Nobody Knows but Croesus" first appeared in *Venture*.

To William Shawn

Contents

CONTENTS

Are You Decent, Memsahib?

A young Malayan belly dancer became a peeress today with the death of Lord Moynihan, a former chairman of Britain's Liberal party.

The new Lady Moynihan is the former Shirin Berry, known professionally as Princess Amina, who was married in 1958 to Anthony P. A. Moynihan, the Baron's son, at a secret Moslem ceremony in Tangier, Morocco.

A year later they were married again in England. Mr. Moynihan, a devotee of rock 'n' roll, resigned his reserve commission in the Brigade of Guards and played the bongo drums at his wife's worldwide cabaret appearances.—*The Times.*

Hᴀᴠᴇ ʏᴏᴜ ᴇᴠᴇʀ ɢᴀᴢᴇᴅ into your mirror, girls, and longed to be dazzlingly lovely, breathtakingly so, no matter how stiff a price you had to pay for pulchritude? Of course you have; nor do you reck that beauty can ofttimes lead to woe. And yours truly has good reason to know, for when the gods lavished their gifts on me, an obscure little cipher from Scranton, Pa., and grafted an angelic countenance onto a physique divine, I sure as hell thought the world was my personal oyster. Which I don't mean that my success was handed to me on a platter—far from it. I had to hustle aplenty to climb that pinnacle. Still and all, I doubt whether anybody who saw Shirley Mazchstyck in pigtails could predict that out of this drab cocoon there would one day emerge a gorgeous butterfly yclept Sherry Muscatel, America's No. 1 stripteuse. Or that the latter would ever blossom forth into an Indian begum with the power of life and death over her subjects. Let's face it—the whole thing was just too fab.

The story of how I climbed the show-biz ladder to its topmost rung has been told so often in *Sizzle, Roister, Smolder,* and the other picture magazines that I don't have to burden your brain with it. Suffice it to say that, thanks to the smartest talent booker any star ever had, Solly Positano, I zoomed into the ace spot five years ago and stayed there. Why do I command top money and pick my engagements, you ask? Pure and simply because, unlike your average strip act, mine has no taint of vulgarity. As Solly analyzed, I give them something artistic that is lacking in their lives, a spectacle they wouldn't be ashamed to take their mother or sister to. The framework that my specialty is built on is the four seasons; i.e., winter, summer, fall, and spring. I make my entrance in winter garb, bundled up in mink, and after gliding around to the "Skaters' Waltz" peel down to fur briefies and matching bra. For the summer bit, I wear like a milkmaid frock of gingham, very demure, with batiste underthings and a parasol. I love working with a parasol; it makes everything you do seem so much more sexy. Anyhow, such is the basic routine, and even family-style resorts like Grossinger's and the Concord consider me so clean and educational that they outbid each other for repeats. From Thanksgiving on, I usually play the Fontainebleau or Eden Roc in Miami Beach, alternating with the Sands or the Desert Inn at Vegas. Even if Uncle Sam and Solly take out a big chunk between them, it is still a very nice dollar.

Well, one fine day last spring, I was laying off for a week at the Americana in New York when Solly phones me—a *megillah* about this inspiration that he and some other bookers had that morning in the steam room. They're going to put on an evening of old-fashioned burlesque in Boston. There used to be a house up there called the Old Howard that was very big in the days of the Columbia Wheel, the Gus Sun circuit, and the Izzy Herk time, but nobody remembers it now except a few elderly gaffers.

"Like you and your cronies," I said fliply. "It'll bomb, Solly. I predict you'll lose your shirt."

"Listen, Shirley girlie," he said. "You've got the best chassis in the business and you can shimmy like my sister Kate, but a predictor you're not. I tell you the public will eat it up. Look at the way they go for the old cars, ragtime tunes, et cetera. Anyway, I penciled you in, so make a note—the fourteenth of next month in Beantown."

I'm a straightforward person, and if I'm wrong I'm the first to admit it. The show was a sensation; we killed the people, we fractured them. God only knows where they dug up the performers from—the baggy-pants Dutch and Hebe comics, the soubrettes, and the crummy tenors with their lantern slides—but they didn't miss a one. And the material! Hokey old sketches like "Irish Justice," routines like "Flugel Street"— the audience was rolling in the aisles. But you should have heard them whistle and stomp when I came on, and the reason why was plain. Most of them were collegians from Harvard and Tufts which, while they bought the corn, secretly hungered for my more sophisticated approach. Well, I don't have to tell you. By halfway through, I had them howling like wolves, and those final bumps and grinds on my exit did the trick. The stage manager had to ring down the house curtain so the show could go on. A very clever team of acrobats, Anaxagoras Bros. & Delphine, followed me, but they didn't get a thing. The kids were too wrought up.

There was such a crush in my dressing room afterwards that when Solly barged in with this Oriental-type fellow and introduced him as Lam Chowdri, a Harvard boy, I thought it was a rib on account of it sounded like clam chowder. But he was legit, all right—a real dyed-in-the-wool Hindu, kind of good-looking in an offbeat way, and, from what Solly said, one of the wealthiest kids in India. He kept raving away about my act

11

and said I reminded him of the native dancers back home on the temple friezes.

"You bet," said Solly, who can't resist a gag. "She freezes our temples over here too, don't you, Sherry? She turns strong men to like stone."

I could see from Lam Chowdri's face that he didn't dig but he was too polite to say. Instead, he invites me to have supper with him, and while I don't as a rule go with civilians, I made an exception. As soon as I heard him ask the maître d' at Locke-Ober's for a private room, I got the message. Oho, I thought, here it comes. Lobsters and champagne, and for dessert a wild chase around the table. Well, I didn't need to worry; he never stepped out of line, not once. It surprised me how American-ized he was. I thought Hindus spent all their time crouching on a bed of nails or worshipping a cow, but not he. He knew the name of every pop singer on TV, he was posted on any current events you could mention, and he was a fluent con-versationalist. I also found out something those graybeards up at Harvard didn't know. He was a maharajah, the head of a section in India called Cawnpone, where his uncle, a regent, was minding the store while Lam finished his education.

Well, talk about your whirlwind courtships—this one was a tornado. For the next three weeks, not a day went by without caviar, orchids, little fantasies from Cartier's to keep your wrists cool, and special-delivery letters that got more excited on every page. I was his meadowlark, his bulbul, his fleet-footed gazelle, everything but his water buffalo. At the time, I was working a string of clubs in the Midwest, one-night stands, and each airport I got to, why, I was met by a chauffeur-driven Rolls that Lam had laid on. (Somebody gave the item to Lennie Lyons, but they had the wrong Indian, and it came out "Cherokee" instead of "Chowdri.") Anyway, the minute my tour wound up in New York, there was Lam waiting to pop the question, and, of course, he has to pick a real kookie locale like the Mayflower Donut Shop at 2:30 in the morning. Love among the crullers. But he was so sweetly sincere that it brought a lump to my throat, and I decided to lay my cards on the table too. I told him about my ex-husbands, the jockey and thȩ druggist—I skipped the brassière manufacturer because we split out after two weeks—and how my search for happiness had failed.

"Oh, moon of my delight," he says, grabbing my hands. "Life has bruised your wings, my little shama thrush. All I ask is a simple boon. Let me spend the rest of my life catering to your smallest whim."

No woman can resist that kind of a pitch, especially if it's a maharajah talking, and twelve hours later a j.p. in Virginia tied the knot. I wanted to call Solly right away so as to give Earl Wilson an exclusive, but Lam talked me out of it. He said we had to keep it dark for a month, till he finished Harvard, and then he would stage a big ceremony in Cawnpone, with painted elephants and sword swallowers and the whole *tzimmas*. Well, that was a bringdown for me, natch, because I had visions of sweeping into Sardi's East, everyone kowtowing and murmuring, "Good evening, Highness. My, what a gorgeous gold sari." Still, rather than launch our honeymoon with a spat, I made like I was ecstatic over the idea, and Lam slipped the judge a deuce to button up to the press. Everything was peachy keen—so I thought.

It was like two days after he went back to Cambridge that I got my first jolt. I walk in the flat one night from Jersey, where I'm headlining the show at the Migraine Room of the Hotel Winograd, in Newark, and there's my royal master, lock, stock, and baggage. He's quit college because he can't stand being separated, but that's only for openers. The real wallop—are you ready?—is that he's gone and renounced his throne because it would always stand between us. From here in, he's devoting himself full time to my career, and, in fact, he's dreamed up a way to weave himself into my act. I was so flabbergasted I could hardly talk.

"Wait a minute, Buster," I said. "A maharajah can't quit like a short-order cook. Don't you have to go back to India to renounce your title?"

"No, I renounced it on the phone," he said. "But that's only a detail. Listen to my idea for our new act."

In my turmoil, I didn't follow too closely, but the *drehdel* was that he would be costumed like an Indian snake charmer, in a turban and a diaper, kneeling on the floor in front of this large basket and playing a flute. And pretty soon, after the applause for his solo dies down, out of the basket would come you-know-who and go into her number. Except that it wouldn't be a strip exactly, more of a slow cooch.

Well, I knew I couldn't handle the situation alone, so I ran to a guy whose business was trouble—viz. and to wit, Solly— and spilled the whole story. I must say he was a doll. Never a word of criticism; only trying to be helpful. He came up with a solution pronto.

"I got the perfect identity for him," he says. "A candy butcher. In between your changes, he circulates around the floor with an old-fashioned spiel: 'Ladies and gents, if I may have your kind attention. Introducing America's biggest-selling candy, Greenfield's Confections, a prize in each and every package.' It's a great comedy touch, Shirl, and we can get a million tieups with Loft's, Whitman, whoever. And think of the publicity! 'Sweets for the Sweetie. Ex-Maharajah Vends Bonbons for Love.' "

It sounded like a natural, but when I sprang it on Lam he blew his stack. Nineteen generations of royalty would revolve in their grave if he became a hawker. Solly was a cheap vulgarian, he stormed, and then, like *that*, he suddenly has another brain wave. Why not let him represent me instead of Solly and save all that commission? I almost told him that those nineteen generations would spin like a Waring mixer if he went into the agency racket, but I was afraid he might slap me across the chops. When those Hindus get angry, man, it's Amoksville. So I pretended his notion was marvy but I needed a few days to mull it over. And that very evening Mr. Nuroddin checks in from Cawnpone.

Mr. Nuroddin is what they call a Parsee, this very high-toned sect of fire worshippers that almost every one of them is a rich, influential banker or merchant. He's the family lawyer and he's been sent over by Lam's uncle, the regent, to rescue the boy from my coils. Well, the scene he put on was right out of *East*

Lynne. Within two minutes, he's using words like "adventuress," and when he brought out his checkbook and asked "How much?" I really let him have it. I called him every name I could think of, I threw a jar of Albolene at his head, and I made such an uproar that he ran out quaking like an aspirin. But if you think that was the end of him, you don't know Mr. Nuroddin. He starts showing up at a ringside table every performance, sending me mangoes and skirt lengths of madras and mooning around till after my late show. At first I thought it was like a ruse to break up Lam and I. Then I realized the old *nudnik* is serious, for God's sake. He's carrying a torch, but he's not worshipping *it*—he's idolizing *me*. I chewed him out good and proper.

"Why don't you act your age, Nuroddin?" I said. "You ought to be ashamed, a man of your standing in the legal profession behaving like a stage-door John."

"I can't help it, O beauteous one," he snuffles, wringing his hands. "To me you're the sun in the morning and the moon at night. I adore you, my little nightingale."

My life isn't complicated enough already; now I have an old Parsee mouthpiece to contend with. "Listen, Clyde," I said to him. "You better watch out or you'll be wearing a silk thread around your larnix. Lam's getting suspicious—he asked me when you were going back home."

Then the stove explodes. "I'm not. Never again," he says. "I just sent off a cable to Cawnpone resigning from my law firm. From now on, every ounce of my being is devoted to serving you."

"Are you out of your *mind*?" I said. "What about your family? Don't you have any wives?"

"None to compare with you, my ringdove," he says. I was beginning to feel like a zoo. "Let me do your bidding, my lovely tigress. Walk on me, tread on me."

Well, what could I do? I told Lam I needed a secretary and I took on the old buzzard—not that a stripper has that much paperwork, but like Solly said, it was good publicity. I guess he was right; Louis Sobol wrote that I was the only ecdysiast on record with a Zoroastrian amanuensis. That didn't sit so well with Hubby, Nuroddin crowding him out of the spotlight, and the two of them started catfooting around, exchanging these vicious little digs—in Hindi yet. If it was in Scrantonese, which I'm fluent, I could have coped, but they drove me right up the wall. So that's how matters stood when Uncle Nooj, the regent, blows in.

You'd have to see this joker to believe him—he's right out of *The Arabian Nights* or some pageant Sol Hurok imported. A skinny little man with a big bugle, which one flange has a diamond the size of your pinkie welded into it. He has on a shift embroidered with rubies, and around his neck five strands of pearls like Mary Garden or Schumann-Heink in the *Victor Book of the Opera*. But there the resemblance ends; he's got a high, squeaky voice like a peanut whistle and he beams it straight at me. Well, brother, you could write the dialogue. I'm Valerie Vampire, and what kind of a hex did I put on his nephew and his legal eagle? They must have drunk a love filter I prepared, whatever the hell that is. He's going to annul the marriage if it takes Louis Nizer's weight in platinum, and in the meantime he's got a table next to the band that night to watch me work my voodoo.

Well, do I have to spell it out? It was love's old sweet song, and I'm the gal who put the sex in sexagenarians. As I ran off in my birthday suit with the peasants yelling, I look back and there's Nooj standing on the table, squealing for an encore, but in my dodge you have nowhere to go, as they say. The flowers and the trinkets started arriving on schedule, and if you never saw an emerald the size of an Idaho baked potato, neither had I. I don't know who was ruling over Cawnpone while Nooj was absent, but whoever it was, they kept the supply lines open. Solly used to come by nights in an armored car to haul the stuff to the bank. You can imagine how Lam and Nuroddin reacted to Nooj. It's a wonder they didn't drop a krait down his peplum or something. And the topper, of course, was the matinée that he shows up in a business suit too large for him and a tweed cap cocked over one eye. He looked like a pinboy

I used to go around with in Scranton. "I have a very startling piece of news for you, my eaglet," he says, undressing me with those goo-goo eyes.

"Don't tell me—let me guess," I said. "You went and renounced your title. You're over here permanent from now on."

His jaw dropped with such a clang you could almost hear it. "How did you guess?"

"Well," I said. "It's becoming pretty common around here. Do you know anything about how to use Carbona?"

"I never heard of it," he says. "What is it?"

"Well, you better find out," I said, "because from now on you're in charge of all my cleaning and pressing. Here's a key, and you can use the locker right next to Lam and Nuroddin. Good luck."

That's what I told *him*. But I was the one who needed it.

Reunion in Gehenna

THE ENVELOPE beside my plate the other morning, addressed in a florid feminine backhand, was tinted the particular robin's-egg blue reserved for babies' bassinets. As I slit open the flap, I stole a furtive glance at my wife across the breakfast table. Her classic features, frequently confused with Katharine Cornell's, betrayed such martyrdom that, given chain mail and a wooden sword, she could have played St. Joan in any little-theatre production in America.

"Well, go ahead and read it," she challenged. "Who is it from this time—some overblown carhop with a platinum rinse?"

"I haven't the faintest clue to what you're foompheting about," I said with hauteur.

"Fancy," she said. "Then suppose I blueprint it for you. I find this correspondence you persist in conducting with other women in abominable taste. Humiliating, in fact. Utterly and unspeakably degrading."

Rather than bandy words with a person patently corroded with jealousy, and lacking, moreover, the words to bandy, I retreated into dignified silence and made a quick scrutiny of the letter. "Well, stap my vitals!" I exclaimed. "It's an invitation from Lorna Dabchick, the secretary of my high-school class. They're holding a forty-second reunion. And you know something?" I added reflectively. "I've got half a mind to attend."

"That's just about all you'd need," she observed. I raised one eyebrow in the manner of William Powell—ironical yet quizzical—but made no comment. "Yes," she went on. "I've felt for some time that you were aching to spend an evening with a lot of rheumatic old fogies, cackling over the pranks you used to play on your algebra teacher. It's senile dementia, dear—second childhood."

The implication that I was an imbecile wounded me in my Achilles' heel and I became quite emotional, if not altogether coherent. "Right! Right!" I bellowed, reddening with anger. "I'm a sentimental fathead, an irresponsible dotard, but let me tell *you* something, Mrs. Wisenheimer. There are still a few other values in life besides yours. There's love, and there's friendship, and—and there's loving friendship that money can't buy!" I rose and, overturning the coffee cup to underscore my words, swept from the alcove.

My passionate sincerity must have convinced the woman how futile was protest, for inside forty-eight hours I found myself aboard a crack train of the New Haven system, speeding through southern New England. Any doubts I may have entertained about my ability to recapture the past were dispelled at New London. The train butcher who embarked there was the very same one I had encountered four decades ago on my maiden journey to New York, and he still displayed the same formidable case of rhinitis. "Chickid, hab, ad peadut-butter sadwiches, folks!" he intoned, weaving his way through the steam cars. "Get your cold bilk here!" It was inconceivable that forty years had wrought no change in his status or mucous membrane, but there he was, as woebegone and infectious as ever.

The Lobster Pot, the roadhouse where the alumni of Dropsical High were congregating, housed eighty or ninety oldsters in paper hats, who, on my arrival, were noisily acquiring a skinful. Between the clash of bridgework and the drumfire crackle of arteries snapping like pipestems, the place was indistinguishable from an encampment of the G.A.R., but after a spell faces began to take on a dimly familiar look. What struck me as totally inexplicable, though, was how my contemporaries could have become so senescent while I had remained vibrant and arrowy. I noticed a good half dozen clutching to themselves phials of adrenalin, nitroglycerin, and similar restoratives, and I gave them a wide berth lest they topple onto me during a seizure and wrinkle my suit.

Within minutes, it developed that the chairman of the assemblage—the party, in fact, who had conceived and organized it—was a retired podiatrist named Dr. Harry Samovar. Harry had distinguished himself in youth, I recollected, for his forensic powers, singlehandedly vanquishing the debating team of the Lizzie Borden High School in Fall River on the proposition "Resolved, that the initiative, referendum, and recall constitute an arrant menace to the body politic." Whereas Demosthenes had improved his diction by holding a pebble in his mouth, Harry was more favored by fortune; when he spoke, the words rippled from his tongue as if strained across an entire creek bed of gravel. Tonight, plucking a microphone out of thin air, he bade us address ourselves to dinner and explained that the impetus for the reunion had come to him while he was convalescing from a stroke. Barely had he conceived the idea, however, when a second one laid him low; still, this provided him with the leisure to work out the details. After his third stroke—apoplexy hounded Samovar, apparently, much as head colds did my train butcher—he heard the swish of Father Time's scythe and hastily began rallying his classmates. Although nobody at my table appeared to be following his discourse, appetites suddenly started to flag and I felt an overwhelming urge for a cigarette. A buxom, grandmotherly lady on my left, whom I had idolized throughout the whole four-year term without disclosing my passion, scrabbled in her handbag to supply me with one and inadvertently exhumed a tin of BiSoDoL tablets. The realization that my goddess had, so to speak, feet of clay affected me keenly, and I lapsed into a reverie finally broken by the voice of Lorna Dabchick, the class secretary, beamed across the table.

"And what have you been doing all these years, Sol?" she inquired chattily.

I replied that since the death of Moriarty at the Reichenbach Fall I had travelled for two years in Tibet and amused myself by visiting Lhasa, spending some days with the head lama. I had then passed through Persia, looked in at Mecca, and paid a short but interesting visit to the khalifa at Khartoum, the results of which I had communicated to the Foreign Office. Returning to France, I had then spent some months in a research into the coal-tar derivatives, which I conducted in a laboratory at Montpellier.

Lorna listened with rapt interest. "You always had itching feet," she recalled. "Tell me, did you ever get married?"

"No," I confessed. "To me there will always be but one woman—Irene Adler."

"A lovely person," she agreed. "She was coming to the reunion, but she had an attack of gastritis—that is, she *said* it was gastritis—"

I would have loved to hear more about Irene's internal arrangements, but Dr. Samovar, occupied meanwhile in sorting a number of packages, rapped for order. "The prizes we're awarding fall into three categories," he announced. "First, for the couple here wed the longest. Is there anybody married a hundred years? . . . Ninety-five? . . . Ninety?" The search eventually produced a pair of lovebirds—regrettably, no longer on speaking terms—who had gone straight from Dropsical to the altar, and who drew a carving knife suitable for disembowelling each other. The prize for the graduate travelling the greatest distance to the banquet—a ceramic kangaroo with a pouchful of wooden matches—went to a cotton-waste dealer from Woonsocket (a singularly appropriate choice, inasmuch as he had twice been convicted of arson). As for the five-hundred-dollar award to the most distinguished retired podiatrist in the class, that posed the knottiest problem, until Samovar, over his furious protestations, was ultimately prevailed on to accept it.

These preliminaries disposed of, we were ready for the main event of the evening. A sugary-sweet matron in harlequin glasses, her nose sharpened from poking it into other people's business, rose and identified herself as our schoolmate Elise Grabhorn, currently an interviewer on a local radio station.

She graciously offered to quiz volunteers on their most arresting experience after graduation, and selected as her first candidate a nearly spherical lady in dotted swiss who spoke in a penetrating, squeaky treble.

"I'm Olive Moultrie," the latter piped. "Olive Krebs when I was single. I don't know if you remember me before I put on so much flesh."

"We certainly do, my dear," said Miss Grabhorn with a vinegary smile. "I'll never forget what a kissing bug Olive was in those days, will you, gang? Now, what was your most unusual experience?"

"Well," began Olive, "Nathan, my hubby—Nathan Moultrie of Peets & Moultrie, Meats & Poultry—was always crazy about my veal birds. He used to say, 'Olive . . . ' He used to say, 'Olive . . .' He used to say, 'Olive' "—Miss Grabhorn clapped her hands sharply, and Olive wrested herself from the groove she had slipped into—" 'Olive, I never can get enough of your veal birds.' "

"And did he?" asked her inquisitor.

"Did he what?" Olive repeated adenoidally.

"Get enough of your veal birds," Miss Grabhorn snapped.

"Uh-uh," said Olive. "He passed on four years ago last August."

"Well, you certainly have the sympathy of each and every one of us," said Miss Grabhorn, waving her into oblivion. "Now, who else? I think I see Everett Eubanks over there with his hand up."

"My Uncle Clint was a railroad man," declared Eubanks, a dried-up little man with watery eyes, "and the day I got my diploma he gave me a good timepiece, because, being a railroad man, he had to rely on a good timepiece—you know what I mean? Well, I carried it for nearly twelve years, and one day after I was out fishing for squeteague off Barrington I couldn't find it. Hunted high and low, but nary a trace. So about a month later I was fishing for squeteague again off Gaspee Point and I hauled in a real beauty. And what do you think was in the belly?"

"The timepiece!" several voices chorused.

"No, just a lot of grits the size of your pinky," said Eubanks. "My wife found the watch on a window sill in the attic. Must of laid it there when I put away the screens."

"Thank you, Olive Moultrie and Everett Eubanks," said Dr. Samovar, rising briskly, "and a special thanks to Elise for her brilliant job as m.c. This has been a truly memorable occasion. And now, if you will repair to the Ragtime Room adjoining, Chalky Aftertaste and his Musical Poltroons will cater to your dancing pleasure."

To the strains of "I've Got a Bimbo Down on a Bamboo Isle," "Would You Rather Be a Colonel with an Eagle on Your Shoulder, or a Private with a Chicken on Your Knee?," "Arrah, Go On, I'm Gonna Go Back to Oregon," and a host of similar favorites, I spent the next half hour impervious to aught save the worship of Terpsichore. If I say so myself, I was the cynosure of all eyes. At the behest of my powerfully muscled arms, each of them easily larger in diameter than a pencil, my partners curvetted in figure eights, whirled and skimmed like swallows; in and out of the throng we dipped and swung, shaking our bacon. And then, yielding to the entreaties of my onlookers, I consented to demonstrate the Camel Walk, my interpretation of which had electrified the Senior Prom in 1921. But in choosing Olive Moultrie to share the limelight with me I made a fatal miscalculation. As I was bending her backward in a dizzying tango glide, her weight overbalanced me, I rolled under her, and she fell solidly on my thorax, full fifteen stone. The impact must have knocked me galley-west, for when I regained consciousness I was spread out on a divan like a starfish and Dr. Samovar was distractedly canvassing the bystanders for some hint as to my next of kin.

Luckily, a bit of diathermy, a week of bed rest, and a fortnight at New York Hospital soon put me right, and my account of the train derailment near Westerly was so vivid that my wife completely forgot about the forty-second reunion. And so will I, by the time the eighty-fourth rolls around. I expect to build up quite a head of new nostalgia by then.

23

Palette and Tureen: Notes for a Life of Marc Grosgrain

ABOUT SIX MONTHS AGO, a very accomplished textile designer I know was approached by J. C. Phrensy & Company, a firm of nationwide chain stores, and presented with a challenge; she was asked to create a tablecloth, primarily intended for breakfast nooks, to retail at $1.79. The problem, outwardly simple, proved more complex when expounded. In quality and aesthetic appeal, it was explained, the cloth would fall midway between two others—a cheap version at $1.24 and a de luxe one at $2.37. It must be made of that grisliest of fabrics, oilcloth, to withstand punishing wear; its background, while emotionally stimulating, should be neutral-colored in order to camouflage bacon-grease and egg stains; and finally, it must embody a gay floral centerpiece—something redolent of lark song and a joyous spring morning—research having established that the average housewife can rarely afford the luxury of fresh-cut flowers. Except for the proviso that the tablecloth should have the sparkle of costly British chintz, launder in a trice, and, however daring, not alarm conservative tastes, the purchasing agent put no curb on the designer. Fling convention to the winds, he urged—let the imagination ride free, but remember, nothing too startling.

A disciplined and serious artist, Lena Pettengill—whose given name derived from her father's obsession at the bap-

24

tismal font with a song called "Lena Was the Queen of Palestina"—retired to her studio and labored hard and long. She ransacked her files for days, tracking down every conceivable domestic motif, and made endless sketches that ran the horticultural gamut. Invariably, her client found fault. This design was too formalized, that too naïve; hollyhocks were corny, violets suggestive; the cloth should be dynamic, modernistic, yet should at the same time exude a warm Victorian glow. As the weeks wore on, Lena began to experience all the sensations of nightmare. Her hands trembled so violently that she had trouble laying in a wash, and one evening, while playing the harpsichord to steady them, she toppled off the bench and had to be revived with stingers.

The day at length dawned when every objection had been stilled. Acres of Bristol board had been frowned over, rivers of water color expended, and warehousefuls of cigars chewed to pulp. The design had been imprinted on fabric, and Lena, flanked by Phrensy's senior vice-president and the purchasing agent, stood contemplating the finished product spread out on the floor of her studio. The vice-president chewed his lip meditatively.

"Excellent—first-rate," he pronounced magisterially. "Tell me, Miss Pettengill—would you say that with this design we have achieved perfection?"

Lena slowly detached her gaze from her handiwork and, wheeling, surveyed him intently for a full fifteen seconds. "Mr. Flatulenko," she returned, "when you use the term 'perfection,' do you mean it in the Chinese sense of perfect philosophical balance, or in the Christian context, which implies a hint of martyrdom? Or," she went on, grasping his cravat and pulling his face up to hers, "are you asking whether you can stamp out five million of these abortions and fob them off on the housewives of America?" Her eyes had contracted to pinpoints and she was enunciating with difficulty. "Because, my dear sir," she rasped, her voice cleaving him in two like an apple, "if the last is what you indeed mean, kindly let us have no more ——— nonsense about perfection."

The career of Marc Grosgrain, whose retrospective show of

hand-painted ties is currently attracting crowds to the Museum of Modern Art, seems to me to typify equally well the perpetual conflict between artistic integrity and commerce. No doubt many are drawn there by the legends that have sprung up about his eccentricities rather than by the matchless purity, the exquisite harmony, of the ties themselves. But the fact that he is reputed to have cut off the end of his selvage and mailed it to a lady of easy virtue, or that he led a life of Bohemianism at variance with polite standards, should not blind us to his genius. Grosgrain came along at a point when the hand-painted tie had fallen into decadence. Dull stereotypes like flamingoes, sunsets, Spanish moss, and wigwams were the only sop necktie manufacturers could offer the masculine craving for pageantry; their poverty-stricken imaginations, no longer capable of truly creative symbols, were coupling incestuously to produce arid zigzags and meaningless whorls of color. Grosgrain blew a fresh breath of life into haberdashery. Scorning the clichés that held the four-in-hand prisoner, he threw away everything but the solar spectrum and fathered a new philosophy for the male cravat. It is to his pioneer daring that we owe the whole concept of nonobjective neckwear and its elevation from apparel into a work of art. Incidentally, too much stress cannot be placed upon the sympathetic, tasteful display the directors of the Museum have given the exhibition. The counters piled with cut-rate shirts, porous-knit underwear, and bathrobes provide an ideal background for Grosgrain's originals, and the inspiration of presenting the attendants as floorwalkers was a singularly felicitous one. Perhaps the most ingenious touch, though, was the hanging of several especially celebrated collectors alongside their acquisitions. As one sees Mr. Joe Levine, for example, twinkling down from beside such superb abstractions as "Kaiserschmarrn" or "Breakfast with Toots," tie and tycoon blend into a unity that exalts the gallerygoer's heart. Here, at last, is a fusion Van Dyck—not to say Van Heusen—never dreamed of.

It is difficult, within the confines of an informal biographical sketch, to distinguish apocrypha from fact in Grosgrain's trajectory to fame. We know, nevertheless, that he was a Troy man and that his proximity to collars, both starched and semi-soft, did much to prepare the soil for the seed fated to germinate in it. That he harbored any artistic bent or preco-ciousness of whatever sort was not apparent to his classmates. At the age of eleven, from all accounts, he was a stolid, bourgeois boy, already married to an ultra-respectable girl with strabismus who regularly presented him with a child a year; indeed, his offspring were so numerous at Grosgrain's graduation from grammar school that the principal was con-fused as to which member of the party had earned the diploma. By the time he reached fifteen, however, some sort of creative yeast was stirring in the adolescent youth. He had begun to dabble with paints, realizing a few crude neckties which evoked universal derision from the townsfolk. "Marc's Neckties," as they were mockingly referred to, became a huge popular joke; his sportive elders were wont to inquire patroniz-ingly when he proposed to quit his aimless Cubistic scribblings and settle down. (Ironically, it was one of these selfsame "scribblings" that last week brought an undisclosed sum from a wealthy unidentified collector at a private sale in the Anderson Galleries.) At any rate, the jeers and hostility of the Philistines finally became insupportable, and one day, out of the blue, Marc abruptly abandoned his family, came to New York, and took a furnished room in Greenwich Village. He had been reading *The Moon and Sixpence* rather intensively, and he suspected that some friend or other of his wife's would seek him out to demand an explanation of his outrageous behavior and urge him to return home. Nothing of the kind happened; he sat in the room until his vision fogged, but nobody came near him. At the end of two weeks, he saw the handwriting on the wall and decided to bury the past. This may be said to conclude what has been called the Troy phase.

The story of the next twelve years is sufficiently familiar to avoid being retold—his long, arduous apprenticeship as a stockroom boy at Budd's and Sulka's (from which he was summarily discharged for sneering at a foulard), the first tentative experiments with phosphorus which foreshadowed his discovery of the necktie that glowed in the dark, his growing absorption with nonrepresentational design and *trompe l'oeil*, and his emergence at twenty-seven as the *deus ex machina* behind Bronzini and Countess Mara. Yet throughout all the success, the adulation of jobbers and the acclaim that rang from the Garment Center at each successive triumph, Grosgrain was tortured by a sense of unfulfillment. Again and again his artistic conscience whispered that though his hand-painted ties stood as far above his competitors' as a Giotto above a Landseer, they produced no genuine catharsis in the onlooker. Restlessly cruising from "21" to Sardi's, from Lindy's to Lüchow's, he studied the leathery, imperious executives sporting his cravats and asked himself wherein the final effect fell short. Functionally, the ties were unexceptionable; they screened the shirtfront from flying saliva and bits of food, and they afforded a welcome pool of color on which the eye could fasten when it tired of the jowls above. But no matter how well-worn or saturated with gravy, the tapestry remained a thing apart from the wearer, a separate entity. It did not reflect his distinct individual personality and the dishes he preferred; for all the pains Grosgrain had lavished on it, it was as atypical of its owner and devoid of character as a cheap umbrella. If only a union could be arranged, he thought wistfully, some way of inextricably yoking the two. . . . The answer, so lucid and unequivocal that it might have fallen from the lips of the Muse herself, came to him one midwinter night at Toffenetti's.

On the evening that was to prove a turning point for male plumage, Grosgrain, en route to the theatre, was hurrying through dinner in that midtown rendezvous when a passing waiter inadvertently tilted a heavily loaded tray. A rivulet of ravioli in tomato sauce, interspersed with peppercorns, flooded down over the artist's dove-gray tie. The waiter, in an agony of contrition, blurted out profuse apologies and dropped the tray into the lap of a neighboring old lady, explaining that he was slightly drunk; but to everyone's bewilderment, Grosgrain sprang up and embraced him joyfully. In the rich pastiche soaking into his bosom, he beheld the clue he had vainly sought for months—not a sterile painted naturalism, but (as he later defined it) "accidental neo-objective suprarealism." Pressing a munificent tip on the menial, he sped to his workroom overlooking Bryant Park and labored until dawn, feverishly preserving the design with fixatif and jotting down notes for future compositions. It was this necktie, "Ole Parmesan's Got Me," now in the possession of Mr. David Merrick, that charted the course Grosgrain was to follow the next three years.

And what a course it was, we marvel to ourselves as we survey the spectacular bows and scarves, glowing like Byzantine mosaics, that light up the walls of the Museum. Here is "Saraband on Second Avenue," the pastel in gefilte fish, cheese blintzes and sour cream that took so much patient stalking at Ratner's; "The Fall of the House of Chan," a macabre arrangement of shark's-fin soup, crisp noodles, and soy bean conceived in that renowned Chinese restaurant (not to be confused with Lum Fong's, where the equally brilliant "Egg Roll Round My Shoulder" was dashed off on Grosgrain); "Variations on a Bream," a stylized fish piece garnered at Sweet's, skillfully mingling chowder, pilot crackers, and a side order of smelts; and scores of others, each a testimonial to its creator's gusto and boundless invention. Like every innovator before him who has dared to challenge existing shibboleths, Grosgrain was reviled at first as a madman. Academicians joined with wholesalers to dub his soaring masterworks "dippy," and it was smugly predicted that no well-groomed man would ever be induced to appear in public with table leavings on his tie, irrespective of what pleasing arabesques they formed. Then, imperceptibly, the tempest abated. Sporting figures and theatrical producers, innately sensing how apposite it was to stroll into the Brass Rail or Gallagher's with a collage of pastrami or hamburger at the throat, began commissioning Grosgrain to do special orders; Igor Cassini electrified the Colony with an ascot featuring an entire tomato surprise; and when the Chief Executive himself invaded Harvey's in Washington in a dazzling salmagundi of shrimps, avocado, and apple pandowdy, the vogue spread like wildfire across the nation.

Had Grosgrain been a cynical man and less of an artist, he would have been content to commercialize his success, to engage assistants to substitute for him in the restaurants where his inspiration flowered. Characteristically, it was his lifelong unwillingness to compromise that brought about his undoing. Fortuitous situations like the Toffenetti incident grew harder to find, and in time it became necessary to contrive them; he took to jostling waiters deliberately, provoking them both verbally and physically into upsetting their burdens over him. On several occasions he narrowly escaped bodily injury, and toward the last, in order to function at all, he had to resort to a multiplicity of disguises. His tragic destiny overtook him at Keen's Chop House during a noonday rush hour. Just as he had interposed his leg in the path of an overladen busboy and was extending his tie in readiness, a lynx-eyed headwaiter sprang forward and capsized a salad bowl on Grosgrain's head. Whether it was the latter's weakened condition due to nervous strain, suffocation caused by the tightly fitting bowl, or both, the coroner was never able to decide, but, at best, it was a wholly technical point, for the noble, sorely tried spirit had forever shed its mortal husk.

So passed Marc Grosgrain, a victim of the very yahoos for whom he had striven to capture a moment of beauty. No splendid cortège or honeyed valedictory marked his leave-taking, and yet in many a delicatessen and tavern the city over, men who knew Tabasco best paused to pour a spoonful of it on their neckties or drench them with bouillon to keep his memory verdant. The heritage he left behind in Fifty-third street is not mere garbage; it is an eternal—well, practically eternal—reminder of the degree to which the common stuff of life, its humblest meat and drink, can sustain and enrich the graphic artist. And as for the dollar cleaner, you wouldn't believe the figures if I told you.

Nobody Here 'cep' Us Riffraff

Those interested in "making," or, at any rate, "digging" (two slightly different things), the American Literary Scene to-day would be well advised to cultivate the acquaintance of George A. Plimpton and Robert B. Silvers, the two young men who run a regular fortnightly literary salon in the offices of the *Paris Review,* which also happens to be the apartment of George A. (Robert B. having a smaller one in the same building). . . .

Who will you meet there? First of all, to stave off disappointment, I had better tell you right away who you won't meet. You won't meet Faulkner, Hemingway, or Salinger (sorry). . . . Another interesting omission at these particular soirées is literary ladies. . . . In my two years' attendance I have yet to come across Mary McCarthy, Eudora Welty, Carson McCullers, or Katherine Anne Porter in these rooms, not even the special darling of the intellectuals, Lillian Hellman. . . . —*Elaine Dundy in the* London Observer.

MARCH 16

LONDON! Dear, grimy, historic old London, with its fobs and its boggies— Oh dear, I'm so thrilled at just being here that my thoughts get all scrambly. I meant to say its fogs and its bobbies and its pageantry and—oh, everything I've longed for since I majored in Eng. Lit. at Wellesley three long years

31

ago. Wouldn't Boots Hochstetter and Gloria Zenk and the rest of that Wordsworth seminar be consumed with envy if they could see me now, in my own bed-sitter at Filbert's, so thoroughly English and reeking of tradition? Mummy will have kittens, I imagine, when she hears I'm staying in a fall-down place instead of the Park Lane or the Connaught, but I happen to know this is Cyril Connolly's and Elizabeth Bowen's and John Wain's favorite hotel, though they almost never come here, and you're liable to meet anyone from Ian Fleming to Ionesco in the lobby. This morning, while I was having my elevenses in the lounge—I must be as British as possible if I'm to get into the swim here—the sweetest old gentleman sat himself down nearby. He had a steamer shawl over his shoulders and was carrying a green baize bag. I practically fainted; E. M. Forster, my second day in London! Well, I took my courage in both hands and told him that the central portion of *Howards End* was perhaps my most moving experience next to *Wozzeck,* but he didn't seem to comprehend. It turned out he only resembled Mr. Forster; he was actually a poultryman from Leeds. Still, there was something charming and Old World about it, whereas had it taken place in America I would have felt like a goop. It's the difference between two cultures.

As soon as I get my bearings, I intend to find out where the real literary lights congregate. When I was working for *Seedbed: The Journal Vernal* last winter, Mr. Ramiswam Chowdberry Lal said that most of them clustered around Dame Edith Sitwell, if I could find her. However, she clusters around somebody else I can't remember, so it may not be easy. The difficulty is that I don't know anyone here, outside of Webster Fife, who is crass beyond belief. All he's interested in is my body and Time, Inc., and since I flatly refused to discuss either in New York, I can't very well enlist him. I suppose, basically, that association with a person of Ramiswam Chowdberry Lal's stature spoils you for mere journalists. I remember how wrought up, almost mesmerized, he used to become when he and I chose poetry for our quarterly issues. His eyes blazed

with me to lend him fifty pounds for his rent. Fortunately, my escort whispered into my ear that Derek was the most notorious sponge in the United Kingdom, which convinced me that I must be more wary in future. The advice certainly came in handy. We'd barely gone a block before he, too, this poet who as far as I knew wasn't even published, burst into demands that I give myself to him. So angry and disillusioned was I that I came within an ounce of slapping his face. I made him drive me straight to my hotel.

"I suppose you'd like a little loan also," I said cuttingly as we pulled up in front.

"Well, I *could* use a few quid to tide me over," he said. "A couple of fivers'll do handsomely. And don't forget the cab fare, will you? It's these small extras that chip away at a chap."

I wonder whether he and Derek are representative of the local literary scene. No, I shan't succumb to cheap cynicism. That would negate every ideal Ramiswam Chowdberry Lal tried to implant in me.

APRIL 5

It's happened—I've crashed the Sitwell circle! Or at least I've met their bosom friend, which is tantamount to the same thing. And not just an intimate of the trio, I may add, but an altogether charming, civilized, and superior being, totally without affectation yet a man of the world. His name is Lionel Weems-Horsfall, and he himself is involved in belles-lettres, though in what precise capacity I haven't established. We became acquainted, oddly enough, through a jesting remark of the hall porter at Filbert's yesterday. Whilst handing me my key, he inquired in this droll way he has—sort of respectful and teasing at the same time—whether I'd caught up with Sir Osbert or Dame Edith. I wasn't aware anyone had overheard, but shortly afterward Mr. Weems-Horsfall approached me in the lobby.

"I say, I hope you'll overlook my cheek," he apologized. "As a bosom friend of the Sitwells, I felt obliged to enlighten you." All three, apparently, have an inflexible rule never to turn up

35

at Filbert's, and to spare me further search he revealed that they were cruising in the Adriatic at the moment. "In their absence, however," he finished gallantly, "may I offer you a sherry to palliate your disappointment? I know they'd want me to."

No American could have put it so engagingly, and in donkey's years (a peculiar expression they employ here for "the twinkling of an eye") we were ensconced in the bar, chatting away like old cronies. His directness and honesty were refreshing after those scroungers at the Prospect of Whitby. An attractive girl of my background, he declared, could easily captivate any salon in London she chose to; she merely needed proper sponsorship, a requisite he was prepared to extend. In the meantime, he hoped I might dine with him tonight at Quaglino's, where we'd draw up a list of salons and select those he thought suitable. Need I add that I jumped at the invitation?

That tiresome Webster Fife! I knew it was only a matter of time before he'd track me down, and, furthermore, in the sneakiest, most devious way possible—through Mummy. He cabled her asking where I was—oh, those *Time* correspondents —and, the second he heard, began hounding me. Great vulgar bouquets of roses, appeals to lunch, the old mustache-twirling routine. As if I can't divine his motives. He must think I'm Nellie Naïve indeed.

APRIL 10

Well, it goes to show how overwhelmingly, blindly mistaken one can be about human nature. I thought I was a pretty shrewd judge of character, but this week was a bringdown. Fakery, deceit, betrayal—that's the keynote of the whole literary scene, our own as well as the British. And then the very person I most distrust proves my salvation. I'm still looping.

First, the unspeakable Lionel Weems-Horsfall. Our evening at Quaglino's started off rapturously. He'd ordered the dinner in advance, and superb it was, too, with just the right vintage wines, and a lovely corsage, and the manager personally supervising the crêpes Suzette. Lionel effervesced all over the place. He had an epigram for everything, sometimes two, and finally I was so convulsed with giggles I had to beg him to stop. As the meal wore on, he neglected to broach the list of salons we were to discuss, and, not wishing to seem opportunistic, I didn't press it. At last, after innumerable brandies, the check arrived, and, to my dismay, Lionel handed it to me. It appeared that he'd left his wallet in another suit, but if I advanced the cash we could stop by his flat in the Edgeware Road and he'd repay me. There was no suggestion of giving myself to him, he continued, inasmuch as he was already in love with the wife of a prominent M.P.; the loan was a straight business proposition. I was just seething, but what could I do? The instant we got outside, I expressed my disbelief that he had any connection with the literary world.

"You're wrong there, pet," he said with this brazen smile. "I'm an expert typewriter repairman."

"So that's where you learned the touch system," I said scathingly, and left him standing there.

Back I flew to Filbert's, determined to tell the hall porter what sort of leeches infested his hotel, and there I got my second surprise. Who should be awaiting me but my old mentor, Ramiswam Chowdberry Lal, fresh in from the States. We fell into each other's arms, for he was exactly the confidant I needed to unburden myself to. Dear Ramiswam—he was sympathy itself, with his quaint, flowery language and his promises to introduce me to the real literati. In fact, he was a little too compassionate; all of a sudden he said something in Hindi I didn't quite understand. I asked him to translate.

"I—er—I was seeking to consummate our union," he explained slyly.

I replied as unpriggishly as I knew how that we could proceed only on a Platonic basis.

"O.K., you're the engineer," he agreed, in a slangy way that struck me as new and alien to his personality. "Then how's about putting up the scratch to revive *Seedbed* over here? Or, failing that, a bit of walking-around money?"

37

I realized with an acute pang that he had become tarnished since our last encounter, and, assuring him I would think it over, I withdrew. Early the next morning, I moved bag and baggage to the Park Lane and immediately phoned Webster Fife. I found to my delight that he's grown astonishingly mature. He's leaving Time, Inc., to return to his family's leather business, and we've been out dancing the last four nights without a single pass. So I may just conceivably call up Mummy this weekend and announce our engagement. . . . Does one regret all the people one never met when one quaffed the Pierian spring? Very likely, but perhaps I've matured, too.

Walk the Plank, Pussycat— You're on Camera

I'VE SAID IT BEFORE and I'll say it again—I love the editors of *Time*, the weekly news magazine, all two hundred of them, and I don't care who knows it. Given a hammock large enough to accommodate us, I'd willingly snuggle in their arms till homeward came the cows while someone in snowy flannels plunked out "Carolina Moon" on a round-bellied mandolin. Now, it's self-evident that when you love two hundred persons that deeply, you're a cinch to be disillusioned, and it was small wonder I felt heartsick recently when their choice of Man of the Year turned out to be a soldier. A soldier, indeed. Standing in the wings was one of the great pioneers of our time, a man fit to rank with Rudy Gernreich and Clarence Birdseye—a chap whose dazzling accomplishment in 1965 may eventually transform all human relations—and they gave him the mitten. I refer, of course, to television's Nick Adams.

I must confess, in all conscience, that I never heard of the *boychick* in question until I read of his achievement in the New York *Post* the day afterward. The account, in part, ran thus: "Actor Nick Adams revealed to a nationwide television audience last night that he and his wife are divorcing. His wife, Carol, in Hollywood . . . commented: 'That's Nick for you. He called me up this afternoon and told me to watch the show and please be understanding . . .' Adams, best known as television's 'The Rebel,' used the Les Crane show over ABC-TV to take full blame for the breakup of the marriage.

'I'm inconsiderate,' he said . . . 'I'm a horrible guy to live with.' . . . Sandy Sheldon, a writer on the Crane show, met with Adams yesterday at Sardi's, where Adams earlier had held a press conference to plug a new movie. . . . Sheldon recalled that Adams told him: 'Listen, I got a scoop for you. How would you like to have me announce on your show that I'm getting a divorce?' . . . 'He wanted to let his wife know as he tells America that he really does care for her and that—like it or not—he's trapped by his drive to be successful and he feels at this point he's about to make it big and can't neglect it—the price of it being his wife's good will,' Sheldon said."

Arresting and unconventional as was Adams' coup, the implications were so profound that the dentures rattled in my head. Whether he realized it or not, this gifted youth has stumbled on an entirely new potential of television—an amalgam of exhibitionism, red-hot newscasting and public purification. Marrying the confession box to the gossip column has gestated a framework for even the lowliest to bask in the spotlight and unzip his psyche, communicating to an enthralled audience sweetmeats hitherto reserved for the bedroom and the law courts. Any day now, we may expect a proliferation of programs in which married folk joyously shuck off their partners, blurt out all sorts of piquant katzenjammer, and shrive themselves of guilt. One such I envision, for example, would look something like this:

MODERATOR: Good evening, and welcome to *Run Off at the Mouth,* the only show that guarantees its participants complete immunity from their peccadilloes. Well, viewers, if any of you have lips, get ready to smack 'em, because we're in for some pretty salty revelations. Let's hear first from Mrs. Friedl Henbane, this charming lady on my right.

MRS. HENBANE: I don't know about other husbands, but mine never gave me a minute's peace. Always pawing me, hugging and kissing. So I started giving him these powders I bought at the druggist.

MODERATOR: What sort of powders?

MRS. HENBANE: Search me. Smelled like peach-pits.

MODERATOR: It wasn't arsenic, was it?

MRS. HENBANE: That's the name.

MODERATOR: Did you get any relief?

MRS. HENBANE: I hope to tell you. He keeled over flat as a flounder.

MODERATOR: You called a doctor, of course.

MRS. HENBANE: Yeah, but the line was busy. So after a while Porphyrion quit twitching, and I buried him in the basement. He would have wanted it that way.

MODERATOR: It must have been a fearful ordeal. I mean, lugging him downstairs and replacing the cement.

MRS. HENBANE: Nah, Virgil did that—the young fellow I've been cavorting with. We're planning on getting married, soon as he disposes of his girl friend.

MODERATOR: And good luck to you both. Next, Mr. Hunyadi, the gentleman across the table. Your occupation, sir?

MR. HUNYADI: I'm with the Predators' & Skinflints' National, in charge of their safe-deposit vault.

MODERATOR: I think the folks would like to hear about the new technique you've evolved.

MR. HUNYADI: Well, it's really a pipe, once you get the knack of it. A customer hands me his key so as to fetch him his box. What he don't know is that I keep a little dab of beeswax stashed in my pocket.

MODERATOR: In which you take a quick impression of the key —correct?

MR. HUNYADI: Reet. Then I make up a duplicate in my home workshop, and when things are slow, why I comb through the valuables. Like shooting fish in a barrel.

MODERATOR: I would imagine the cash is useful in playing the track, purchasing liquor and flowers, and so forth, but what about negotiable bonds?

MR. HUNYADI: I work with a fence out of town that sells the

originals and gives me copies to substitute. With rings and watches, you just slip in 10-cent-store phonies—nobody'd ever think to scan them carefully.

MODERATOR: Any reactions qualmwise from your peculations?

MR. HUNYADI: Day and night, but I'm helpless. Without I'm a big shot, life is as sounding brass and a tinkling cymbal.

MODERATOR: The Biblical reference suggests that you have a strong religious bent. Do you visualize ultimate reformation?

MR. HUNYADI: Yup, in about six months. Soon as I beat the ponies, I'm winging off to Andorra, a small country near Spain where they got no extradition proceedings.

MODERATOR: And then you'll send back whatever you glommed.

MR. HUNYADI: Let's cross that bridge when we come to it.

MODERATOR: A safe journey to you and a snug anchorage. Our next guest is Barbara Buxom, an attractive dietitian who moonlights nightly as a masked stripper at the Kamasutra Club. . . .

Now, juicy as are the possibilities of such a show, it lacks two elements—it doesn't fully satisfy the libido of the audience, its innate voyeurism, and it fails to sprinkle salt on the victim's wounds. The ideal format, clearly, is one wherein we witness the actual events motivating the divorce or whatever the electrifying disclosure. Perhaps the ensuing vignette may serve as a guide to some creative producer.

SCENE: *The kitchen in the residence of Newt Thigpen, a prosperous hardware dealer. Wanda Thigpen, a weathered matron in pink curlers faintly reminiscent of a demented chicken, is preparing dinner, oblivious of the television set brumbling in the background. An announcer materializes on the screen, features suffused with the spurious excitement requisite in such enterprises.*

ANNOUNCER: Howdy, people—all set for our weekly *Thunderclap Show?* The first recipient of stupefying news this evening, whose reactions are brought to you by the wizardry of the concealed camera, is Mrs. Wanda Thigpen, of 223 Hosea Avenue in Ecstasy Park.

WANDA (*awestruck*): Why, that's me! Oh, dear, and I'm so unkempt—I must put on some lipstick.

ANNOUNCER: No, no, Mrs. Thigpen—no furbelows, please. We want the viewers to see you precisely as Newt does—in all your inadequacy, as it were. O.K.? Then here's lovely Jinx Auerglass, your husband's sweetie, to deliver the bombshell in person.

JINX (*a blond cupcake in a black negligee that barely imprisons her charms*): Hiya, Wanda baby. Well, Newt certainly was right. You *have* let yourself go.

WANDA: It's the overhead fixture . . . I look much better by candlelight. . . .

JINX: Knock it off, honey, this is woman to woman. With a cannelloni roll around the hips and crow's-feet like yours, you get to spend a lot of time at home, don't you?

WANDA: Well—uh—Newt doesn't take me out much.

JINX: Natch. And therefore you wouldn't have spotted us the past few months, roistering around the taverns and living it up. Oh, what a ball we've had.

WANDA: Newt's a real frisky one. He makes things hum.

JINX: Yes siree, no flies on him. And let's face it, a guy like that needs a person with the physique and talent to keep him happy. Now, I'm 39-24-32, I cook like Irma Rombauer and dance like Killer Joe Piro, and I've got an IQ of 187. (*To corroborate her statement, she encircles herself with a tape-measure, confects a chocolate soufflé, executes a step or two of the Monkey, and recites a stanza of "The Eve of St. Agnes."*) Well, lambie, do I have to spell it out?

WANDA: I'd sort of like Newt to give me the heave-ho himself, for old times' sake.

JINX: I'll see if he can talk. He's pretty hung over. (*Sounds of contention off screen, and Newt, puffy-eyed and wheezing bourbon, appears shakily.*)

NEWT: Ur-r-rch. Listen, Wanda, I want the whole world

43

through the medium of Telstar to know one thing—I'm
crazy for you. Do you believe that?

WANDA: Papa, I've always known it, under the hide of me.

NEWT: Then get this through your thick head. A boat can't
sail with barnacles on its keel. I'm scraping you off.

WANDA: You mustn't blame yourself, sweetheart. You could
have been the biggest retailer in the community if I'd of
kept pace with you.

NEWT: No, I'm a louse, but I'm not going to welsh on my dear
ones. How many children have we?

WANDA: Three, I think.

NEWT: Well, Jinx and I will need the house, but why don't
you all just move in the garage? There's a room there with
running water, and you're welcome to our table scraps.

JINX: Now, don't go signing your life away, you big boob.

WANDA: Oh, don't worry, we'll make out somehow. I'd take
in washing if it meant Newt's happiness.

NEWT: You bet it does—and to show there's no hard feeling,
I'm starting you off with a free box of clothespins.

WANDA (*choking up*): Gee whillikers, it—it kind of restores
your faith in human nature. Bless you, Daddy. (*Newt,
beaming, enfolds Jinx in his arms, Wanda beats her head
against the wall, and as the audience, cleansed and up-
lifted, wriggles its toes in enjoyment, organ sting, commercial, and out.*)

Hail to the Chief, at Two-Thirds Off

On a Monday forenoon four or five years ago, a well-fleshed, convivial friend of mine, returning from an intemperate Nantucket weekend, found himself at a very low ebb in New Bedford. It was raining cats and dogs, he had a grisly hangover, and he had missed his Boston train connection, necessitating a seven-hour wait. Desperate for diversion, he recalled mention of a unique whaleship on view at the Bourne Whaling Musum and, prompted by despair rather than nautical curiosity, decided to pay it a visit. Whether he knew that the vessel was a half-sized replica didn't emerge from his subsequent chaotic account, but, once aboard her, he began to experience palpable tremors. The rigging, longboats, and deck gear seemed disproportionate—Lilliputian, in fact—and, as he squeezed down the hatchway to the officers' quarters, instinct warned him that he was compounding a disaster. The premonition was correct; as he ducked to enter the captain's cabin, his forehead collided with the lintel and he pitched forward heavily onto his knees. When his eyes returned to focus, they caught sight of a bunk barely three feet long, a tiny pillow at one end, and a bijou copy of Bowditch's *Practical Navigator* spread open on the counterpane. It was the thought of the skipper's half-sized head reclining on the half-sized pillow, asserted my friend, that undid him. With a shriek, he clawed his way up the ladder, hurdled the bulwarks

45

like a Thomson's gazelle, and sped back through the downpour to the railroad station.

The incident lay encapsulated in my memory until a while back when an advertisement in the *Times* for Wallachs, a chain of men's clothiers, broadcast further word of a shrinking universe. Announcing a window display of thirty-one small models of United States Presidents, it supplied the following apocrypha on their origin: "Back in the thirties, Paramount Pictures needed a complete cavalcade of Presidents for use in a film. They had to go to Berlin to get the models made at a reputed cost of $20,000. After the picture was finished (we haven't yet been able to discover the name of it), the models were sold to an enterprising gent who toured the country with them. . . . It is true," conceded Wallachs, scrupulously acknowledging another distinctive collection, "that they are not as big as Mme. Tussaud's figures. They're about one-third life size, which adds to their fascination." Perhaps "fascination" wasn't the most felicitous word for the copywriter to have chosen; the secondary meaning of its verb is, I discover, "to deprive of the power of resistance, as through terror." If this was indeed the effect of the wee manikins, the sidewalk outside Wallachs, dotted with petrified people, must have been a memorable sight.

It was the double-talk about that Paramount film the models were made for, though, that really brought me up short. Why, if the picture was finished, was Wallachs unable to discover its name? There was a furtive connotation in the phrase—an implication that, like Holmes' Giant Rat of Sumatra, it was a story for which the world was not yet prepared. The longer I thought about it, the less credible it became. After all, how many movies embodying cavalcades of little American Presidents had Hollywood produced? I seriously wondered if Wallachs hadn't, so to speak, confected the yarn out of whole cloth. And then, abruptly, a long-shuttered casement in my past flew open, and I was pitchforked back a quarter century to the Paramount lot—to Archibald Spontoon and his voluptuous private secretary, Helga Nethersole.

46

The dozen producers functioning at that studio in 1935 fell into two categories—"showmen" and "college-bred" executives. The showmen, Neanderthal and subhuman types who stumped around on their knuckles, turned out "meat-and-potatoes" pictures—i.e., program movies with basic themes like mother love, Navy heroics, and canine loyalty. Their literacy was minimal; they had enough schooling to comprehend trade papers and the digests prepared by the story department, but they privately considered learning effete and anyone who possessed it a sexual deviant. Three of the dozen producers excited particular suspicion among their colleagues because they held—or, more properly, flaunted—college diplomas. These peppered their speech with polysyllables, sponsored movies built around psychoanalysis and similar unwholesome subjects, and altogether gave themselves insufferable airs. It was through the most pretentious of the trio, Archibald Spontoon—possibly one of the most pretentious men in the whole world—that I first heard of the little Presidential cavalcade.

A bumptious, aggressive hop-o'-my-thumb whose expression of benevolence concealed overweening ambition and the ferocity of a stoat, Spontoon had latterly bought an original, so called, about the French fashion industry, entitled *McGillicuddy in the Haute Couture*. It concerned an Irish playboy's inheritance of a bankrupt Parisian dress house, and the plot, a dizzying goulash, embroiled the roistering hero in scrapes innumerable with his mannequins and with apaches bent on stealing his designs. By a series of ingenious twists, however, McGillicuddy (meaning Errol Flynn, of course) extricated himself from his troubles, restored the establishment's former glory, and won an American heiress. To adapt this nonesuch to the screen, Spontoon chose Gerhart Hauptmann and Jean Cocteau, cabled them princely offers, and, receiving no answer, straightaway engaged me. At our initial meeting in his executive suite, he discoursed at length on my exceptional qualifications for the job.

"The average writer in this town is a peasant—a hick," he said contemptuously. "He hasn't got the faintest concept of

47

what goes on in Europe—like, for instance, that Anatole France authored a work named *Penguin Island* or that Joseph Conrad was a Polack. His real name was Korzeniowski," he continued, tamping a mixture of Barking Dog and Imperial Cube Cut into his Dunhill. "Now, you knew that. You've travelled—you're cosmopolitan. That's the feeling I want in the script, and nothing should mitigate against it. It's got to have a smell of sophistication."

"Of worldliness," I supplied. I had been out of work for months and was anxious to make good.

"Yes, but not too cynical," he warned. "I'm sticking my neck out as it is, entrusting a valuable property to an unknown, and I'll get hell from the front office if it's just a series of Noël Coward wisecracks. Keep it down to earth—human. Maybe McGillicuddy should have a dog."

Promising him a feature that would at once tug at his heartstrings and tickle his risibilities, I repaired to the hutch allotted to me in a nearby warren, and there proceeded to give birth to a screenplay. Every fortnight or so, I was summoned to my superior's office, ostensibly to report progress but actually to receive some additional nugget of literary information he had unearthed. Was it not shameful, he demanded indignantly, that nobody in this supposedly cultured community knew that Herman Melville had finished life as a customs inspector, that the pseudonymous character known as Saki was really H. H. Munro, that T. S. Eliot once worked in a bank? I had a strong conviction that Spontoon secretly wanted these gems woven into the script, but, short of incorporating them in a recitative for McGillicuddy to chant while the mannequins paraded his gowns, I could think of no feasible way to arrange it; so, feigning renewed morale, I would thank him effusively and hasten back to tend my nursling.

One morning, I reported to Spontoon's office for my bi-weekly session and found his secretary, an auburn-haired goddess with a penchant for knitted jersey that set one's blood on fire, in a state of agitation. Miss Helga Nethersole (or Ginger, as she allowed me to call her) was leafing frantically through the Los Angeles *Examiner*. Beside her desk, on a bamboo easel, was a map of Abyssinia speckled with colored pins denoting the relative positions of the Italian invasion forces and Haile Selassie's troops. Sensing a dilemma, I asked if I could be of service.

"Oh, would you? Could you?" Ginger begged, tears of gratitude dimming eyes as wide-set and melting as a Jersey's. "I'm supposed to change the pins every morning so Mr. Spontoon can tell at a glance how the war is going, but I can't follow these creepy names—and he's due any second—"

I soothed the poor distraught child, and in jig time reconciled the battle lines with the latest dispatches—a not inconsiderable task, by the way, as the latter were confused with details of the Santa Ana baby parade. Before I could nerve myself to exact a kiss as payment, Spontoon bustled in, a portentous frown in the area where electrolysis had given him a forehead. He scrutinized the map closely. "Hmm, so they've tried a flanking movement around Aduwa," he muttered, echoes of the great von Clausewitz in his voice. "I would have expected a pincers thrust toward Gharama. Ah, well," he said, forcing himself back to mundane affairs, "*revenons à nos moutons*—let us return to our muttons. Any calls?"

"Mr. Paltry arrived," said Ginger. "He's at the Beverly Wilshire."

"My breeches-maker, from London," Spontoon confided. "The only guy in Europe that knows how to design a decent pair of jodhpurs—he's pacted to me on a loanout from Darryl Zanuck. Anybody else?"

"Yes, Max Zukunft, in the transportation department," she replied. "He needs at least two trucks to carry the models."

"Models?" her boss repeated abstractedly.

"The cavalcade of little Presidents they're moving to your house," Ginger explained. "He said they counted thirty-one figures in all—"

"God damn it!" Spontoon bellowed in a sudden inexplicable access of fury. "Didn't I tell you to keep your bazoo shut?"

Ginger crimsoned with guilt. "I—I'm sorry, sir, I forgot," she stammered. A look of such utter penitence overspread her classic features that I longed to clasp her in my arms and comfort her.

"I'll deal with you later," Spontoon growled, and motioned into his chamber. It was one of those dramatic moments my training as a scenarist had taught me to recognize—a choice between love and duty. Here was the woman I adored, every line of her exquisite, rippling form in its knitted jersey sheath cowering in humiliation before a tyrannical brute. Ought I to knock him senseless with a single blow and sacrifice my future, as would fiery-tempered George Brent, Nelson Eddy, or Warren William, or was it my duty, rather, to contain my rage and, combining business with pleasure, to woo the lady and elicit Spontoon's secret from her? Swifter than a falcon plummeting to the kill, I made my decision and followed him into his sanctum.

Six nights later, in a secluded booth in one of the Southland's most exclusive eateries, Ziegler's Steak Grotto, Ginger and I dallied over our pousse-cafés, breathing those intimacies that only hearts attuned to each other understand. For the past week, I had deluged her with flowers, candy, and inexpensive jewelry, used every resource of a well-lined purse and a passionate nature to convince her of my devotion. We had dined and danced endlessly, attended the preems of several hi-budget flicks, taken long hikes through the canyons, even journeyed to Santa Monica to watch the annual spawning of the grunion by moonlight. On closer acquaintanceship, I sorrowfully had to admit, Ginger fell short of my ideal; despite her figure, which was just as inflammatory in voile, chiffon, organdie, peau de soie, and black taffeta, she had a fundamentally shallow nature, an instinct for triviality that forbade the communication of serious abstract ideas. At this instant, for example, she was expatiating in wordy fashion on the virtues of the charge-account system.

"I never realized you were such a mule," she chided me petulantly. "Suppose a person wanted a smart cocktail jacket for these cool evenings, like, or a fur chubby. They could step into I. Magnin's or Bullock's, and—presto—"

"Yes, yes," I interposed. "Look, sweet, there's something I've got to know if we're to go on together—something I'd never dare ask if we were just two strangers meeting over a sirloin." Panic, swift and unreasoning, seized her as I revived the episode of the little Presidential models. "What did it mean?" I demanded. "Where did they come from, and how did they concern Spontoon?"

"Oh, lover, don't," she whimpered. "Ask me anything, but not that. He—he'd kill me!"

Painful as it was to withstand the entreaty of those delectable coral lips, that tumultuous bosom, I nonetheless remained inexorable and managed in the end to extract the story. It was a bizarre yet strangely touching tale, a record of human fatuity at its most arrogant. Until two months before, the head of the studio had been a micromorph named Ignatius Brogan, a man hardly five feet tall. Sensitive to the point of neurosis about his height, Brogan had secretly imported the cavalcade of Presidents from Germany to bolster his ego. It was housed in an alcove adjoining his office—a species of safety valve for Brogan's frustrations. Whenever the pressures of existence threatened to swamp him, he retired into the *musée* and lorded it over the models. "Think you're big shots, do you?" his secretaries used to hear him cackle. "Well, get this straight—I'm twice as big as you are, and I got ten times the brains!" When, unhinged by his *folie de grandeur*, Brogan was deposed and removed to a tiny bin, Spontoon snapped up the collection at a tithe of its value.

"And now he's driving his wife dippy," concluded Ginger tremulously. "He stays up every night arguing with Lincoln and Grant. He says he could have won the Civil War in two years."

Well, so much for the window display at a certain New York clothing store. As for Ginger, she began exhibiting symptoms of a disorder quite as dire as Spontoon's—*folie de mariage,* characterized by a scenting of nonexistent orange blossoms—

and had to be forcibly disillusioned. I never see a knitted jersey dress but that I dream— What? *McGillicuddy in the Haute Couture?* Oh, sure, it was made, all right, but in a somewhat different version from mine. In theirs, this swashbuckling young Navy hero who's devoted to his mother, played by Alan Ladd (the hero, that is), inherits an obedience school for dogs.

Caution—Beware of
Excess Prophets

Wе converged in the middle of the East Fifty-seventh Street sidewalk, a disturbingly lovely lady inside a magnificent broadtail coat and I unfortunately on the outside, and the mazurka we executed trying to pass each other would certainly have convulsed bystanders had there been any. As we seesawed left and right, colliding and muttering apologies, my nostrils were ravished by the delicious scent she exuded; in the momentary glimpse afforded me of her ivory pallor, I beheld wide-set sloe eyes (the legacy of some remote Tartar forebear?), accented by a mouche. An instant later, she was gone and I was staring down at the card she had pressed into my palm. It read, "Madame Myosotis, Spiritual Reader and Adviser. Speaks several different languages. Will help you on problems such as love, marriage, business. She will bring you happiness. One visit will convince you. All readings private. Satisfaction guaranteed. If you are troubled in any way, don't fail to come and see her now." The sibyl's address was close by, hardly a stone's throw off Park Avenue, and yet it might just as well have been in Tananarive or Valparaiso for all I cared. Whatever thirst I had for divination was effectively slaked years ago, thank you. Soothsayers, stay away from my door.

Stripped of excessive detail, the particulars were these: In mid-February of 1963, I was tarrying briefly in Nairobi, about to consummate a long cherished dream of visiting Seychelles, the Indian Ocean archipelago a thousand miles east of Mombasa. So beautiful was Seychelles, reputedly, that many authorities located it as the original Garden of Eden. It was also said to be the last stronghold of British colonialism, full of Edwardian eccentrics and remittance men—a paradise, in short, calculated to pique anyone's scholarly interest. Owing to its rugged terrain, there was unfortunately no air service, and accommodations aboard the monthly steamer out of Mombasa, crammed with Indian refugees from Angola, were at a premium. Through the intercession of a government official, however, whom I convinced that I was a potential spark in the Kenyan powder keg, I ultimately procured a one-way passage. But this essential was merely a prelude to the mechanics of embarkation that had to be arranged in Nairobi—the visas, the bedding one needed for the overnight train journey to the coast, the meal vouchers, the myriad clearances, declarations, and affidavits mandatory for admission to the Garden of Eden. Then, just as my preparations were complete, a shattering cable arrived from Toby Swingler in New York.

Toby was much more than a theatrical agent; he was guide, philosopher, and friend—an ebullient, warmhearted chap who was shepherding a play that had bubbled out of my inkwell the previous autumn and was currently visible on Broadway. Nearly a month had elapsed since Toby's last bulletin, but that had radiated such optimism, with its talk of road companies, movie sales, and the like, that it never occurred to me anything was amiss. Today's tidings, though, were unequivocal: PRO-DUCER DEFENESTRATED SELF INTO 45TH STREET LAST NIGHT. CAST EXHIBITING WONDERFUL PLUCK NONETHELESS. SOME PERFORMERS HOARSE BECAUSE OBLIGED TO PROJECT TO HANDFUL OF PATRONS IN BALCONY BUT MORALE UNIMPAIRED. EARNESTLY ADVISE YOU LENGTHEN VISIT SEYCHELLES AS UNDERSTAND BREADFRUIT PLENTE-OUS AND AGGRAVATIONS MINIMAL.

Once the significance of Toby's message sank home, it abruptly dawned on me that I was in a devil of a quandary. If the show was about to expire, as appeared likely, it would be callous to sequester myself on an atoll in the Indian Ocean. On the other hand, would it actually benefit anybody if I jettisoned the Seychelles trip and hurried back to attend the obsequies? Lacking any intimate in Nairobi to counsel me, I decided on an expedient I had never resorted to before; namely, astrology. A gentleman named Mohandas Ghanef—a renowned stargazer, according to his advertisement in the East African *Standard*—invited the perplexed to consult him. I rang up forthwith, and was greeted by the sage himself in a loud, jovial voice. He seemed agreeably devoid of humbug, and, having ascertained my birth date, he arranged to receive me within the hour at his chambers in Vasco da Gama Road.

The quarter where Mr. Ghanef practiced was largely given over to bicycle-repair stores, Indian groceries, and shops displaying an impressive array of aphrodisiacs. His inglenook, two flights up a dark and clangorous stairway, consisted of a bedroom, half of whose floor space had been preëmpted for a reception area. Seated cross-legged on the floor was a portly gentleman with a liquid eye, studying a pattern of chicken bones strewn over a towel.

"Good morning, good day!" he shouted, springing up with the grace of an antelope. "Mohandas Ghanef here! You are the Aquarian who phoned me just now?"

I nodded, and he conducted me into his boudoir past a gray enamelled gas stove on which were ranged a dozen works of the late Elbert Hubbard in limp leather, surmounted by a human skull. Bidding me sit on the edge of the bed, he drew up a chair opposite, jotted several columns of figures on a clipboard, and, after a close scrutiny, emitted a grunt of satisfaction. "Capital, my dear sir!" he said. "I perceive that I am dealing with a most remarkable individual. A man of deep wisdom, one who has been tempered in life's crucible. As his system is alkaline, he tends to be ascetic in his relations with women, in which respect he resembles William Ewart Gladstone. Above all, a man of fantastic generosity. Am I correct?"

I acknowledged that my largesse was often princely, and he continued on a note of admonition. "Your chief trouble is that you are too mushy, too softhearted. Be on the alert for

55

sharpers, persons with oily tongues seeking to fleece you. Also guard against rheumatism and fried foods."

I promised to be vigilant, and inquired what course the planets dictated in my present dilemma—ought I press on to Seychelles or return to New York?

Mr. Ghanef became wildly animated at the disclosure that I was a playwright. That was his avocation, he exclaimed; in fact, he had just completed two acts of a comedy he would be delighted to read to me—a rattling good love story that poked fun at various human foibles. Unluckily, I was too distraught to hold still for a Hindu version of *Springtime for Henry*, and was forced to decline. Mr. Ghanef accepted my refusal with a fatalistic shrug. Perhaps it might clarify the decision, he suggested, if I chanced to have a handwriting specimen from someone connected with my play. It happened that I did—a grisly picture postcard Toby Swingler had sent me in Paris of Doris Day costumed as a *torero*, with a rose in her teeth.

A frown corrugated the seer's forehead as he studied Toby's inscription. "Whoever wrote this is a trickster, a double-dealer," he declared flatly. "With every hour that passes, he betrays you anew. Chastise him, smite him hip and thigh, cast him into the sea with a rock attached to his feet."

A suspicion began to take form in my mind that Mr. Ghanef's pipeline to the infinite was clogged, and, tendering him his fee of forty-three East African shillings, or roughly six dollars, I cleared off. That evening, over a sundowner at the New Stanley with some British residents of the colony, I recounted my experience. To a man, they chided me for having impulsively sought out a mountebank. The ranking astrologer south of the Sahara, the foremost wizard in the protectorate, was Ibn Momzeyrim, an oracle whose prescience was so uncanny that persons from every walk of society, even government Ministers, flocked to consult him. Several Greek and Syrian millionaires, uncommonly flinty types, had been known to risk fortunes on the basis of his predictions, and no prospective bride would dare approach the altar without his prenuptial horoscope.

With such a clear mandate, hesitation was unthinkable, and the next morning found me nervously awaiting my turn in Ibn Momzeyrim's outer office at Vedic House. The atmosphere was humdrum, totally devoid of any suggestion of the sorcerer's cave; the matronly *Hausfrau* in printed cotton, her scrawny husband, and the two giggling schoolgirls were straight out of any dentist's anteroom in the States. In due course, all of them were processed, and a high-pitched, impatient voice inside bade me enter.

Mr. Momzeyrim, a plump, button-eyed Pakistani, was seated behind a modernique kitchen table with a Formica surface, in an ambience where every visible object was synthetic. He wore a pair of outsize spectacles with fake tortoiseshell rims and was garbed in a suit of some Dacron-like material, from the breast pocket of which three ball-point pens protruded. A blue plastic vase containing a red plastic tulip stood at his elbow, and he was bawling into a Bakelite phone. "No, no, I absolutely forbid you!" he was shouting. "Hold on to those securities till Mercury replaces Saturn—do you hear? Otherwise you court bankruptcy, ruin, starvation!" He slammed down the receiver and pointed at me. "What time is it?"

"Why—er—ten past eleven," I said, glancing at my watch.

"Wrong," he returned triumphantly. "Only eight past, and those two minutes make all the difference in a horoscope. Everything in your past, present, and future is governed by time, my friend. Give me the exact hour and date you were born."

In the next quarter of an hour, I learned a number of things about myself I had never suspected. I had a strongly sensual nature and tended to throw my cap over the windmill at the sight of a pretty ankle. The second of my wives—I appeared to have been married three times—had deceived me repeatedly with a rake on the order of Blazes Boylan, sporting a black beard. The four coming years, it seemed, promised to be the most fruitful in my life. I was slated to amass wealth beyond the dreams of avarice—provided, of course, I kept a tight rein on my satyriasis and stuck to my knitting. Throughout the session, at intervals of thirty seconds, phone calls poured in from a wide spectrum of folk—horseplayers, seafarers contemplating voyages, the lovesick of both sexes, and merchants convinced that their partners were mulcting them. To all of them Momzeyrim snapped out advice without an instant's hesitation, but when I broached my own immediate problem, he countered with the windiest of generalities. A dark Sagittarian—not unlike Toby Swingler, from his description—was exerting a malign influence over my future. Notwithstanding, I must pretend to accede to his wishes until Jupiter was in the ascendant, when I should be amply revenged. In view of the urgent circumstances, I implored Momzeyrim to give me more specific guidance.

"That's what everyone wants," he said peevishly. "What business are you in?"

I decided that if he was as clairvoyant as represented, it was up to him to find out. "Well-l-l." I hesitated. "It's kind of related to the theatre."

"Yes, yes," he said, closing his eyes in concentration. "I see row on row of chairs full of people clapping. Oh, yes indeed, we have a dandy success here—cornucopias full of money, steam yachts, female caresses galore. But wait a moment—what is this? All is changed. The people have disappeared—only the chairs are left. Yes, and some scenery being lifted into lorries. . . . What is this legend I read? It says 'Cain's Warehouse.' . . ."

He was bent on describing a few other things he saw, but I cut short his balderdash. I had suddenly had a bellyful of their auguries—of Mohandas Ghanef and Ibn Momzeyrim and the whole blasted lot. After all, why should I hire Indian fakirs to dream up disasters for me when I was perfectly capable of doing it myself? I knew now where my duty lay—not on an island paradise eating lotus but patrolling Times Square, where I could keep an eye on chisellers named Toby Swingler who betrayed a man the moment he turned his back. I nipped around the corner to the shipping office, traded my Indian

Ocean ticket for one to New York, and left on the wings of the morning.

Dreaming when dawn's left hand is in the sky, I sometimes wonder whether I'll ever get to visit Seychelles. Maybe I ought to look up a really reliable fortune-teller—someone like Madame Myosotis, say—and see what the future holds.

Tell Me Clear,
Parachutist Dear,
Are You Man or Mouse?

"WEE, sleekit, cow-rin', tim'rous beastie," sang Robert Burns, dipping his pen into triple-distilled schmaltz to apostrophize a mouse, "O what a panic's in thy breastie!" That the little creatures are capable of inducing similar and immoderate panic in someone else's breastie is, of course, a commonplace, but until quite recently nobody seems to have had the imagination to use them as deliberate instruments of terror. The first inkling I had of their conversion was in a dispatch to the *Times* from Britain about a year ago. "Rita Houlton, a clerk, was alone in a small shop in the London suburbs," it said. "Two young men entered, one carrying a paper bag. Without a word, the youth placed the bag on the counter and opened it. Out scampered four white mice. Out of the store scampered Rita, in shrieking flight from the mice. The youths then stepped out a side door, got into the shop's delivery truck, and drove away." Soon afterward, another blitz involving rodents, this time political, occurred in the Iberian peninsula. During a concert in Madrid by a group of singers and dancers from Havana, according to the *Times* of London, a group of Cuban exiles created an uproar by shouting abuse at the performers, hurling stink bombs, and showering the audience with leaflets. "The release in the stalls of mice—and some claim there were a few rats," the correspondent noted with relish, "added to the confusion as women screamed and shrieked." It took an equally volatile but more enterprising race, the Italians, however, to perfect the weapon. *This Week in Rome,* a bulletin of convenient information for tourists, reported that Luigi Squarzina, author of a play called *Romagnola,* had filed suit against a clutch of Neo-Fascist hoodlums for attempting to sabotage its première. Two other disturbances from the same source made news, continued the item, "one particularly on account of the fact that mice were let down on parachutes from the balcony into the stalls."

The selection of mice staunch enough to become paratroopers, their indoctrination, and the Commando training requisite for such warfare are too complex for anyone less than Hanson W. Baldwin to explicate. Nevertheless, one aspect of the subject cries out—all right, whimpers—for clarification. The artisan who confects these minuscule parachutes—what manner of chap is he? What specialized problems and stresses confront him? Rather than indulge in windy hypotheses, let's slip into something brief and gossamer-sheer, like a playlet, and see if we can't gain an insight into his temperament and associates. Settle down, please—curtain's up.

SCENE: *A workroom in a fifth-floor tenement in the Trastevere quarter of Rome. In the weak light filtering through the windows at rear, nearly opaque with dust and accumulated spiderwebs, two small figures are dimly visible, seated cross-legged on a bench. They are apparently occupied in some form of invisible weaving, for each squints through a magnifying lens as he plies a needle, threaded with filaments imperceptible to the naked eye, through minute scallops of nylon. Baldassare Volante, the elder of the pair and boss of the firm, is a wizened Tom Thumb who, poised on tiptoe, would measure a scant forty-eight inches. Scarcely a head taller is Beppo, his apprentice, a robust cockerel in his twenties with unruly blond curls and a dimple sufficiently like Kirk Douglas's to flutter any feminine heart.*

VOLANTE (*tossing a finished parachute onto a pile*): Basta!
There—that's thirty-five, and with your fifteen, the Twen-
tieth Century-Fox order is complete. Yes siree, Beppo—a
few more commissions from minority stockholders bent on
disrupting their annual meeting and we'll be on Via
Agiata (Easy Street).

BEPPO: With respect to that, Signor Volante, and with all due
respect to yourself, may I respectfully speak what is in my
heart?

VOLANTE: Respect, respect—take the polenta out of your
mouth! What are you trying to say, man?

BEPPO: Just that my conscience impels me to warn you,
padrone. Our business is in mortal peril.

VOLANTE (*agitatedly*): You've overheard some rumors . . .
some gossip . . .

BEPPO: No, no—

VOLANTE (*seizing him by the throat*): Somebody's betrayed us
to the police, to the Ministry of Sanitation! Who was it?
Spit it out, you dog!

BEPPO: Sir, I entreat you on my sainted mother's virtue—
your fears are groundless—

VOLANTE: It's Serafina, that old hag of a *portiera* downstairs.
She offered me her body eighteen years ago, and I recoiled in contempt. Now she's brought an information
against me.

BEPPO: But you forget, *commendatore*—there's nothing illegal
about our product. We furnish little parachutes to anyone
who needs them.

VOLANTE: Why, that's right, come to think of it. We're a
service organization, aren't we?

BEPPO: Nothing more. And are we responsible if they're used
to create disorder? When some elderly virgin, unhinged
by jealousy, hurls a phial of acid at a voluptuous nude by
Titian, is the apothecary who sold it to blame?

VOLANTE: Of course not. A brilliant analogy, Beppo. I never
realized you had a poetic gift.

BEPPO: Coming from one in whose veins there flows the blood of Dante Alighieri, that is praise indeed, *eminenza*. I thank you humbly.

VOLANTE: Yes, you'll go far in this business, my boy. But tell me—what, then, is the danger you speak of?

BEPPO: Overspecialization, sir. We must branch out, I beseech you. In the hurly-burly of modern combat (*nel chiasso del combattimento moderno*), the airborne warrior requires a modicum of equipment to survive, be he man or quadruped.

VOLANTE: Now, don't start that stuff again. We're not tooled up to produce little jump suits and shockproof watches.

BEPPO (*pleading*): But a pair of boots at the very least, sir, if only for the psychological effect. It vitiates all the menace to drop from the sky with four naked feet.

VOLANTE: (*shortly*): If naked feet were good enough for Icarus, they're good enough for a mouse. Let's have no more schmoos.

BEPPO: I defer to your vastly superior judgment, Excellency. I spoke as youth is wont to, in a freshet of impetuosity.

VOLANTE: I sensed that, *figliuolo*. In any case, I have other matters to occupy me. This is a red-letter day, Beppo. As all the world knows, my beautiful daughter Ippolita, who has just graduated from Perugia U., is due home momentarily, and I must hie me on down to the *drogheria* to buy some cakes and wine for a celebration.

BEPPO: Maestro, I shall defend the premises with my very life till you return.

VOLANTE: Never mind the rodomontade—just keep your paws out of the cash drawer. (*He exits.*)

BEPPO (*chuckling*): *Che riso sardonico!* Little does the old pantaloon suspect that Ippolita and I have been secretly affianced for months, that we daily exchange burning epistles, and that I would enclasp her hair in a snood of stars, so enslaved am I by her charms. (*He stiffens at the sound of a soft, repeated knock on the window at rear. As he hastens to it and raises the sash, Ippolita, a toothsome*

*blend of Claudia Cardinale and Anouk Aimée, whose eyes
bespeak intelligence on a par with Amy Lowell's, is disclosed on the fire escape, suitcase and diploma in hand.*)
Ippolita *carissima!* What are you doing there?

IPPOLITA: This is no time for chin music (*stridore di denti*). Lift
me down. (*Beppo complies—not without visible effort,
since she towers above him.*) Listen, I must have a word
with you before my father comes back. A serious crisis is
imminent.

BEPPO: What's wrong?

IPPOLITA: Have you ever heard of a publishing firm in America named Barber & Farber? Concentrate—rack your
brain.

BEPPO: Let me think. I seem to recall . . . why, of course—
that big package there on the shelf! I was just shipping
them a consignment by air express.

IPPOLITA: Of two hundred chutes. Am I correct?

BEPPO: (*bewildered*): Yes, but how on earth did you know?

IPPOLITA: Because Barbara Sparber, my roommate at Perugia,
is the daughter of Marboro Sparber, the distinguished
New York publisher who is their deadliest rival. Do you
follow?

BEPPO: I . . . I think so.

IPPOLITA: Good. Well, late last night, Marboro Sparber tele-
phoned Barbara that his firm's best-selling novel, *Scar-
borough Harbor*, by Sahbra Garber, was a certainty to
win the National Book Award next week. . . . Why do
you look so puzzled?

BEPPO (*faintly*): Er— Nothing, nothing. Go on.

IPPOLITA: Now, attend me closely, for here comes the wienie.
Marboro Sparber has been tipped off that a moment
before the award is announced in the grand ballroom of
the Hotel Astor, hirelings of Barber & Farber are going to
strafe the assemblage from the mezzanine. At a given
signal, the lights will be extinguished, and two hundred
mice, dipped in phosphorus to glow in the dark, will
flutter down on the guests, ninety per cent of whom are

female. The veriest donkey could divine the consequences.

BEPPO: (*duly divining them*): It will be a catastrophe—*un panico universale!*

IPPOLITA: That's for sure. The resultant melee will discredit the National Book Award, make my Barbara's father a laughing stock in Publishers' Row, and wash up her engagement to Tabori Czabo, a Hungarian boy at Harvard she's mad about. Beppo, this rotten stratagem must be thwarted at all costs.

BEPPO: Shucks, honey, what can *I* do? I'm only an obscure apprentice—

IPPOLITA: Simpleton. Idiot boy. Don't you see? You and you alone have the power to knock the whole scheme into a cocked hat.

BEPPO: (*cunningly*): You mean, by not sending the chutes to Barber & Farber?

IPPOLITA: Nothing of the sort, stupid. Ship them, by all means —but first, prick each and everyone with a needle so they'll collapse in midair!

BEPPO: But how does that help matters? The mice would plummet down with even greater force on the target.

IPPOLITA (*carelessly*): Oh, once the element of showmanship is removed, the audience, already narcotized by the speeches, will hardly notice. Well, how's about it?

BEPPO: Ippolita—do you realize what you're saying? You're asking me to sacrifice your father's reputation. He's built up a clientele by years of hard work—

IPPOLITA: *Ach*, can the sentimental slop. I'm offering you a choice.

BEPPO: I . . . I don't understand.

IPPOLITA: Between love and duty, you clod. Either do as I ask or it's all over between us—*capisci?*

BEPPO (*with a nobility Sydney Carton would have envied*): Very well, then. Bastinado my feet, reduce me to mincemeat, boil me in Vesuvius—I shall never betray Baldassare Volante. Goodbye.

VOLANTE (*flinging open the door*): Bravo! What did I tell you, Ippolita!

IPPOLITA: Beppo, *angelo mio*—come into my arms! (*She stoops, sweeps him up in an embrace.*) Oh, darling, how happy you've made me!

BEPPO (*flummoxed*): Is this all a dream? Am I in Paradise? What's happened?

VOLANTE: Merely that you've passed our test with flying colors. I wanted to be sure of my future son-in-law.

BEPPO: Then—the whole thing about the publishers was a confection?

IPPOLITA: Totally. Papa and I made it up between us, every bit.

BEPPO: But I *know* the Hotel Astor exists. I once smoked a cigar by that name.

IPPOLITA: A coincidence. I can assure you that there's no such thing as the National Book Award—and even if there were, a few mice here and there wouldn't make a scrap of difference.

BEPPO (*emotionally*): Signor Volante, I'd like you to know one thing. You haven't lost a daughter, you've gained a son.

VOLANTE: I withdraw what I said earlier about your poetic gift. (*Resignedly.*) *Allora,* take her, my boy, and one of these days, no doubt, there'll be another little warrior descending from Heaven—but this time a biped with no strings attached. (*Maidenly blushes from Ippolita and suitably hymeneal music.*)

CURTAIN

Sex and the Single Boy

Let's see now—exactly what do we know about Phil? He's twenty-five years old, he's an investment broker, and he went to Yale. We know he likes girls, because, by his own candid admission, he's got a little black book carefully dividing them into four categories—"pretty," "great to go to bed with," "nice to take to parties," and "nice to talk to." Any chap with that many categories, it follows, must be darned attractive, and Phil doesn't bother to deny it: "I average a couple or three calls a night from girls. . . . They're all the same old girls. But they call. Sure, they'll come over and cook your dinner, and sure, they'll stay all night, and sure, they'll move in if you want." Yes, indeed, he's quite a tiger, is Phil, as he emerges from that tape recording. Ah, but I'm getting ahead of myself. You haven't a glimmer as to what tape I mean, or how it evolved—right? Permit me to sketch in the background.

Well, sir, it all originated in some fertile editorial brain over at *Mademoiselle*, which was celebrating its thirtieth anniversary with a number roguishly designated "Man Talk Issue." The notion, in brief, was that five young men-about-New York should freely discuss the strategy and techniques they use to artfully entangle unattached women. In the resulting twenty-one-column symposium, "How Do Bachelors Get Away with It?," the quintet of participants, shepherded by a moderator, included Spencer, an advertising man; Tom, an airline employee; Max, a magazine editor; Larry, a municipal-bond trader; and the aforesaid Phil, the fiddler with feminine virtue. On the face of it, the juxtaposition of such divergent stags might be expected to produce at least several novel methods of conquest. What actually eventuated, however, was a vast quantity of flatulent chin music, studded with words like "communication," "relationship," and "chemistry." Spencer, for example, advanced a master plan of enticement based on three dates with his quarry, as follows: "The first evening you have quite a good dinner somewhere, where the opportunity essentially exists to talk a great deal and get to know the person. . . . The second date is usually a very offbeat sort of thing. It may be a hamburger or a Forty-second Street movie. . . . The third date is: I cook dinner in my apartment. . . . I happen to be a very good cook." This culinary approach, presumably, creates such ardor that on the fourth date the two reach fulfillment in *her* pad, sleeves rolled up and exchanging recipes like mad.

Phil's reaction to so premeditated a campaign, it appeared, was contemptuous in the extreme. "My life is such that I take it as it comes," he said, doubtless fingering a hairline mustache in the manner of the late Lew Cody. To illustrate, he evidenced the case of a recent amour that flowered from a haphazard encounter with a lady whose party he chanced to attend: "She was a very honest and shy little girl, so the next week I called her up for a date. It was a week night. I wanted to have a football pumped up. [A not unreasonable yearning in one recently graduated from Yale.] I had a friend who had a football pump, and we went over and pumped up the football and then went out and had a drink." Whether Phil's *petite amie* was subsequently classified under his "great to go to bed with" heading he was too gallant to divulge. Perhaps he had a secret fifth category—"nice to pump up a football with."

While *Mademoiselle's conversazione*, by and large, added nothing of significance to the technique of seduction, it did produce one blockbuster—a generalization about womankind that struck me as revolutionary. It was expounded by Phil, never a man to mince words: "I find that they hop into bed with you a lot faster if they really think you are interested in them as human beings, even if you are not. . . . Unless you really try to be nice to them and treat them as human beings, you won't get anywhere."

The magnitude of Phil's discovery, the sheer audacity of his postulate that women belong to the same species men do and must perforce be regarded as hominoids, transfixed me in my chair. I daresay that although the transcript gives no hint of it, there was an instant of stunned silence among his confreres. The question that immediately springs to mind, of course, is how Phil came to arrive at this conclusion. Was it the end product of painful trial and error or a sudden blinding revelation? I suggest that we might possibly derive some clue from portions of what I imagine to be his diary. It's worth a few moments' study.

FEBRUARY 25

Another rough day at the office. The minute I walked in this morning and the new girl at the switchboard saw me, I knew I was in for trouble. Her first response, I could tell, was one of incredulity—I mean, she'd probably seen fellows like Robert Goulet or Marcello Mastroianni on the screen, but to have their actual flesh-and-blood counterpart materialize before her was to her magical. I stood there, cool and amused, while she fought to regain control, and then asked her if she had any messages for me.

"Oh, golly," she said faintly. "Your voice is just what I expected it to be—sort of husky yet caressing. What are you doing for lunch?"

"Easy does it, sister," I said, stopping her. "Take your place in line. I'll let you know when there's a vacancy."

"I'm available day or night, on very short notice," she said. "My, I wish somebody'd pinch me to see if I'm dreaming. Would you mind?"

I was strongly tempted, but my life is complicated enough already, God knows. "Sorry, little one, you're not my type," I said. "Now, then, who phoned?"

"A party named Vivian Reifsnyder," she said. "She wants to come over this evening and cook your dinner. Oh, yes, and another—a Miss Foltis, or Poultice. She offered to stay all night."

I told her not to put through any further social calls today, no matter how urgent, and went along to my desk. Less than an hour later, she buzzed me.

"Phil, darling?" she said. "This is Sondra, on the switchboard. I hope you don't mind my calling you that."

"You're a pretty fast worker, I'd say."

"Pappy, I've only started," she said. "Look, I've been thinking—you're a Yale man, and you must have a lot of dusty pennants at your flat that need washing. I have a friend who's got a washing machine. Why don't we take them around there tonight, and afterwards go out for some drinks?"

Well, if I do say so myself, I'm a fairly sophisticated guy, and plenty of girls have tried to pull the wool over my eyes, but this was such an unusual pitch that I nearly fell for it. I sat there trying to figure out what the catch was, and all of a sudden it dawned on me. I didn't have any pennants in my flat; therefore, how could they be dusty? The whole thing was a ruse Sondra had dreamed up, a pretext to get me sufficiently stoned to be easy prey for her wiles. Rather than humiliate the kid by accusing her, though, I played it cagey. I advised her to quit acting ape and said she was a no-good little tramp who didn't fit into any of my categories. That slowed her up, by jingo. She gave a strange little whimper like an animal, except that it sounded—well, almost human, though, of course, that couldn't be. I guess I've been working too hard.

MARCH 1

I wonder if people ever stop to think what a drag it is to be criminally handsome, to have every damned salesgirl and waitress and receptionist slavering over you, trying to date you up and get your phone number. It really drives me up the wall to hear those females whinnying and whistling when I walk down a subway platform. And they're even worse on a bus, where they swarm around you like flies, mooning over your profile and ignoring the driver's pleas to move to the rear. I often ask myself, Are these birdbrains members of my own species?

Take this Sondra effect, for instance. I thought I'd squelched her for good that first go-around, but after a day or two she was on the make again—not openly but in a sneaky, underhanded fashion I didn't dig right off. One afternoon, on returning from lunch, I found her crying her heart out at the switchboard. She had a hankie crumpled against her lips and she looked so woebegone that, against my better judgment, I asked what was wrong. Boiled down to essentials, her problem was that the Miss Subways contest, in which she was a finalist, required a set of her measurements, and, living alone as she did, she didn't have anyone to help her take them accurately. The poor creature was desperate, I could see; she had all the necessary equipment—the tape measure, the pad and pencil— and yet, without somebody to assist her, she was likely to be disqualified. Suddenly, as we were mulling over her predicament, an inspiration seized her.

"Why didn't I think of it before?" she burst out. "Oh, Phil, couldn't *you* do it—just as a favor to me? I realize you hate me . . ."

"I don't hate you," I corrected her. "You merely don't exist, as far as I'm concerned."

"I know," she said humbly, "but the contest means so much to me. *Please.* I'll never ask another thing of you." She unclasped her pocketbook and plucked out the tape measure. "Now, wind it here."

I was complying with her instructions when, without any warning, she wriggled around with the agility of an eel and, gluing her mouth to mine, imprisoned me in a kiss. It took all my strength to uncoil her arms from my neck and thrust her away. I guess the shock of my rejection and her disappointment were more than she could stand, because she keeled over in a dead faint. Now, fundamentally, I'm a decent guy; the sight of anybody in distress bothers me, and I'll go out of my way not to step on a worm if I can avoid it. I thought of getting someone to throw a pail of water over Sondra or chafe her wrists, but the truth was she didn't deserve it. After all, she'd put me in a hell of a spot, deliberately tying up the switchboard to block any incoming calls from girls who wanted to cook my dinner and spend the night. So I just let her lie there and work it out as best she could. It's a funny thing, though—my Puritan conscience, or whatever they instill in you at Yale, kept gnawing away at me the rest of the day. Maybe my whole scale of values was gaga and this kook was a real person—not altogether human but struggling to be. . . . No, it was too fantastic. I wish I knew more about biology.

MARCH 3

Well, I suppose I had it coming to me and I should have been prepared. I notice that every time I'm riding high and start to congratulate myself Fate throws me a curve. And boy, what a lulu this one was! I've lost my little black book. Why a tiny mishap like that should throw me is beyond my ken, but the minute I discovered it was gone I got panicky. Not that I needed the twenty or thirty phone numbers of those various dolls; I was fairly confident they'd check in soon enough, for the simple reason that they couldn't get along without me. My headache was how the devil to remember their categories— which I just talked to, which I allowed to shack up with me, etc. A fine investment banker I must be, investing years of effort in tabulating those chicks and ending up with a bunch of ninepins nobody could tell apart.

Then a very odd thing happened. My entire stable began phoning me, all right, but the calls were short and each had the same refrain—"Goodbye forever." You never heard such fury. "So I'm pretty, but not the kind you take to a party, eh?" they hollered. "O.K. to climb into the sack with, but not to talk to—is that the idea?" One after the other, they crucified me, ordered me to get lost, or, still better, drop dead. I could almost swear they knew how I'd rated them in my book. It was uncanny.

Anyhow, for the time being, my life's much less strenuous. Now I can relax at home and watch TV without some silly dame tousling my hair or messing around in the kitchenette. I get sort of restless once in a while, and I walk up and down the room a lot, but that'll wear off. I may even get a cat or a dog for companionship.

MARCH 5

There comes a point when a man has to face up to himself, and thank God I'm big enough to admit it—I was wrong. Sondra is a human being, just like me. Perhaps her brain isn't as well developed as mine. Perhaps it never can be. Nevertheless, in the light of what happened last night, my whole concept of her has undergone a change.

I was pretty bushed when I got home after work, and, to tell the truth, I was still brooding about the loss of my address book. As I closed the door and pressed the light switch, this peculiar feeling hit me that there was someone else in the room. I whirled around, and my hunch was right—it was Sondra. She was holding a big bag of groceries in one arm and had a nightie folded over the other.

"What are you doing here?" I started to say, and then, Lord only knows why, the riddle that was bugging me was solved in a flash. "It was you!" I cried out. "*You* stole my little black book, didn't you? You called those girls!"

Her eyes filled with tears. "Yes," she said. "Oh, Phil, it was a rotten, a contemptible thing to do, but I had to convince you I was a woman. I had to prove there were no lengths I wouldn't go to in order to win you."

To my surprise, tears sprang to my own eyes, hardened cynic though I am. In her blind, fumbling way, Sondra had risked everything to express her devotion. Was I worthy of it? Or was I only a heartless Don Juan who rode roughshod over his casual loves? It was up to me to show her my true stature, and I did. I took the groceries from her very gently and cooked dinner for us both. Then I put my bed at her disposal, tucked her in, and contrived a shakedown for myself on the floor. Tonight we're going to have a meal out, at some place where we can communicate and discuss our relationship and chemistry. . . . Can this be love? I don't know. Given two human beings, anything can happen.

If a Slicker Meet a Slicker

I shall always remember the day I purchased my first Burberry. The moment I slipped it on I suddenly knew we were going to be inseparable companions. I can only liken the feeling to the way some men respond to a car; or a favorite pipe or hound. Well, sir, I just put it on and that was that. What a time we two had! Slogging through the heaviest English downpours. Never fazed us. Then off to the Possessions and the wars. My Burberry and I made a bit of history at Somaliland. Kenya. Ypres. Gallipoli. We knocked about in almost every corner of the Empire. Then . . . home again. I sometimes think the Burberry took it all better than I. My friends at the club began calling me a sentimental old duff. Rightly so, I expect. Because I just couldn't bear to part with my old friend, the Burberry. After so many years, so many adventures, a part of my life had become woven in that cloth. But, heaven knows, we were both showing our age. Finally I decided it was high time to retire myself and my good old Burberry and get another.—*Adv. in* The New Yorker.

O<small>H, HE'S A FINE</small>, substantial figure of a man, to be sure, is Mr. Julian Vicissitude, lounging there in that new mackintosh of his, a high-grade hat in one hand and a smart bamboo stick in the other, smirking into the camera as though

74

the earth was his own private crumpet. A typical empire builder, you'd say—one of those solid, foursquare chaps you'll meet along Threadneedle Street of a morning, brisk and yet twinkling, because he's just brought off this little deal, don't you see, whereby forty thousand quid gives birth to eighty and nobody the wiser, tee-hee, especially the Department of Inland Revenue. I mean, the sort of old reliable family friend you wouldn't hesitate to trust with your investments or your niece, and then one fine day the news item datelined Hendaye about the Spanish authorities having detained a certain prominent industrialist and his blond companion for questioning. Ah, yes, the butter hasn't been churned yet that would melt in Mr. Julian Vicissitude's mouth. As for that new raincoat draped over his body, so crisp and sweet, every blessed button in place, well, I wish it joy of him. Wait till he starts showing his true colors; wait till he repays its years of devotion as he did mine. I was the only waterproof he ever loved, he used to say, and I was fool enough to believe him. Oh, I know how bitter it sounds, but as long as he's washed his hands of me so publicly, he needn't expect me to remain silent. So I'm just an old bit of rainwear to be exploited and cast aside, am I? We'll soon see about that.

I may as well begin with the way we first met, the day he "purchased" me, as he calls it—and there's a bloody euphemism if ever I saw one. The plain truth is that I was hanging in the cloakroom of Iscariot's, this Cypriot restaurant in Soho, scarcely an hour after an overseas visitor had bought me at a shop in Shaftesbury Avenue. He was a rancher—an Australian, I gathered from his accent—the big, beefy kind that rips apart your shoulder seams unless you're double-sewn, as I am. Well, halfway through lunch I felt a hand stealthily rummaging through my pockets, and a second later I was unceremoniously whisked from the hanger, folded over someone's arm, and carted off. In that position, naturally, I'd no clue to where I was being taken or by whom, but I wasn't left in doubt very long. All of a sudden, a brash young gent in a thirty-guinea suit, with a larcenous glint in his eye, was shaking me out in the middle of Vigo Street and holding me up for inspection. "Well, you're a dandy all-weather mackintosh, as sure as my name's Julian Vicissitude," he crowed. "A bit ample, perhaps, but then a wide boy like me needs a roomy garment, what?"

That anybody should abstract another's apparel in broad daylight and, furthermore, openly gloat over it seemed such brazen impudence that I was rendered incapable of reply. Within a couple of days, however, I learned that my new owner was, as he'd proclaimed, a wide boy, a real layabout. He manifestly had no fixed profession or business, because he stayed up till all hours and never rose before noon; and yet, judging from the wad of banknotes he slipped into me now and again, he was in easy circumstances. At the outset, I reckoned him for a retired jockey or a tout, as he was forever haring off to race meetings at Goodwood and Newmarket, but he also liked to hobnob with pressmen in the Fleet Street pubs and tipple in those bars around Hatton Garden where jewellers congregate, so I couldn't rightly figure his pitch. I got his measure, finally, from the pack of cards he kept secreted in one of my sleeves. Obviously, Vicissitude was a citizen who lived by his wits, and since my destiny had been forcibly intermingled with his, I had no choice other than to close a hook-and-eye to his capers.

How right I was the events of the very next Sunday proved. Vicissitude was weekending with one Gerald Peach-Wintergreen, a rich wool factor up in Essex, just outside Finchingfield, and from what I was able to piece together—I wasn't eyewitness to it, of course, since he rarely wore me indoors— his host was mad keen on backgammon. After losing a few games to whet the fellow's appetite, Vissy moved in for the kill. When the score was totted up eventually, Peach-Wintergreen was loser by seven hundred pounds. Unhappily, just as he was scribbling his cheque, a set of loaded dice tumbled out of Vissy's trouser cuff. Ten minutes afterward, the boss described a somersault down the front stairs into the gravelled drive, where his bag and I had landed moments before. Apart from having his *Sitzfleisch* peppered with buckshot, I don't suppose he sustained any actual damage from the shotgun blasts I heard, but he seemed much more subdued thereafter. He'd none of that devil-may-care aplomb, that honeyed charm, that he used so effectively to lull his victims.

It was soon after this contretemps that his fortunes took a sharp turn, largely through the agency of an uncle, Sir Isaac Mangrove. Apparently, the old party had somehow got word of his relation's exploits, for one morning Vissy hurriedly pulled me on over his pajamas and answered the doorbell, which was buzzing like a hornet. The chap outside was a real museum piece—cavalry mustache, single eyeglass, gray cutaway, the lot—and he was in a fearful wax. The whole family'd been disgraced, he bellowed; generations of Vicissitudes past and unborn were doomed to eternal shame on account of one black sheep. Having worked himself up to the verge of apoplexy, Sir Isaac delivered an ultimatum: his nephew would emigrate immediately to Mombasa, in which outpost a job in a shipping firm awaited him, or a detailed account of his chicanery would be handed in to Scotland Yard the next morning, with a recommendation that he be given six dozen of the best and transported to Botany Bay. Swayed by the generosity of the offer as well as by the prospect of new fields for his talent, Vissy gratefully assented. Inside a fortnight, we were speeding eastward to Aden aboard a Union-Castle liner.

Since the weather was clement most of the trip, Vissy had little need of me. Nevertheless, several gleeful remarks he addressed to the shaving mirror—I was swaying on the bathroom door at the time—indicated that he was paying court to an Italian beauty from Somalia, the wife of a wealthy date merchant there. I naïvely supposed it was an innocent shipboard flirtation until a chance reference of hers, to the effect that her husband was passionately addicted to bridge, enlightened me. With the aid of a couple of Drambuies and an obliging full moon, Vissy obtained his objective, an invitation to dine with the pair at Mogadishu. While I myself wasn't taken ashore that evening, the sheaf of Somali shillings he brought back plainly signified what a coup he had scored. Just as he was cackling over his haul, though, the bombshell burst. A launch full of excited officials swept alongside, and Vissy panicked and flung the money out the porthole, only to discover that the authorities were hunting for a stowaway. You should have seen him rage up and down the cabin, smiting his forehead like some Old Testament boffin and groaning. It was immense.

By the time we reached Mombasa, the monsoon rains had set in, so the two of us practically lived together. The berth Sir Isaac had secured for the scapegrace was a clerical one—copying into ledgers endless columns of figures on the coffee, pyrethrum, and sisal the firm exported. It took him a day or so to learn his duties, and another to practice imitating the manager's signature on his checks. Then he removed his sleeveguards, took me from the peg, and went down to the Old Port, where he concluded a pact with three Arab highbinders to smuggle ivory by dhow to Madras. One of the trio, unfortunately, was a police informer, and within the hour Vissy and I were sharing a cell in Fort Jesus with a family of sixteenth-century Portuguese fleas. Thanks to an urgent collect cable Vissy was allowed to dispatch, Uncle Isaac managed to pull wires in Whitehall, and the next morning we were hustled onto a tramp steamer bound for Marseille.

If Vissy was disheartened by the ensuing period in Paris, when he was scrounging barely enough to exist on, it didn't seem to diminish his bounce. Not one of the schemes he evolved to line his purse materialized; but one evening he held a long, whispered conference in a *zinc* off the Place Denfert-Rochereau with a flashy type sporting a black monocle, and I sensed that something big was in the wind. The following day, the two bore me to an obscure tailor's shop in the Saint-Denis quarter and arranged to have a number of extra pockets sewn into my interior. It was a touchy business, crossing the Channel with six dozen Swiss watch movements stuffed inside me, and they shook like bloody castanets, what with Vissy aquiver and all of a muck sweat as we went through the customs barrier. However, I knew enough to keep a stiff upper fabric, and we ultimately passed the consignment to the proprietor of an *espresso* bar in Wardour Street. And then, just as Vissy was skipping out of the place, his wallet as fat as a Strasbourg goose, treading on air at the way he'd handled the deal, he got his comeuppance. Two stern-faced men were approaching us on the pavement, deep in conversation. As one of them looked up and saw Vissy, he gave a violent start. "That's him!" he exclaimed. "That's the one!"

"By George, so it is!" said the other, thunderstruck. "Quick—don't let him get away!"

Under the circumstances there wasn't any alternative except to bolt, and off we went, dodging through the complex of streets around Charing Cross Road with the pair in hot pursuit. Somewhere to the north of Trafalgar Square, my boss's wind gave out and they closed in on him. Between his fright and the general uproar, he couldn't understand at first what they were saying, but they finally got it across. They were television folk from the States—a producer and director, I believe they called themselves—and they urgently needed someone to play a Scotland Yard inspector. It didn't matter two straws to them that Vissy was no actor and that he exuded about as much menace as boiled haddock. The main thing was that I was ideal for the role, and these chaps, being true professionals, had the insight and the sensitivity to recognize it.

It always used to fracture me, after I scored an international success in the *Itching Trigger* series and the one that followed, *Code in the Head*, to listen to the rot Julian Vicissitude dished out to interviewers. From his account, he'd been cradled in a theatrical trunk, appeared in pantos at the age of seven, trouped all over the U.K. with his own repertory company, and given Gielgud and Olivier their earliest comprehension of Shakespeare. Not once did he bother to acknowledge his debt to me, who'd lifted him out of the ruck and assured his climb to the heights. Oh, he was meticulous enough about having me dry-cleaned and replacing my snaps

—I was his bread and butter. But companionship, snuggling up together as we'd done back at Fort Jesus? That was ancient history. Nowadays, I was beginning to embarrass him ever so slightly; he'd outgrown me, as one of your *nouveau-riche* baronets has his old lady who served as barmaid in his first taproom. Time and again, I caught him gazing into gents' furnishing shops, pretending to examine a robe or cravat but secretly eying some sleazy mac in the back. His conscience, of course, wouldn't permit him to discard me out of hand, so he chose the coward's way: he deliberately set out to lose me. But it wasn't all that simple; my audience was as big as his and just as loyal. His first try, when he left me behind on a Paddington bus, misfired ludicrously—the conductor spotted me straight off and I was back at the studio early next morning. Then he did me up in a brown paper parcel, checked me at Waterloo, and threw away the claim ticket, but I was picked up by the C.I.D., along with a number of similar parcels containing a deceased lady, and the police, who modelled their techniques on those we used on our telly program, returned me to him with a note of apology.

The cream of the jest was that we finally parted just as we'd met; one of the light-fingered gentry, a souvenir hunter more than likely, filched me from the cloakroom of the Ivy whilst Vissy was lunching there. He set up a great hue and cry, offered a reward, pretended his career was ruined without me, and got hell's own amount of publicity out of the affair. By then, though, I was swinging on a rack of derelict rainwear in Seven Dials, bleached oyster white and flaunting a sign that read "Nobby Value—16 Shils." And here I expect to remain until fortune's wheel revolves again. My current owner is a perky little toff with the red-rimmed eyes of a stoat, a detestable spiv who'd slit your bloody weasand for a florin, but he hasn't an ounce of pretense. You know where you stand with him—which is a damn sight more than can be said for nature's nobleman and jolly good fellow, your television idol and mine, and may a pox fly away with him, Julian Vicissitude.

Once Over Lightly, and Please Hush Your Bazoo

Hᴵɢʜ ᴏɴ ᴛʜᴇ ʟɪsᴛ of topics about which I unhesitatingly rate myself an ignoramus is the British press. I take in—largely to overawe the postman—an English newspaper or two and a couple of weeklies, I glibly misquote clerihews culled from the *New Statesman* competitions, and I carry around a copy of the London *Times,* folded to the agony column, on the off chance that some pretty bus passenger sharing my seat might need a conversational gambit. The economic, sporting, and financial news in these publications, though, could just as well be printed in Pushtu or Volapük for all the benefit I derive, and it's only when I encounter a basic, easily digestible subject, such as the hairdressers who cater to the social and artistic élite of London, that I feel other than a moldy fig.

A good example of the sort of tonsorial feature I mean, containing plenty of resonant names and scads of tradition, appeared in the *Daily Mail* a while back. It was embodied in an interview with Prince Philip's personal barber, at the shop the latter managed in St. James's. In recognition of his dexterity with the shears, the establishment had been awarded its fifth Royal Warrant, and everyone was bathed in gratification. Without impugning the manager's artistry, however, the reporter pointed out that his predecessor, a Mr. Topper (*sic*), had been quite as gifted, his clients on his demise, at seventy-two, having included the Duke of Windsor, the late Duke of Kent, Mr. Harold Macmillan, Nubar Gulbenkian, Earl Mountbatten, and Sir Gordon Richards. But even *he*, it emerged, was a gosling compared to the ninety-two-year-old barber who still periodically trimmed Sir Winston Churchill. An absorbing account in every way, though I feel it would have rounded out the picture to learn who cut the hoary hairdresser's locks.

Another pastiche on the same order, but stressing a more cultural aspect, materialized in the *Observer,* which found copy in the memorabilia of a renowned playwright. "Some of Bernard Shaw's hair and whiskers came up for our inspection last week," it announced, with quiet pride. "The property of Mr. Henry Mulcrone Edwards, aged sixty-five, a barber, who now works in a saloon at the back of the American Cigar Stores behind St. Martin-in-the-Fields. Mr. Edwards, who cut Shaw's hair regularly at Whitehall Court, keeps these valuables wrapped up in brown paper labelled 'Bernard Shaw. Hair and whiskers. October 14, 1943. Time 4:45 P.M.' He explains: 'It may not seem anything much. But I had all the dealings with his hair and beard for a long time. And with the times we're living in these days it is rather interesting.'" From his Olympian vantage as Shaw's hirsute counsellor, Mr. Edwards proceeded to evaluate him professionally: "'His hair was whiter than his beard. The beard kept its colour more and was what we call ginger in the trade. Actually, the hair was rather coarse. Quite common in itself. You wouldn't call it anything special in the hair industry.'" In other words, Mr. Edwards seemed to be saying that however adept his client may have been at fashioning situation and dialogue, however brilliant his unorthodoxy, he just didn't shape up hairwise. I stiffened in expectation. Could this be the prelude to important new sidelights on Shaw's character? Disappointingly, Mr. Edwards chickened out and hid behind biographical glucose: "'But a wonderful man underneath it. Never any trouble. Made no appointment. Came in casually like anyone else. A great memory. After a month he'd come back and converse on the same subject he'd been speaking on before. We'd be speaking about apples, say. He'd come back to apples the next time I cut his hair.'" Evidently deciding that these fruity colloquies were of no transcendent importance, the interviewer inquired whether G.B.S. knew that Mr. Edwards was saving his hair. " 'No,' " the barber answered. " 'But he said he often wondered what became of it.' "

With the curious persistence Life often shows for copying Art, it chanced that shortly after I read the preceding I ran into a worthy whose recollections equal, and possibly dwarf, those of Mr. Edwards. The hamlet in rural Pennsylvania where I procure sterile lawn seed and toothless hack-saw blades contains a barbershop I have patronized intermittently for thirty years. Its service, hygiene, and prices were, in my experience, maladroit, questionable, and exorbitant, yet every so often direst necessity impelled me back there. My misgivings as I approached it this time, though, were partly allayed by the sign UNDER NEW MANAGEMENT in the window. The disgruntled, lard-faced pair of attendants I remembered had yielded to a fine old patriarch in a surgical smock, who was vigorously massaging tonic into the scalp of a high-school youth. Picking up a tattered photo album, I mused over the tribulations of a bevy of French models caught in a chiffon shortage until the barber's voice dispelled my fantasies.

"You certainly were immersed in that portfolio, sir," he remarked as he enveloped me in an apron. "Had quite a time bringing you out of it."

"Yes," I confessed. "I don't get over to France nowadays as much as I'd like to, and I want to keep up with the trends."

He clucked appreciatively. "Intellectual curiosity," he said. "There's precious little of it around these days, if you ask me. You been interested in women long?"

"Only since boyhood," I said. "Forty-five years at most. How about you?"

"Well, I go back a bit further than that, frankly," he said. "I'll be a hundred and thirteen next March, though I may not look it. And I'll tell you this—these modern women are a joke. All padding and zippers, no real meat on 'em. You take Margarete Matzenauer and Emmy Destinn, for instance." He molded expressive patterns in the air. "Now, *there* were a couple of big strapping girls. Plenty of brisket fore and aft."

I expressed chagrin at never having known any opera stars—or, indeed, any women—of such magnitude, and observed that he must have met a host of celebrities in his career.

"Sometimes I can barely remember their names," he said. "I learned my trade in the downtown financial district of New York back in the seventies, starting as a brushboy at nominal wages. All the high mucky-mucks used to come into the shop— Jay Gould, Boss Tweed, Richard Canfield—and when they saw what a wide-awake lad I was, they soon took me into their confidence. Incidentally, Tweed's one of the most misunderstood men in history. Sure, he had a bluff, rugged exterior, but behind the mask there was an idealist, a bold and original thinker."

"I guess certain individuals just naturally attract legends," I hazarded. "That story about his looting the public funds—"

"Balderdash," he said contemptuously. "Lies from beginning to end. He was railroaded by a pack of do-gooders and wild-eyed spinsters. Look, sonny, keep your head still, will you?"

"The clippers hurt my neck," I complained.

"Probably a little rusty," he said, tapping them on the headrest. "I laid 'em up on the porch roof to air out and it came on to rain. Well, as I started to say, I was a bright kid and I knew enough to get out of Wall Street while I was still ahead. I went out West and panned gold for a spell with another youngster, by the name of Bret Harte, but he was bitten by the journalism bug, mooned around and couldn't keep his mind on his work, so I sold out my interest and drifted over to Utah. Did all right there, too," he added reminiscently. "I was the youngest elder in the Mormon Church by the time I was eighteen. I had five wives, and whenever anything went wrong in the Tabernacle, it was yours truly they sent for. Then one day I came to my senses. 'You're a chump, Billy Watson,' I said to myself. That's my name— Billy Watson. They used to call me Sliding Billy, because I slid around from one occupation to another. 'Is this your idea of success—a Mormon trouble-shooter?' I knew I'd never make the grade again as a brushboy with five wives, so I settled a goodly sum on each of them and lit out for Europe."

"Er—excuse me," I broke in. "Don't cut it too short in front, will you?"

"No, I see you roach it down to give the impression of a forehead underneath," he said, with a sympathetic nod. "By the way, did anyone ever tell you that you're his spit and image?"

"Whose?"

"Why, Robert Ingersoll's, of course," he replied. "The great agnostic. You're as alike as two peas in a pod. You sure you're not related?"

"Well, I *was* kind of influenced by his ideas in school," I admitted. "I wrote an essay my senior year, called 'Science Versus Religion,' that was pretty outspoken for a boy with no forehead."

"There, what did I say!" he exclaimed triumphantly. "No wonder I spotted the resemblance. Many's the time I appeared on the same lecture platform in Chautauqua with Colonel Ingersoll and Houdini and Thurston—all those escape artists. Anyhow, where was I? . . . Oh, yes, Europe. Well, on account of I was a hot-blooded young fellow, I eventually gravitated over to Paris, and, first thing you know, I was mixed up with the whole bohemian crowd around Maxim's—Victorien Sardou, the Lefcourt brothers who wrote that journal, Liane de Pougy, and Jack Offenbach, the composer." He chuckled reminiscently. "He was a real swinger, that Offenbach. I well remember the time he walked in and offered thirty thousand dollars, which was a lot of mazuma in those days, to anybody that could think up a dessert named after Nellie Melba."

"Peach Melba?" I asked. "I thought it was—what's his name?—Escoffier who invented that."

"You bet it was, kiddo," he asserted, "and I was sitting right there in Maxim's with Count Boni de Castellane and the

Czarevitch when he did. But, as I said before, I was too restless to stay put very long, so I pulled up stakes. Came back home and went into business with a party named Haldeman-Julius, out in Kansas, publishing those five-cent classics in blue covers. We had a bright bunch of lads in that organization—Brann the Iconoclast and Lafcadio Hearn, among others—and we were coining money hand over fist when along came an opportunity that fired my imagination. The group that controlled the Hotel Astor barbershop back East was selling out, and, knowing that I wanted a good central location—"

"How did they know that?" I queried.

"Through the grapevine . . . the newspapers—How the hell should I remember?" Watson retorted impatiently. "Don't interrupt. Well, it was a tough decision, but I shook hands with Haldeman-Julius and bowed out. As luck would have it, though, I lost my bankroll on the train somewhere outside Chicago, playing klabiatsch with a couple of strangers, and I didn't have the wherewithal to consummate the deal. Fortunately, a few of my old Wall Street acquaintances, like Henry Clews, Russell Sage, and the Van Sweringens, rallied together and chipped in the needful. That place was a bonanza, my friend. In the fifty-two years I managed it, every luminary on the Gay White Way was a patron of mine, from Ira Gershwin to Ira Wallach, from Jerry Kern to Jerry Robbins, from David Belasco to David Merrick. The next time you're over in New York, drop around to the Public Library and look at the Watson Hair Index in the theatre collection."

"You mean to say you kept a record of all those people's hair?"

"Not a *record*, bub," he said with disdain. "The hair itself—over six hundred actual specimens, each in a separate glassine envelope, autographed and witnessed by a notary public. It's practically an encyclopedia of show business. I was offered a fortune by Sardi's and various other restaurants, who wanted to use it for display purposes, but I felt it had to be preserved for future generations of research students. Well," he concluded, as he whipped off my apron and backed off to scrutinize his handiwork, "there you are. Nothing to brag about, but a lot better than you could do yourself."

"It certainly is," I agreed, and handed him a twenty-dollar bill. All of a sudden, the import of his words struck me. "Wait a minute, Mr. Watson," I said quickly. "Are you implying that a person could cut his own hair if he had to?"

"Why not?" he returned. "I've been doing it ever since I was ninety—nothing's impossible. . . . Here, young fellow, don't you want your change?"

"No, thanks," I sang out from the door. "You keep it. You just gave me a honey of an idea."

And he had, believe you me.

A Soft Answer Turneth Away Royalties

Please don't give it another thought!" I shouted at my vis-à-vis over the uproar of the cocktail party. "It's perfectly all right!"

"I can't hear you!" she shouted back, her nose wrinkling in frustration. "What did you say?" She was an angular hyperthyroid in green herringbone, with a fur piece slung across her jib, and we stood glued to each other amid the crush like lovers in an Indian erotic sculpture, but without intimacy. My left sleeve, down which she had just emptied two-thirds of her highball, was waterlogged, and a fearful premonition gripped me that I might spend eternity bonded to this afreet unless some miracle intervened. Providentially, it did; somewhere in the hurly-burly a drunk sank to the floor, the axis of the party shifted, and I found myself confronting Stanley Prang.

Though we had caromed into one another intermittently around New York over the past couple of decades, all I really knew of Prang was that he did editorial work for some major publishing firm and, I distantly recalled, kept his finger on the British literary pulse. Since he, in turn, always exhibited equal incuriosity about me, our encounters had been lubricated with an exchange of grins or platitudes on the weather. Today, however, I seemed to produce an effect like adrenalin on the chap. His pupils distended to the size of agates, and, seizing my arm, he wrenched me into an adjacent hallway. "I want you to read something," he said, feverishly extracting an envelope. "In twenty-three years of working with authors, nothing like this has ever happened to me." I reached for it, but he struck aside my hand, determined to finish his preamble. "Of all the ingrates on earth," he declaimed, "of all the crabs, malcontents, and faultfinders, writers are the worst. You coddle them, correct their grammar, soothe their wretched little egos, turn yourself inside out to please them—and what do you get? A kick in the head. Not one speck of gratitude, appreciation—just more bellyaches. Well, anyhow," he broke off, obviously conscious of his failure to ignite a pile of wet leaves, "that's why I'm going to frame this document. It's historic!"

The letter, a barely decipherable scrawl on pale violet notepaper, was the handiwork of an English lady novelist too eminent, asserted Prang, to have her identity noised about. Its tone was emotional, almost elegiac. Acknowledging the receipt of a romance of hers he had just issued, she hailed it as a masterpiece of the bookmaker's art, a milestone in publishing. Everything about it—type, format, binding—bespoke the most refined taste; indeed, she declared, the setting was so exquisite that she feared it shamed her poor bauble. The beauty of the end papers was only rivalled by the ingenuity of the chapter headings, and, as for the dust jacket, she planned to have its breathtaking design duplicated on a negligee. True, the publisher's blurb was a bit fulsome; she could not truly regard herself as the peer of Dostoevski, Dickens, Balzac, Flaubert, and Zola, but perhaps such encomiums were necessary to stimulate sales.

"And that isn't all!" Prang added vehemently. "On publication day, she cabled flowers to the entire editorial staff, and begged us to cut her royalties in half because she felt our advertising appropriation was overgenerous."

"Jiminetty!" I said. "Well, I hope you send me a copy. Good book, is it?"

"Unreadable," he snapped. "A bomb. That's not the point, though. This dame's behavior throws a brand-new sidelight on authors." He shook his head perplexedly. "Maybe the bastards *are* human, after all."

For a moment, I thought of vindicating my profession dramatically with a right cross to the man's jaw, but it occurred to me that he might vindicate his with a right cross to mine, and I forbore. Reviewing the episode later, however, I wondered if the lady's testimonial, while magnanimous in the extreme, may not be fraught with perilous implications. Across the years, publishing has come to expect—in fact, to predicate its very existence on—the author's mistrust, his rancor and perversity. If suddenly he were to start fawning on his sponsors like a coach dog and rhapsodizing all over the place, his *amour-propre* would vanish overnight, a generation of executives trained to grovel and demean themselves would become obsolete, and the whole structure of the business might disintegrate. As a corrective to any such trend, as well as an illustration of how one creative artist combatted it, I submit a brief correspondence between Marshall Crump, a prominent New York publisher, and Cyprian Wynkoop, a fledgling poet:

FEBRUARY 13

MY DEAR MR. WYNKOOP,

I guess each one of us gets tongue-tied when writing to his idol, be he Joe Blow scratching out a fan missive to Sinatra or a prominent New York publisher lauding a genius like yourself. This is the third stab I have made at expressing my homage to you; I tore up the other two stabs, because, frankly, I was afraid you would deem them a bit overboard. Nevertheless, and at the risk of earning your ill will, I must speak my piece. In my humble opinion, Cyprian Wynkoop is destined to rank among the literary greats of all time. He stands like a colossus among his contemporaries, already enshrined on Olympus albeit he is very much alive and at the pinnacle of his powers. To his detractors (not that you have any, Mr. Wynkoop—a mere figure of speech) I say, show me one scrivener fit to tie Wynkoop's shoe. They cannot, by George, and I will tell you why. Because he is a giant among pygmies.

I can just picture a sardonic smile wreathing your physiognomy as, meerschaum in hand, you peruse these lines in your study. I can just hear you speculating, how does a roach like him have the crust, the presumption, to approach an immortal! The answer, sir, is that I refuse to be muzzled any longer. There is a conspiracy of silence aimed at keeping you in the dark, and I will not be a party to it. Your present publishers, Winograd & Totentanz, are crucifying you. All unbeknownst to you, they have dumped your latest brilliant compendium of poems, *Arabesque for a Gay Hetaera*, in a cut-rate drugstore off Nassau Street. A fine comment on our time—the American Keats remaindered for thirty-nine cents by a couple of pitchmen that I happen to know began their career demonstrating silver polish on the Atlantic City boardwalk. To such lengths will hoodlums go to clear their inventory.

Well, just wanted to pass along this tip in return for the profound sock you hand me whenever I run across your work, which will be quite often now that it is retailing for thirty-nine cents. Incidentally, if you feel restless for any reason in your current publishing setup, we certainly would mortgage the old homestead to have your clever pen in our stable. How are you fixed for lunch Tuesday? If agreeable to you, let's meet at the Puritan Doughnut Shop, at Ninth Avenue and Twenty-eighth Street. I usually eat at the Plaza or "21," but if some columnist spied us in a huddle, Winograd & Totentanz might do a burn, and the way things are breaking for you, you need all the friends you can get.

Cordially yours,
MARSHALL CRUMP

FEBRUARY 22

DEAR MR. CRUMP,

The noise in the cruller shop the other day was so deafening that I did not understand your proposition too clearly, and the cigar stump you chewed throughout lunch did nothing to clarify your diction. Hence, I am rather confused as to whether you offered me a twenty-five-thousand-dollar advance to show you the first twenty-five pages of a novel or twenty-five dollars for the first twenty-five thousand words. In either case, I carried away the impression of a glib trickster who would bear watching, and your frantic insistence that I pony up eighty-five cents for my share of the check further disturbed me. Please note that whereas you consumed a London broil with mashed turnips and beets, cabinet pudding, and coffee, I ate only two jelly doughnuts and a cup custard. If your firm has published all the best-sellers you claim, why should our initial meeting leave me forty cents the loser? It seems a poor augury for business relations.

On the other hand, Mr. Crump, despite the revulsion you filled me with, I have decided on mature reflection to flout every dictate of common sense and let you issue my next book. The financial details are inconsequential; my basic motive is altruism, the *réclame* your paltry imprint would acquire by publishing me. What consternation this has evoked in my circle I need not describe. To a man, my friends predict disaster, excoriating you as sneak thieves, pushcart peddlers, and worse. I, too, sense my utter folly but, quixotic simpleton that I am, rush headlong into the abattoir. With best wishes and no illusions whatever,

Yours,
Cyprian Wynkoop

February 27

Dear Wynkoop,

Sorry to have been out of the office when you visited us yesterday. The mixup about our twenty-five-dollar check bouncing was a stupid clerical error, and I assume complete responsibility. Miss Overbite, our bookkeeper, had drops put in her eyes for new glasses and on the way home from the specialist took a bus to White Plains by mistake. When she didn't come back after lunch, I naturally thought she had absconded, and stopped payment on several items. If you will deposit the check again in two weeks—three weeks, to be on the safe side—it should breeze right through.

And now for the big news, my boy. I stayed up till after two this morning reading the eleven pages you brought in of the new novel. I'm a pretty tough audience, Wynkoop, but this is perfection—this is the jackpot. There isn't an extra word, or comma. Except for the hero, the girl, and her parents, none of whom really come off, it's the merriest, most tragic, searching, and yet least depressing thing I have glimpsed in many a moon. Even if you never added another line, it would stand as a complete work of art—and right here is where my keen publisher's instinct bids me speak up. Let us not tamper with it, I say; let us bring out this sterling prose fragment as a novella that will sell like hot chickpeas now and whet the public's appetite for the finished product next fall. The idea had such a sensational impact around the office that a couple of the staff could hardly speak for a few minutes. Anyway, the book is already at the linotypers and you will have proofs inside two weeks. The only hitch I foresee is getting a classy enough portrait of you for the jacket. Could you possibly fly up to Canada this weekend and be photographed by Karsh? If the old writing schedule is too tight, of course, just holler and will get Karsh flown down to you. Meanwhile, best personal regards from

Your devoted fan,
MARSHALL CRUMP

MARCH 15

DEAR MR. CRUMP,

It took me the better part of an hour yesterday to decode the hysterical phone message you left here with my Lithuanian cleaning woman. I finally gathered that Hollywood was offering three hundred and fifty thousand dollars for the screen rights of my novella, that it had been chosen by both the Book-of-the-Month and the Literary Guild, and that William Inge and Gore Vidal were vying with each other to dramatize it. Whether the foregoing had actually happened or was imminent, I was unable to tell, owing to my handmaiden's tendency to scramble past and future tenses. One conclusion, neverthe-

93

less, was inescapable—that by bandying my work around the market place you have cheapened and degraded it beyond repair. All your vaunted reverence for my talent, your sycophantic flattery, is nothing but camouflage for your real purpose—to emblazon my name on the best-seller list, hamstring me with adulation and pelf, and convert me into a hack.

The attorneys I have retained to collect damages for the humiliation and loss of ego arising from your indignities are confident that any jury would instantly indemnify me to the tune of half a million dollars. Rather than expose your villainy in open court, though, I herewith offer you a proposal. Withdraw the novella from general sale and issue instead a limited edition, for collectors only, of one hundred copies on Japanese vellum. While you have permanently blasted whatever hope I cherished of attaining the status of a cult, I may yet regain the integrity I once had.

Yours truly,
CYPRIAN WYNKOOP

MARCH 28

DEAR CYPRIAN,

I apologize for not answering before; I have been laid up with a small stroke that hit me the day I got your letter. (Please do not feel you are responsible in any way—just overwork, aggravation caused by other writers, etc.) Owing to my absence, there was a little slipup in the office. My assistant, Miss Overbite, forgot to notify the printer of your wishes, so the original trade edition of thirty-five hundred copies was shipped to the bookstores. Of course, I fired her, also stopped payment on the printer's check, but, after all, nobody is superhuman. In my condition, I did the best I could.

Fortunately, I have good news, too. The critics must have guessed our predicament and decided to let you down easy, because not one of them reviewed the book. How is that for professional courtesy? Only a man of your stature gets a break like that, and maybe the ball-point pens I distribute annually to the press don't hurt, either.

On the sales front, we anticipate plenty of action, as there is a terrific word-of-mouth across the country. To nudge it along, we are remaindering the book for thirty-nine cents in a few key spots like bus terminals, drugstores around Nassau Street where the brokerage crowd lunches, etc. Well, baby, so long for the present, and any time you're near the office, drop in and chew the fat with us. It should be Old Home Week for you now that we have decided to merge with Winograd & Totentanz.

Yours ever,
MARSHALL CRUMP

MARCH 30

DEAR MR. CRUMP,

To say that you have hoodwinked me and undermined my self-respect, forever destroyed any claim I may have had to artistic purity, would be the palest simulacrum of the truth. I have just come from Brentano's, where with my own eyes I saw half a dozen copies of my novella sold in as many minutes. The sight of those brutish, dishevelled customers pawing my work as if it were dress goods so revolted me that I groaned aloud. "Stop!" I wanted to cry. "Don't you realize you're stealing my birthright, you Philistines—that every book you buy diminishes me that much more?" That is what I wanted to cry, but somehow I could not.

Perhaps this nightmare in which you have embroiled me was a necessary ordeal; perhaps I shall emerge the nobler artist for it. In any event, this letter formally dissolves our association. I have just signed a contract with an altogether obscure publisher of chess books and almanacs in Philadelphia. He may not have a fancy office, a scapegoat like Miss Overbite, and a pair of unprincipled yahoos as partners, but at least he has facilities for keeping his author's books out of the hands of the public. Wishing you every conceivable tribulation, I am,

As always,
CYPRIAN WYNKOOP

95

Eat, Drink, and Be Wary

Had anyone pressed his nose against the windows of our brownstone late yesterday afternoon—a feat requiring no more than a nineteen-foot ladder and the agility of a Blondin—he might have beheld a scene that, while it lacked a hay wain and browsing cattle, rivalled in tranquillity anything Constable ever painted. The sleeper recumbent on the davenport, his diminutive chest wheezing as rhythmically as a bellows, was an individual on whose brow not a single trace of care was discernible. Here, even Ralph Waldo Trine would have hastened to proclaim, was a man altogether in tune with the infinite, a person unmistakably proof against all the petty anxieties of existence. And then, in almost the very next breath, the pastoral confronting the observer was annihilated in a single stroke. A part-time maid, bearing a tote and the equivocal name of Bonanza, appeared in the doorway. "I stuffed the chicken and put it in the range," she announced, as she prepared to vanish into the gloaming, "but tell the Missis I couldn't find the needle and thread."

The instant the door of the apartment slammed behind her, I sat bolt upright, prey to a gnawing, inexplicable disquiet. The first part of the message was plain enough, but there was something furtive, if not sinister, about the rest of it. With a premonition that much more than a fowl was cooking, I got up and made for the kitchen. A rich, flavorsome scent emanated from the stove, and everything appeared to be in apple-pie order. Just as I turned to leave, though, my eye fell on a bulky volume lying on the breadboard. It was Irma S. Rombauer's classic, *The Joy of Cooking*, spread open to an entry, under "Dressings for Meat or Fowl" and headed " 'Dry' Dressing," that ran as follows: "This name is given by my cook, Sarah Brown, to a dressing she frequently makes, which is by no means dry when served." There then followed directions for making it so dry as to practically crackle, concluding, "Fill the cavity lightly with the remaining dressing and pour the remaining butter on it. Sew up the opening." It was that laconic final sentence that brought the whole thing into focus and snapped my head back. Bonanza had tried to fulfill Mrs. Rombauer's instructions faithfully enough, all right, but in her haste to leave, and possibly distracted by rock 'n' roll, she had mislaid the needle and thread. It was careless—an oversight anyone might have committed, except for one detail. *She* knew, and I knew as I stood there aghast, where it was. It was inside the dressing.

For a moment, as the significance of her blunder trickled into my consciousness, a wave of dizziness swept over me and I felt my knees buckling. Then some gyroscope deep inside righted itself, and I realized the need for swift, decisive action. To pluck the bird from the oven, excise the stuffing, and laboriously comb it for the needle was inadvisable, not to say beyond my powers. However, if I could still recall Bonanza . . . I sprang down the hallway toward the front door, but before I reached the first landing it struck me how futile was pursuit. By now she must be miles away, roaring uptown on the Broadway-Seventh Avenue express and well on her way home. The sensible, the rational, course was to reach her by phone, explain that I did not hold her culpable in any way, and solicit her advice. After rummaging through my wife's address book for an eternity, I found the number of a beauty parlor on West 136th Street through which she maintained a tenuous link with Bonanza. The party who answered spoke in tones so velvety with mistrust that I finally threw circumlocution to the winds.

"Listen," I said, my voice shrill with impatience. "I can't stand here jawing with you all night. When she comes in, tell her that the needle's in the dressing and that she has to help me get it out—is that clear?"

"Yes, *sir*," he replied, with the alacrity of one suddenly comprehending everything. "I certainly will, but you better get to the clinic real fast."

A foreboding that I could look for no further aid from that quarter began to loom, and, hanging up, I pondered the next move. Perhaps the needle had already worked its way out; I remembered hearing of numerous instances in which objects of the sort had magically reappeared after making a complete circuit of the human body, and a chicken, after all, was minute by comparison. A quick glance into the stove disposed of any such likelihood, and the wave of heat that gushed into my face warned me that further exploration was perilous. I sat down and methodically tried to reconstruct what I knew of our schedule for the evening. Some couple or other was coming to dinner; just who, I couldn't recall, but I distinctly remembered my wife's injunction not to stray off with any cronies. It was pikestaff-plain, therefore, that she herself had been detained somewhere, and that the only recourse left was to alert her to the situation while there was still time to resolve it gracefully. I flew into the bedroom and again began thumbing through the names in her address book.

It was nearly six o'clock, and my voice had dwindled to a croak, when I finished canvassing the list of relatives, friends, and acquaintances, each of whom had failed to encounter my helpmate that day. Most of them, sensing the urgency of the call, tried to find out what was amiss, but I took care to divulge it to only the trustworthy few who promised to respect my confidence. Oddly enough, several of these, whose judgment and lucidity had always impressed me hitherto, persisted in trying to apply logic to the mishap. If Bonanza had actually sewed up the opening, they argued, how could the needle and thread have remained inside? I quickly cut short their sophistries, conveying, as delicately as I could without wounding them, that in their stress they could hardly be held accountable for talking nonsense.

98

The protracted ring of the doorbell, just as I was feverishly completing my toilet, reawakened my hopes; my wife was back, heaven be praised, and would know intuitively how to cope before our company turned up. To my consternation, it was the guests themselves, a pair named Pettijohn, to whom we were incomprehensibly wedded because we rented adjacent cottages at Martha's Vineyard. Robin Pettijohn, a corpulent hyperthyroid in his late forties, was a self-styled dramatist, none of whose plays had been produced as yet but who was rumored to be vastly gifted. His spouse, Vida, was a fierce little polecat with burning eyes that transfixed everyone she addressed, contentious and given to quoting statistics from the latest Consumers Union bulletin. They had just attended a cocktail party and were slightly gassed, a circumstance that heartened me measurably; perhaps if enough anesthesia were forthcoming they might overlook any surprises that popped up during the meal. To this end, I brewed a pitcherful of Gimlets so potent that they brought tears to my eyes and plied the two, bombarding Pettijohn meanwhile with oversolicitous questions about the progress of his newest play. I could see that modesty forebade his making any extravagant predictions, but as the grog took hold he dropped his domino and confessed that the new work was touched with genius.

"What are you calling it?" I asked inattentively, my ears straining for my wife's footfall on the stair.

"Well, I can't decide between 'Finders Keepers' and 'Keepers Finders,'" he said, "but Vida claims it cries out for something lighter—more comedic."

"Yes, like 'Needle in a Haystack,'" she said. "How does that strike you?"

I succumbed to a coughing fit so violent that the Pettijohns became visibly concerned, but I ultimately managed to regain control. From the repeated glances Vida had been casting toward the bedroom, it was evident that she was perishing to know what had become of the mistress of the ménage. So was I, and, to add to my tribulation, the pungent odor of burning chicken now assailed my nostrils. At this juncture, the Furies must have decided to grant me a breather, because the door burst open and my wife plummeted in, one cheek distended as in the advertisement for Dent's Toothache Gum. She had just undergone a fearful session in the dentist's chair, it appeared, lasting two solid hours. The Pettijohns cooed their sympathy, but when I proffered mine it was brushed aside.

"Didn't you get my message to turn off the stove?" she demanded, and raced on before I could reply. "The nurse kept calling, but the line was busy, busy, busy. Good grief, who were you talking to?"

"The—uh—roast— I mean the Coast," I floundered. "Look, there's something I have to tell you—"

"Later—not now," she cut me short. "I've got to see to the dinner. Give Vida and Robin a dividend while I go look."

I complied numbly, hoping that a pretext, however trifling, would arise for me to slip into the kitchen. None did, and, to thwart me further, Vida insisted, over my protestations, on absenting herself to lend a hand with the cuisine. Pettijohn, growing more expansive by the moment, was sounding new depths of fatuity; he embarked on a scornful denunciation of the Broadway theatre, slashing left and right at its banality and commercialism. Perhaps his artistic standards were too lofty, he conceded, but he would sooner lay down his pen than cater to the degraded tastes of a bunch of cloak-and-suiters. I stared at the man frozenly, longing to tighten a bowstring around his neck, to somehow quench his babble forever, but on he boomed, impervious to all save the music of his own voice. By the time we finally sat down to eat, a deep fatalism suffused me. I had done everything imaginable to avert a catastrophe, and my tocsin had gone unheeded. If someone wound up skewered from end to end—Pettijohn, by choice—at least my conscience was clear.

The dinner that ensued, while not quite as harrowing an ordeal as a meal I once shared in the Uganda saw grass with the sixteen members of an all-girl safari, was nevertheless a lulu. My heartbeat, I was convinced, was sickeningly audible as I spooned out tiny portions of the dressing in the flickering candlelight; at any instant, I was braced for the metallic glint, the strangled cry, and the whole calamitous hurly-burly that would follow. Insofar as one could exercise a degree of caution, I did my utmost, carving paper-thin slices of the bird, screening each one painstakingly, and even mashing down the cranberry sauce to make certain it harbored nothing lethal. My consort must have instinctively sensed the trepidation I felt, for within minutes her perplexity yielded to irritation. "Why on earth are you fiddling around there?" she demanded. "Give Robin and Vida something to eat. Those portions wouldn't feed a sparrow."

"I'll say," Pettijohn chimed in. "I think he's hoarding it for himself. Come on, fella," he urged, extending his plate in a humorous imitation of Oliver Twist, "I'm a big boy and I want my vittles—eh, Vida?"

"Oh, Robin, don't be a pig," she rebuked him, snatching the words out of my mouth. "As a matter of fact, though, I will have another wee bit of the stuffing." She threw the hostess a bright smile that was stiff with insincerity. "It's really scrumptious, darling—do tell me what went into it."

I could have told her, and for a fleeting moment had to fight off a wild impulse to do so. Finally, and agonizingly, however, the crisis passed; the main course ended without any lesions and we segued into the dessert. The strain I had undergone predictably produced its reaction, and if I was a bit prodigal with my own tot in serving the brandy, I needed a shield for the pyrotechnics I knew were inevitable when the Pettijohns left. They erupted promptly.

"*Well*," said my wife, her arms assuming the posture traditionally known as akimbo. "Before I comment on your behavior tonight, would you like to make a short, bumbling statement?"

"You're damn well right I would," I said, and launched into a heated résumé of the events of the afternoon.

Her face softened as I concluded. "Mercy, but what anguish you've been through!" she sympathized. "If you'd only seen the note I left on the drainboard."

"Note?" I repeated faintly. "About what?"

"The buttons I asked Bonanza to sew on your shirts," she said. "*She* saw it, even if she couldn't find the needle. In fact," she mused, "Bonanza sees everything that goes on around here, and sometimes I wonder how she stands it."

Curious creatures, women. Always coming out with these elliptical remarks, and the devil only knows what they're driving at. Ah, well, perhaps they're just trying to needle you—to pin you down—to keep you on tenterhooks . . . Oh, bother, you know what I mean.

A Walk on the Sweet Side

STICKY GOES WALKIES . . . AT £5 A DAY. Eighteen inches of well-groomed dog called Sternroc Sticky Wicket yesterday went walkies with his mistress. And just behind, and costing about £5 a day, was his own personal 6 ft. 2 in. private detective. Sticky is the only dog in Britain with a human "tail." He is the American champion of the Schnauzer breed, a wire-haired terrier-like dog, and is insured in the U.S. for £1000. Every time Sticky makes more than a brief appearance among the ordinary canines of the world he must have a private eye shadowing him. Otherwise, says his English-born owner, Mrs. Pamela Cross Stern, people might feed him sweets. "You only need a few people a day to stuff Sticky with titbits and his championship qualities would be ruined," said Mrs. Cross Stern.—*London Daily Mail.*

I MUST have worked my way through half a dozen copies of the *Tatler,* and was thoroughly briefed on the activities of the gentry—all their hunt balls, cotillions, and débutante parties—when the door opened and Mr. Hawfinch bustled in. He was a stout, breathless chap in a pepper-and-salt tweed, quite unlike my notion of a fancy bespoke tailor, but then I'd never had much traffic with the breed, always having bought my clothes off the peg. What I mean is, if you're the sort who can afford to spend fifty guineas for a suit, that's splendid, and God bless; in my line of work, one wants a serviceable, inconspicuous garment that doesn't stand out in a crowd.

"Ah, good afternoon, Piggott—have I the name right?" he puffed. "Hadn't meant to keep you, but I've been rushed off my feet with fittings. Here, let's have this door closed. It's a—well, a rather confidential matter."

"It generally is if I'm called in," I said. "Nothing serious, I hope?"

"Heavens, no—not in the least," he said. "Just a curious situation we've run into that requires a bit of skilled assistance, as it were. Can I rely on your discretion?"

I could see the man was uneasy about getting entangled with a professional sleuth, so I reassured him straight off. I hadn't any police affiliation or formal detective status, I explained. I was merely a private operative licensed to protect property or individuals, and such work as I did nowadays was largely humdrum—guarding valuables at society weddings, discouraging shoplifters at Harrods in the holiday season, and the like.

"Capital," said Mr. Hawfinch. "You're exactly the person we're looking for—someone who can protect a client of ours."

"Against what?"

"His own worst enemy—himself," he replied. "I daresay you've heard many a weird tale in your time, Piggott, but this may surprise you."

He wasn't far wrong. For the past eight years, it appeared, Hawfinch & Mealworm had been supplying the client in question, an American journalist named S. G. Prebleman, with lounge suits. To fit anyone with a melon-shaped paunch and shoulders the size of a pygmy's, declared Hawfinch, was a major challenge, but the cutters had accepted it, and, until recently, no hint of dissatisfaction had arisen. Then a barrage of complaints had begun to bombard the firm from overseas. The clothes were altogether too small, Prebleman complained; the firm had departed from its original pattern, the last consignment shipped him was barely adequate for a midget, he had endured public humiliation and was fast becoming a figure of fun, etc., etc.

"The fellow was fatting up like a Christmas goose, of course," said Hawfinch, "and our staff soon discovered why when he popped in here a fortnight ago to order some new things. He was ravenous for sweets—he'd turned into a sugar addict. Forever stuffing himself with cakes, tarts, pastry, puddings, Lord knows what all. Damned if he hadn't a butterscotch bar in his fist while he was being measured." Hawfinch shrugged. "Well, he was sly at first, but once we taxed him with it, he owned up. A fatal compulsion, he called it. Go out of his head if he was deprived."

"He needs a medico, not a bodyguard," I said. "I don't see how I can prevent him from gluttonizing."

"You can, actually," said Hawfinch. "As a matter of fact, the whole idea of surveillance wasn't ours—he proposed it. It's not mere vanity on his part, you see; it's simple economics. He's investing a couple of hundred pounds in these garments, and should he gain any more weight, they'd be worthless."

"But what am I supposed to do, specifically?" I asked, puzzled.

"Just dog his footsteps the next couple of days, until he leaves for New York," he said. "Censor his diet—jump down his throat if he starts nibbling toffees, desserts, and such. He feels that a bit of really strict discipline might help him overcome his craving. As for us," Hawfinch went on, "our motive in hiring you is pure self-interest. We've a reputation to sustain, and it'd be rotten publicity if our wares appeared to disadvantage in the States."

Well, that was pretty much the gist of it, except for his emphasizing that Prebleman, despite his professed willingness to coöperate, would undoubtedly attempt to trick me. I promised to be ruthless and, pocketing the retainer and his client's hotel address, went back to my cubbyhole in Carstairs Buildings. As I walked along Regent Street reviewing the assignment, I began to have qualms about it. Practically speaking, how could one impose curbs on a stranger's appetite? Moreover, what authorization had I to do so, beyond Hawfinch's word? Denied his gooseberry flan or portion of trifle, Prebleman might decide I was persecuting him and react with violence; people with fixations often behaved unpredictably. I was within an ace of ringing up Hawfinch to chuck the job when common sense intervened. After all, the role he'd cast me in wasn't that of a gadfly or scourge but a good Samaritan; it wasn't my mission to harass the boffin but to pluck temptation from his path, to bolster his morale. The instant I'd rationalized my position, and washed it down with a pint of bitter, my compunctions vanished.

At ten-fifteen the next morning, as I was lounging outside Coxcomb's Hotel, in Duke Street, a plump little gent with a florid complexion, steel-rimmed spectacles, and a piebald mustache came through the revolving door. He looked an unsuccessful tobacconist or a news agent more than a Yankee journalist, but the door porter, to whom I'd slipped half a crown, pantomimed that this was my man, so I followed a few paces behind. Twenty yards along, without any warning, he stopped dead, turned, and waited till I drew abreast.

"Excuse me," he said. "You wouldn't by any chance be the Mr. Piggott who's shadowing me?"

"That's correct, sir," I said. "I take it Mr. Hawfinch's been in touch."

He nodded and, eyes narrowed, surveyed me thoughtfully. "Good choice," he observed. "Typical, but unobtrusive. Fine— let's get started. Mind if I pop into that snack bar on the corner for coffee?"

"Sorry, Mr. Prebleman," I said. "You've already had breakfast—and two helpings of marmalade, I understand. I checked with room service a few minutes ago."

"That was pretty officious of you, I must say," he commented, his face clouding over.

"Merely carrying out orders," I said. "I was told you wanted me to play the martinet."

"Yes, I guess I asked for it," he said resignedly. "Very well, now—look sharp. I'm going down to Fortnum & Mason's. Want to pick up something suitable to wear when I work."

"Like a hacking coat, sir?" I twinkled, nudging him in the ribs. I saw immediately that I'd overstepped, and hurried to apologize. "Just chaffing, Mr. Prebleman," I assured him. "Please go wherever you would normally, and I shan't interfere unless I deem it urgent. Fair enough?"

He agreed, and away we went. Everything was jam until we got inside the shop. There was such a crush of folk boarding the lift that we became separated, and by the time I reached the men's-wear section it was all too plain I'd been given the slip. Luckily, I didn't lose my head. Hurrying to the grocery division, on the main floor, I surprised Prebleman just as he was clawing open a tin of Canton ginger. He'd already choked down half a box of arrowroot biscuit, and a saleswoman was busily wrapping a parcel of barley sugar and chocolate creams. My quarry blushed scarlet with shame when he saw me. He mumbled some bilge about a dispatch case containing official secrets that he'd forgotten in his Daimler, pressed a ten-bob note on the astonished clerk, and bolted up Piccadilly toward Hyde Park Corner. I clung to him, and a proper chase he gave me, doubling back along Berkeley Square up Hay Hill into Dover Street. From there into Bond Street was clogged with pedestrians and I was fair winded getting through, so intent on keeping a tight rein on him that I never tumbled to his destination—the Pembroke Tea Salon, close by Aspinwall House. Before I could remonstrate, he'd popped inside, leaving me high and dry. A sedate place like that, full of old ladies, I didn't much fancy the idea of creating a row, so I just lit my pipe and settled down to wait. When he skipped out a quarter of an hour later, all bland and pious with currant jelly on his mustache and his pockets bursting, I dropped down on him like a Brahmany kite.

"Look here, old boy," I said. "It's your waistline, and once you're back home you can get as gross as Falstaff, but right now I call the tune. Will you hand over the stuff you bought or do I have to search you?"

"You wouldn't dare," he said, backing away. "Don't you touch me, you big bully. I—I'll scream!"

Well, that was sheer bluff, of course—the sugar in his system talking—and he turned into a lamb the moment I found the pressure point in his wrist. It seemed a pity to jettison all the macaroons and ladyfingers he'd laid in; still, as I warned him, if he repeated such a performance I'd have to dress him down publicly, no matter what embarrassment it might cause.

"You're dead right—absolutely," he said contritely. "Piggott, I've been a sneaky, self-indulgent little ass, but I'm turning over a new leaf, thanks to you. To show my gratitude, I'm giving you the rest of the day off."

"That's generous of you, sir, but Mr. Hawfinch's instructions were quite explicit. You're not to be let out of my sight."

"Oh, quite, quite," he said. "However, at the time we formulated our pact, none of us foresaw that I might experience a sudden revelation. I'm completely cured, I tell you. Now, this afternoon," he continued glibly, "I'm just going to poke around galleries and antique shops. I may drop into the British Museum to see the Elgin marble cakes—" He broke off, flustered. "Dash it all, I don't need a nursemaid, you know. I'm a grown man, aren't I?"

I had a strong impulse to retort that, on the contrary, everything about him was infantile—his passion for sweets, his love of clothes, his longing to be considered an adult—but I restrained myself. Obviously, the more I crossed him, the more intractable he was likely to become. If, on the other hand, I pampered him a whit, gave him leave to gorge to his heart's content, he might behave rationally out of sheer perversity. It was worth a gamble, and I took it. Provided he bought no sweetmeats until we met again the following morning, I told him, he was free to do as he pleased, unsupervised. He sprang at the bait, wrung my hand warmly, and departed, doubtless to violate his promise, but I wasn't overly concerned. Deep down in my mind, a peculiar suspicion I couldn't put into words was beginning to gnaw at me. I had some hard thinking to get through in the next hour or two, and I needed the privacy of my office and plenty of cavendish.

At half past four that afternoon, Mr. Hawfinch, his jowls aquiver with anxiety, ushered me into his sanctum and, extracting a handkerchief, sponged his forehead. "See here, Piggott," he snapped. "Let's not beat around the bush—that phone call of yours upset me. Of course you're welcome to examine the patterns of Mr. Prebleman's suits—"

"And all his original measurements," I interjected.

"Yes, yes," he said irritably. "But why? What was your implication, sir?"

"There wasn't any," I said. "Call it an intuition, rather." I lowered my voice on the off chance that some interested ear might be listening at the keyhole. "It's merely that if I'm right it could have a very considerable bearing on the future of this company."

Mr. Hawfinch regarded me fixedly for a good ten seconds. "Well, you've told me nothing, but I've learned this much," he said. "When you've a problem with one eccentric, you don't necessarily solve it by calling in another. Mind you, I name no names."

"You don't have to," I said. "In my business, we're trained to figure out things like that. Shall we go along to your cutting room?"

It was well after nine that same evening when Prebleman, Hawfinch, and I finished our second round of port in the Coxcomb bar, and though my companions had tried to disguise the meeting as a social occasion, I could feel their growing impatience underneath our small talk. Evidently satisfied at last that the amenities had been complied with, Hawfinch took the bull by the horns.

"Now then, Piggott," he began, adopting his most formidable executive manner. "We seem to be involved in a most complex situation—too much so, I may say, for a simple tradesman like me. You were engaged to perform certain—ah—custodial duties on Mr. Prebleman's behalf which, as I understand it, you now wish to relinquish. Why?"

"Because they're no longer valid," I returned. "I regret to tell you, Mr. Hawfinch, that in the course of examining your files today I uncovered what I can only describe as some very damning evidence."

"Of what?" he demanded. "For pity's sake, man, speak up! I've had enough of your precious conundrums."

"Very well," I said, "but since it affects our mutual client, I prefer to tell him directly. Mr. Prebleman, for the last eight years you have been systematically and deliberately hoodwinked by Hawfinch & Mealworm."

Hawfinch started up from his chair. "What the devil are you talking about?" he burst out wrathfully. "Of all the libellous poppycock—"

"You have every right to be upset, sir," I broke in. "Nevertheless, permit me to finish. You yourself have been deceived even more shamefully. You're the victim of a conspiracy without parallel in the annals of custom tailoring—a plot that, had it succeeded, would have shaken Savile Row to its foundations."

As my auditors sat in stunned silence, I drew forth a notebook and marshalled the amazing, the well-nigh incredible, facts. I told them of my sudden wild surmise—based purely on instinct—that Prebleman's girth had not varied an inch over the years, despite his massive intake of sweets, and of my discovery that each successive consignment of clothes shipped him in the States had been made imperceptibly smaller in order to exacerbate and unnerve him. I explained how this had been part of a diabolical, cold-blooded plan evolved by someone close to Hawfinch—a scheme to alienate the American clientele, to ultimately bankrupt the firm and enable its architect to wrest control.

"And that someone is . . . ?" queried Hawfinch, his face ashen at my disclosures.

"Your own partner, Morty Mealworm," I concluded, "working hand in glove with Jack Sugarfoss, your head cutter—who, significantly, happens to be his nephew and the chap who consistently falsified Mr. Prebleman's measurements."

It was characteristic of the latter's magnanimity that though he had suffered beyond recompense, he was incapable of bearing a grudge. "Well, Hawfinch," he said quietly, "I trust this has been a salutary lesson to you. The next time a customer beefs anent a plethora of shoulder padding or tight armholes, don't castigate him for a dingbat but, rather, check out on whether or not there might be sabotage in your own bailiwick."

"I certainly will," Hawfinch assured him with a rueful demeanor, and rose purposefully. "As for those two precious scalawags whose depredations have just been aired, I had best lose no time in laying them by the heels. Well, many thanks, Piggott, old scout, and if you are ever in the market for a good pair of bespoke pants that will wear like iron, we can quote you a rock-bottom price." He paused at the door. "Goodbye, Mr. Prebleman—our travelling representative will shortly be skying Gothamward. Is there any place he can contact you?"

Prebleman smiled and flicked a nonexistent speck of icing from his lapel. "I shouldn't be surprised," he said radiantly. "The nearest Schrafft's."

Hello, Central, Give Me
That Jolly Old Pelf

I WAS teetering on my heels the other evening before our fireplace, quaffing a tankard of mulled ale, puffing on a churchwarden, and waving both in unison to a rousing stave—altogether a frightfully good simulacrum of one of Surtees' English sporting squires—when a wayward spark from the hearth suddenly ignited the skirts of my shooting coat. My whipcords stood out like veins, and in consequence I was obliged to remain *hors de combat* the next couple of days, propped up on my elbows and reading the most mealy prose. The situation might have proved less irksome had I been permitted some real intellectual exercise—I was halfway through Newman's *Apologia pro Vita Sua* and frantic to know how it came out—but my physician, in an effort to immobilize me, had decreed a strict invalid's diet of newspapers and predigested periodicals. The only redeeming feature of the entire affair, in retrospect, was that it enabled me to catch up with a few late developments in the advertising world as seen through the high-powered lens of Mr. Peter Bart, of the *Times*.

Inasmuch as Mr. Bart's column is buried deep in the financial section of the paper, and deals in large part with shifts of advertising appropriations and personnel, the casual reader may easily miss his more delectable tidbits. Typical of these was a report in mid-July of the aggressive strategy agency officials employ to secure new accounts. A couple of them, for example, "arranged to have two athletes in gymnastic attire break into the presentation. One carried a huge steel spike and the other an immense hammer. After one athlete hammered the spike into the floor with a resounding blow, the agency president called out dramatically: 'We can give your advertising greater impact.'" Whether the recipient of these attentions crowed in delight, ground his canines in rage, or merely sank deeper into apathy is not crystal-clear; what does emerge with certainty from Mr. Bart's chronicles is that advertising men stick at nothing in their creative frenzy: "One ad man who had proposed an unorthodox campaign to a prospect . . . rented a horse, painted it blue, and deposited it in the front yard of his prospect's Greenwich, Conn. home. Around the neck of the blue horse was a sign urging: 'Don't be afraid of being a horse of a different color.'" This tactic must have evoked many a chuckle from the owner of the horse and the A.S.P.C.A., to say nothing of anybody conversant with Swift's pungent chapters on the Houyhnhnms and the Yahoos in *Gulliver's Travels*.

Another, and rather more disturbing, anecdote of Mr. Bart's dealt with a new wrinkle for tapping the feminine market—a sort of sinister conversational chain reaction. An agency called Inform Associates, founded by a former schoolteacher named George Levine, has set up a network of housewives in four Eastern cities, each member of the sodality pledged to deliver a hundred one-minute commercials to her friends and acquaintances. "To keep track of their output," the story explained, "the women carry around a pocket-sized meter on which they register their commercials, delivered either in person or by telephone. The women consist mostly of active club members who circulate a great deal in their communities, says Mr. Levine. . . . Some women may be irritated when they find out that their friends are firing commercials at them, but Mr. Levine does not believe this problem to be serious. 'Consumers are so conditioned to constant commercial interruptions on radio and television that, like the Pavlovian dog, they miss them when they are not forthcoming,' he states." Intent on his target, Mr. Levine appears to be blissfully unmindful (or do I mean mindless?) of the hullabaloo, the sheer bedlam, the scheme may result in. However torpid one's imagination, it cannot help but reel at the thought of thousands of scarlet-faced club ladies, their glottises distended and their meters clicking as they bombard each other with panegyrics to their favorite detergent, laxative, or anti-perspirant. Goodbye Walden; hello Donnybrook Fair.

The most provocative item in Mr. Bart's bag of goodies, however, concerned the holiday season looming ahead. "A new service will be offered this Christmas to children who are bored with writing their requests to Santa Claus," he reported. "This year they can talk to Santa directly via something called the Santa Phone. Santa Phones will be set up at banks and department stores. . . . The service works like this: Stores having Santa Phones will invite children to pick up the receiver and talk directly to Santa in the North Pole. Santa, to be sure, turns out to be an employe in the back room who asks the child what he wants for Christmas. He also asks his name and address. This information is duly recorded, and a few days later the child's parents receive an envelope containing direct mail advertising for the products requested by the children. In the end, the children may get their presents, but the parents, not Santa, foot the bill."

That Madison Avenue has at last managed to strip Christmas of all the sentimental argel-bargel that has veiled it and transform the holiday into a pure, unbridled orgy of merchandising is epochal news. Henceforth, children will get the gifts they hunger for, no matter how fanciful, and their parents will be held liable for the cost, however crippling. The simplest way to demonstrate the fiendish beauty of the Santa Phone, I suggest, is to drop in on the household of Roy and Murine Isnook, a representative suburban couple engulfed by the Yuletide and desperately treading water.

SCENE: *The Isnook living room the night before Christmas. As the curtain rises, Roy Isnook, panting with exertion, has just finished gift-wrapping a sizable doll house and a Flexible Flyer in gossamer-thin, billowing pliofilm. His wife is perched on a kitchen ladder, trying to suspend a freshly baked gingerbread man, which keeps crumbling to bits under her fingers, from the topmost branch of their Christmas tree.*

Roy (*with satisfaction*): Well, honey, this is one holiday that won't put a crimp in the family exchequer, by the Lord Harry. Thanks to our native resourcefulness, these presents for our little nippers—Cosette, aged eleven, and Robin, nine—add up to a piffling sum.

MURINE: You mean that you actually fabricated that doll house, indistinguishable from those that F.A.O. Schwarz retails at five hundred berries, out of an old crate you wheedled from our local supermart? And that the sled was a factory second, discarded by the inspectors, which you quick-wittedly glommed from the company ash heap?

Roy: Yes, that is precisely what I mean. Can you blame me for preening myself on my sagacity?

MURINE: No, but I fear lest we may have carried economy too far, as witness this gingerbread man flaking into limbo. Maybe I should have used more cornstarch to bind the various elements together.

Roy: Ah, well, no need to pummel our brains over bygones now that the exposition is complete. Tell me, hon—just for curiosity's sake—did the little shavers happen to mention what they wanted for Christmas?

MURINE: Not directly, but when we were in the bank last week I overheard them speaking over the Santa Phone. Albeit she is still wet behind the ears, Cosette asked for a sable wrap and a baguette-diamond bracelet. Her brother said he was figuring on a sleek convertible—a Rolls, if memory serves.

Roy (*derisively*): Boy, what a couple of boobs. I suppose they think Kriss Kringle or somebody's going to drive up here and bring 'em that stuff. (*The purr of a sleek convertible, scarcely audible to anybody but a dog or a reader of*

David Ogilvy, and therefore more likely than not a Rolls, is heard offscene.) Who in the world can that be?

MURINE: (*peering through the Venetian blind*): Search me. A corpulent individual of executive mien, under whose arm I descry a cardboard box bearing the legend "Revillon Frères," seems to be striding forcefully up to the front door.

ROY: Mr. Follansbee, our bank manager, answers closely to that description, but why should he pay us a midnight call? (*Follansbee, a portly Mr. Gotrox in a befrogged astrakhan greatcoat, his smile reminiscent of a cheese blintz freshly fried in butter, enters briskly.*)

FOLLANSBEE: Evening, all. This the Isnook residence?

ROY: That's right. I'm Roy Isnook, and this is my wife, Murine.

FOLLANSBEE: Glad to make the pleasure of your acquaintance, friends. I'm Hollis P. Follansbee, of the Counterfeiters' and Kiters' National.

ROY: You don't have to tell me. I'm a depositor there.

FOLLANSBEE (*his banker's caution suddenly aroused*): You are, eh? How do I know that?

ROY: Why—er—lemme see. (*Producing his wallet*) Here's a blank check.

FOLLANSBEE: That doesn't make you a depositor, Mac. Anybody can carry around a blank check.

ROY: Are you calling me a liar?

FOLLANSBEE (*His smile reveals four rows of teeth, like a basking shark.*): Not at all. I'm merely asking you to identify yourself.

ROY: O.K.! O.K.! Don't take *my* word for it. Ask her who I am!

FOLLANSBEE: Why should I?

ROY: Because she's been living under the same roof with me for twelve years. She's my missus!

FOLLANSBEE: She is, eh? How do I know that?

ROY (*heatedly*): Would she be standing there holding a gingerbread man if she wasn't?

FOLLANSBEE: Listen, Pappy, when you're in the banking business as long as I am, you get used to some pretty weird sights.

MURINE (*indignantly*): What's wrong with my flannel housecoat?

FOLLANSBEE: The fleur-de-lis device is upside down.

MURINE: That's the way it was in the pattern, wise guy. You think you know more than the Butterick people?

FOLLANSBEE: You bet I do. I hold a second mortgage on their plant.

MURINE: Well, go ahead and foreclose! I hope you drop dead, you rummy!

FOLLANSBEE (*stung*): Look here, madam, I went out of my way this Christmas Eve to bring your children their presents! I drove over icy roads without any chains—

ROY: He's right, dear. The least we could do is show our hospitality—ask him to sit down or something.

MURINE: Well, I don't like his attitude. The man from United Parcel always has a nice smile, even when they're on strike.

ROY (*wigwagging*): But Mr. Follansbee's from the *bank*—you know, the monthly payments on our pool, the refrigerator—

MURINE: Oh, *that* Mr. Follansbee? (*Hastily*) Here, do sit down and have a drop of this leekoor, Mr. Follansbee! They call it Fiore d'Alpi, on account of that little tree inside the bottle.

FOLLANSBEE: No, thanks muchly. I just stopped off to deliver the youngsters' presents so they won't be disappointed in the morning. Here is Cosette's wrap, nestling inside the sleeve of which reposes her diamond bauble. The auto her baby brother specified, needless to say, is purring in the driveway.

MURINE (*sobbing*): To think that practically yesterday my little boy was riding up and down there on his scooter.

FOLLANSBEE: No use hiding your heads in the sand, folks. You

117

can't turn back the clock. (*Extending a delivery slip*)
Here, sign on the bottom.

ROY: Gorry, Mr. Follansbee, you'll never know how happy
. . . (*Gulps*) I got such a lump in my throat I can't even
say it.

FOLLANSBEE: What?

ROY: Those kids'll never believe there ain't a Santa Claus. Of
course, you and I know it's only an employee in the back
room.

FOLLANSBEE: We do, eh?

MURINE (*anxiously*): Of course. Isn't—isn't that what Mr. Bart
had in his column in the New York *Times?*

FOLLANSBEE (*his eyes twin gimlets set rather close together*):
Times? What's that—some tomfool newspaper or other
down there?

ROY: We—we got a fat envelope from you people last Thurs-
day with—uh—some leaflets, like, inside, but I thought—
that is, *she* thought—it was only an ad. (*Whimpering*) It
came third class. . . .

FOLLANSBEE: Yup. (*Extracting a document from his greatcoat*)
Well, just sign this form in triplicate, both of you, and I'll
fill in the details from your installment card at the bank.
The gifts total thirty-three nine hundred—let's say thirty-
five grand for convenience. Added to what you already
owe on the house, your car, the TV, the children's tuition,
the washer, the cruiser, the freezer— Have I overlooked
anything? (*Roy and Murine shake their heads mutely.*)
Wait a minute. Didn't you buy a dog on time? An Irish
wolfhound, from the Bosthoon Kennels?

MURINE (*snuffling*): He was run over by the milkman two
months after.

FOLLANSBEE: Tough luck, but you still owe a two-hundred-and-
twelve balance on him. O.K. Let's say that all comes to
another thirty-five Gs. Add another twenty for interest.
Mmmm. Ninety thousand. Over a twelve-month period,
that works out at seventy-five hundred a month—exclusive
of carrying charges, natch.

ROY: Mr. Follansbee, I make a hundred and twenty-four dollars and fifty cents a week—one hundred and five and eighty-nine cents after deductions—

FOLLANSBEE (*brightly*): Then why not consolidate all your debts? We'll loan you a hundred thousand at twenty per cent—that's a hundred and twenty thousand at forty per cent, or a hundred and sixty-eight at eighty per cent, if we handle the paper. Or you can go to Handelsman Associates, the creative-management group, borrow the money from them, pay us, borrow the money from us, pay them, and amortize the children. (*He sponges the foam from his lips.*) What was the dog's name?

MURINE: Garryowen. His—his great-grandfather belonged to a gombeen man in Dublican. I mean a publican in Dub, a Mr. Kieran.

FOLLANSBEE (*shortly*): I've met the man. We served in the Easter Rebellion together—him and I and Patrick Ahearn, or, as he now likes to style himself, Myles Na gCopaleen.

ROY: Mr. Follansbee, we're giving the presents back! You can't hold us to what a couple of dopey kids asked for on the phone!

MURINE: That's right, Roy—they're minors! We're not legally responsible!

FOLLANSBEE (*silkily*): For a tape recording in which Mrs. Isnook approves the order?

MURINE: I didn't any such thing!

FOLLANSBEE: Let me read you the relevant portion of the transcript. (*Affixes pince-nez to his cheeseparing nose*) As Cosette finishes, ROBIN'S VOICE: "If she gets all that, I'm figuring on a Rolls-Royce convertible!" An adult voice cuts in. WOMAN'S VOICE: "O.K.! O.K.! Come on along!" (*To Murine, pleasantly*) I don't think twelve jurors good and true should have any difficulty in distinguishing that voice, do you, Mrs. Isnook?

MURINE: I was only trying to get those little idiots away from the phone!

FOLLANSBEE (*At his smile, icicles form on the tree.*): That's what the jury'll be called on to decide, Mrs. Isnook! (*Refrogging the shawl collar of his astrakhan*) Well, friends, a Merry Christmas to the four of you, and don't bother to walk me to the bus. I'm as warm as toast. (*He opens the door, admitting a gust of snowflakes and a gaunt, stoop-shouldered individual resembling Eamon de Valera bundled in a worn trench coat and a long green muffler. As the two jockey and sidestep each other, Follansbee starts in recognition, then hurtles out the doorway into the darkness. The visitor blinks at the Isnooks through steam-veiled pebble spectacles.*)

VISITOR: Good evenin' to yez all. Ahearn's my name, Myles Na gCopaleen to my friends, and it's good news I have for someone named Isnook holdin' ticket BNX6556 in the Irish Hospitals' Sweeps. Would annyone here offer a thravel-stained wayfarer a cup of tay?

CURTAIN

Samson Shorn, or
The Slave of Love

Had you been a turkey buzzard lazily circling over Tinicum Township in eastern Bucks County last Friday—a possibility, by the way, that shouldn't be excluded until you can establish proof to the contrary—you might have observed beneath your talons the prelude to a dramatic event that occurred later that morning. A portly householder whose nose resembled an exploded boysenberry was engaged in clearing away the snow piled against the entrance of his stone dwelling, his pulses throbbing in the dry, frosty air like the royal Watusi drums. One two, one two, the shovel flew in a great flashing arc at the behest of arms that put toothpicks to shame. At the count of six he straightened up, exhaled, and, carefully placing the shovel behind a syringa bush where it would be available for spring planting, went into the house.

I describe the foregoing because, in a roundabout way, it gives an insight into the dark intricacies of the feminine mind. Hardly had I scuffed the snow from my boots, brewed a milk punch, and curled up before the fire with Palgrave's *Golden Treasury*, concealed within it a photomontage of Balinese maidens hulling rice, when my wife entered. Before I could wipe the steam from my bifocals, she had launched into a philippic worthy of Cicero or Senator Dirksen.

"I know—I've only myself to blame!" she wailed. "My family saw through all those fine promises of yours thirty-five years

121

ago. They warned me you were a loafer and a Lothario, that you'd never lift a finger around the house. Other women have husbands—I've got a cheap facsimile of George Brent, a cluck too lazy to put up a clothesline."

A less gallant person might have pointed out that he had dug the place out of a blizzard, but I scorn cheap victories. "Goodness, my dear Xantippe, you look upset," I said. "Whatever is the matter—or is it only the ravages of time?"

The woman regarded me with an expression of reproach no St. Bernard could ever have hoped to equal. "How many times have you promised to hang up my moth bags?"

"Moth bags?" I repeated, unable to credit my ears. "A moth couldn't survive ten minutes in this weather. Look at the drifts—it's like the Chilkoot Pass!"

"That's what you said last year," she flung at me. "Next thing I knew, all my dresses were chewed to bits, my Italian stole, my sweaters, my wool hose, everything!" But far worse than my apathy, she rushed on, was my contrariness. "For all you care, the roof could fall in," she snuffled. "I beg you to carry the ashes out of the cellar, to put in a few pothooks, to sweep the leaves off the porch, and what satisfaction do I get? *Nyet*—all you do is lie there guzzling over your pinups while the moths and silverfish eat us out of house and home."

Realizing that the poor soul's obsession might become paranoid unless I humored her, I laid aside my book, procured a bag of camphor balls and ascended to the attic. Even a magpie, and a slovenly one, would have been dismayed by the sight that confronted me. Since 1952, when I had left the place in apple-pie order, some vandal had been systematically creating a replica of the Paris Flea Market. Piles of moldering luggage I had never seen before lay stacked against the eaves; the floor was strewn with an appalling mulch of old fly screens, Victrola records, lamp shades, tennis rackets, overshoes, hot-water bottles, and Ayvad's Water Wings; and to compound the havoc, my wife's discarded finery—which I had painstakingly isolated until fashion made it practical again—had been exhumed from steamer trunks and streaked with rust. Fortunately, my New

England upbringing had taught me never to flinch at chores, however unpalatable. Selecting those key areas in which moths were most likely to hatch, I sprinkled them liberally with the repellent, nailed the attic door shut, and returned to the fireside, where, over the balance of the punch, I pondered my wife's extraordinary behavior and tried to assess two-score years' experience with the opposite gender.

This lacklustre drudge I beheld every morning in my shaving mirror, his forehead corrugated into wide-wale corduroy—could he possibly be the virile, dynamic Casanova, I asked myself, who in youth had ravished so many feminine hearts? Woeful that an Adonis gifted with the intellect of a Gibbon—the historian, that is, not the ape—should have become such a door mat, yet it amply illustrated the power of womenfolk to destroy a man. Even at nineteen, at the dawn of the Jazz Age, I recalled that the comeliest of their sex were already pursuing me, eager for the honey of my kisses. A sophomore at Brown, I used to frequent a pleasure dome called the Arcadia Ballroom in Providence; and when, attired in my green Norfolk jacket and Scotch-grain bluchers with brass eyelets, I toddled to the strains of "Dardanella" and "Stumbling," shopgirls and society women alike turned into bacchantes. So unbridled was their behavior, indeed, that the dean begged me, in the interests of public morality, to restrict my appearances to Saturday nights only. The establishment's receipts, naturally, shrank to a trickle, and in the wave of female suicides that followed my graduation, it was forced to close its doors.

The stripling bent on making his mark as a comic artist who arrived in Greenwich Village in 1925 was too innocent to gauge the perils awaiting him. Wherever I turned, I was beset by women—models, aspiring actresses, rich socialites—all of them hungry for love. In vain I tried to convey to them that my career was paramount, that sensualist though I appeared, I was at bottom deeply ascetic. Deaf to my entreaties, they resorted to every underhand device to beguile me. They bribed my landlady, secreted themselves in closets and laundry hampers, even masqueraded as Western Union messengers.

Ofttimes, striving to work at my drawing board, I would discover two or more of the creatures on my lap, beseeching me for caresses. It was typical of their shallow natures that once they had attained their ends, they cynically cast me aside. Eventually, on the verge of distraction, I washed my hands of the lot and sought refuge in Paris.

Like most impulsive gestures, this one proved a near-fatal blunder. I had not reckoned on the hordes of beauties crowding the French capital, the saucy midinettes straight out of *La Vie Parisienne* swinging their hatboxes, the pert grisettes swinging their derrières, the elegant *poules de luxe* ambuscading me at Maxim's to buy them lobsters and champagne. If I so much as entered the Café de la Paix or Les Ambassadeurs, an uproar of oo-la-la's greeted me and I was smothered with feminine embraces; dry-clean them as I might, my clothes exuded a sickening scent of patchouli, musk and heliotrope. At last my concierge took pity on me.

"M'zoo, you are too patient wiz zem, all zat *canaille*," she said. "Zis godlike beauty of yours could easily *cuire votre l'oie* (cook your goose). *Peut-être* if you tell zem you are passionately *enchanté* wiz someone, zey weel desist."

Relieved, I let it be bruited about that I was head over heels in love with a certain Baronne Solange Finisterre de Couzé, a noblewoman I invented on the spur of the moment. What was my dismay when, the very next morning, a perfumed envelope bearing the Couzé crest—entwined hearts on a field of lilies, with a goat rampant—arrived by messenger. Its contents left no doubt regarding the writer's intentions toward me. With an ardor verging on idolatry, Solange confessed that she had been infatuated with me from the instant I had set foot on French soil. The ecstasies she promised if I granted her a rendezvous (date) made my cheeks flame, and I foolishly agreed to her proposal. While I found her personable—a blend of Sophia Loren and Aileen Pringle, though more voluptuous—the predictable happened: her passion for me grew insatiable. She began babbling my praises so widely through the Faubourg St.-Honoré, the Avenue de l'Observatoire, and even the Bon Marché department store, that her husband's seconds finally waited on me and demanded satisfaction. Inasmuch as I had given the baroness plenty, I felt that I had done enough for the family, and left posthaste for England.

To recount my progress through London, Rome, Madrid and elsewhere would be mere repetition; on every hand I left behind languishing, inconsolable ladies to whom I had at least brought a glimpse of paradise unattainable. Meanwhile, in the fatuous belief that I could discourage their fervor if I chose another identity, I laid aside my velvet tam and Windsor tie, forsook the brush for the quill, and became a writer. The ruse succeeded until 1931, when the wheel of fortune revolved and deposited me in Hollywood, a scenarist for the Marx Brothers. Possibly I was drawn there by boyhood devotion to Billie Dove, Priscilla Dean and, above all, to Corinne Griffith, renowned as "the orchidaceous star" and unquestionably the most beautiful woman who ever lived [with the possible exception of a Eurasian I saw dealing blackjack in Manila in 1949]. In whatever case, I soon discovered that I had leaped from the frying pan into the fire. The ambience of celibacy Groucho had promised me if I worked for the troupe was a fiction made up of whole cloth. As I should have guessed, the man carried with him a pocketful of whole cloth from which he made up such fictions. Our conferences and shooting were constantly disrupted by the shriek of starlets evading Harpo's onrush, and Chico and Zeppo, while not quite so impetuous, also bore little resemblance to Cotton Mather. Small wonder, hence, that, surrounded by honeybuns like Thelma Todd, Lilyan Tashman and Toby Wing, my moral fibre should have begun to disintegrate. Less and less I found myself at home dreaming over Spenser's *Epithalamion* and the essays of Bacon; a strange restlessness gripped me that could only be assuaged by tooling a white Duesenberg along Sepulveda Boulevard at seventy miles an hour with a platinum-bobbed head on my shoulder. It was, as I look back on it, a period of—how shall I say?—self-exploration, of coming to grips with things.

Subtly, and quite without any awareness on my part, the icy reserve I had always shown the opposite sex, a trait doubtless inherited from generations of Spanish hidalgos, began to be undermined. It became manifest when, in 1943, I joined with Kurt Weill and Ogden Nash to fashion *One Touch of Venus,* a musical comedy starring Mary Martin. Never before could wild horses have dragged me backstage; the idea of being pawed and fought over by a corps of scantily clad dancers that included Sono Osato, Pearl Lang, Allyn Ann McLerie and Nelle Fisher would have revolted me to the core. A decade in Hollywood, luckily, had inured me to *zaftig* female epidermis en masse, and so, if I had nothing better to do—which was rare—I strolled into the wings and allowed the coryphées to cosset me. It detracted nothing from me, and it gave them an illusion of bliss they could not otherwise obtain in their drab lives.

Thus it was inevitable, nay, foreordained, that, like Sherlock Holmes' ultimate confrontation with his adversary Professor Moriarty, I should at last come face to face with my nemesis, the Serpent of Old Nile—Elizabeth Taylor. She, whose witchery fuses cash registers to white heat, and I, proud, remote, disdainful, had originally met in the orbit of Mike Todd when I whelped the script of *Around the World in Eighty Days.* Those at the encounter will attest that not a muscle flickered in my lean visage, although her lips parted in stupefaction, enabling her to hurriedly spoon in several gobs of pistachio ice cream. From time to time thereafter our trails crossed and I read fear in those magnificent orbs, the knowledge that I had only to crook my finger and it would stay crooked. To protect herself against that fear, she threw herself heart and soul into an intrigue with an actor named Bolton or Benton, some kind of Welsh *arriviste.* But the day of reckoning was nearing, and it came last summer with thunderclap swiftness.

I was in London, working on a television spectacular for her that narcotized seventy million viewers so effectively that dozens of drug firms have sought to name tranquillizers after me. One evening she and this Buxton party—I can't remember the confounded chap's name—invited me to dinner at her sumptuous pad in the Dorchester. She greeted me in a primrose-yellow lounging ensemble by Dior appliquéd with doubloons, and as I beheld her coiffure, aglitter with gold dust, I was reluctantly forced to admit that she did have a modicum of allure. Our conversation over cocktails was on an altogether impersonal plane; we discussed the new best-seller by Anna Sewell, *Black Beauty*, recalled various Hollywood werewolves we had known, and exchanged an epigram or two that deplorably do not lend themselves to print. Brompton, the Welsh upstart I spoke of, sat nursing his drink a few feet away, his features contorted with jealousy. Suddenly, out of a clear sky, Elizabeth burst into heartrending sobs.

"You *hate* me," she wept, burying her face in hands thickly encrusted with emeralds. "Why? Why? You're always so cold, so remote—like a regular iceberg! I don't believe you have a spark of real feeling!" As I bent beneath her fury, she cried out like a wild thing in pain. "Can't you see I've adored you all these years, you blind little fool?"

To deny the soft impeachment was useless, yet such is the tyranny of tears that momentarily I was struck dumb. Had her woman's instinct detected the chink in my armor? Was I, secretly and deep down, putty in her hands like her myriad male admirers? The next moment was to provide the answer. She extended her glass imperiously.

"Here, get me some more Seltzer water," she commanded, indicating a lowboy on which were ranged vintage carbonated waters from all over the world.

I arose, desperately struggling for self-mastery, but there was a quaver in my voice. "I—I'm not your lackey," I faltered. "Go get it yourself."

"Once and for all, you," she said, her marble brow darkening. "Are you or are you not fetching me that there Seltzer?"

You could have heard a Van Cleef & Arpels pin drop in the stillness as our wills clashed, each straining for supremacy, but the outcome was already written in the stars. "Yes, ma'am," I piped in a humiliating falsetto, and from that moment forward I was ruined, irretrievably lost, *kaput*. My vaunted haughtiness, my Olympian detachment, was gone forever: I was a *schlep*.

In the background Brixton gave vent to a sardonic Welsh

chuckle. "You never had a prayer, Clyde," he cackled. "She gets 'em all."

This, then, had been my downfall, I reflected bitterly as I stared into the embers on my Pennsylvania hearth last Friday morning. An Apollo endowed with gifts beyond mortal ken reduced to the status of an exterminator, a custodian of ashes— O, what a noble mind was here o'erthrown! And who was to blame? Only myself, I and my fellow *schleps* who, out of sheer magnanimity, had enfranchised women and as thanks been stripped of leadership in the family, the professions, and commerce. Pusillanimous, cringing wretch that I was to submit to such infamy . . . I sprang to my feet, boiling with wrath, and addressed a silver standard poodle sprawled on the carpet.

"Look at me!" I bellowed. "The man you own as master—or do you too scoff at him behind his back? Well, get this, Jocko—from now on there's going to be a new deal in this household! No more menial jobs for old Dads, do you hear? I'm through being a slavey in my own home, living on crusts and dressing in hand-me-downs! No more of those TV dinners, those makeshift meals you wouldn't dare serve to a handyman. Henceforth, I'm the big wheel around here, and I demand to be treated accordingly! When the *grand seigneur* eats, it's going to be by candlelight, eight courses and plenty of good, fattening desserts—is that clear? And what's more, the women are jolly well staying in purdah! The day of the matriarchy is over—back to the kitchen where they belong!"

Someone behind me cleared her throat, and I turned. It was my wife, clad in a thousand-dollar Nina Ricci original and an Adolfo hat, and utterly expressionless. She was extending a basinful of green podlike objects.

"Here, clean these limas, Buster," she said laconically, "and if anyone wants me, I'm down at the Chanticler in New Hope playing bridge. Got it?"

"Yes, dear," I squeaked in that same humiliating falsetto. I wonder what *can* be amiss with my voice. Perhaps I ought to consult a specialist.

The Sweet Chick Gone

[*Another Plum from the Anthropomorphic Pie Containing* Born Free, Ring of Bright Water, *etc.*]

T HE FIRST faint flush of dawn silvered the bedroom
windows of my Sherry-Netherland suite this morning as I
awoke, stretched voluptuously, and, slipping into a peignoir,
perched on the vanity. While not given to excessive conceit
—we White Leghorns, if less flamboyant than your Orping-
tons and Wyandottes, take pride in our classic tailored lines—
I was pleased by the reflection the mirror gave back to me.
My opulent comb and wattles, the snowy plumage on my
bosom, and the aristocratic elegance of each yellow leg
adorned by its manicured claws all bespoke generations of
breeding. In this great metropolis that slumbered around
me, was there, I asked myself, one pullet half so celebrated
and successful, a single fowl who could contest my supremacy?
I had beauty, wealth, the adoration of the multitude—and
yet, on either side of my aching beak, I saw tiny telltale
grooves of discontent, and I knew that, despite its outward
glitter, mine was a hollow triumph. I had reached a pinnacle
undreamed of in poultrydom, but at what fearful cost.

With an impatient cluck, I shrugged off my introspective
mood and hopped into the living room. The reek of cigars, the
overflowing ashtrays, and the highball glasses mutely attested
to the parasites—the agents and lawyers, tax experts and
business managers—who battened off me. Here they revelled

away their evenings, sipping my liqueur Scotch and (I ofttimes suspected) jeering at my artlessness. "She's only a silly little White Leghorn," I could hear them commenting cynically to each other. "Better get yours while the getting's good." Well, I reflected, at least I didn't suffer from the illusion that money purchased loyalty and affection; S. G. Prebleman had seen to *that*. At the thought of my first and greatest benefactor, a wave of such intense anguish enveloped me, such acute yearning to nestle in his arms, that I was forced to cling to a drape until equilibrium returned. Then, fluttering to the window sill, I stared down over the greenery of Central Park and surrendered to a train of bittersweet memories.

A yellow ball of fluff cheeping in a New Jersey incubator— why had Fate capriciously singled me out for greatness from that swarming brood? I remembered how anonymous I had felt on my emergence from egghood, deafened by the clamor of my hatchmates, buffeted in the melee around the feeding troughs. Scarcely were my pinfeathers dry when I was swept into a carton with a score of others, whirled through the maelstrom of the postal system, and deposited outside a hardware store in Perkasie, Pennsylvania. Those were halcyon days for us fledglings; basking in the adulation of passersby, simpered at and fawned over, we strutted about like harem favorites, imagining ourselves the hub of the universe. As time wore on, though, I grew increasingly restive at the inane cackle of my companions. Most of them were brainless females, interested only in the narrow, circumscribed world of the barnyard. Their one ambition was to mate with some supercilious rooster, bear his progeny, and lapse into stultified cold storage. A strong dash of nonconformism, inherited from who can say what remote gamecock ancestor, prompted me to cavil with them, and when—to my surprise as much as theirs— I found I could put my rebelliousness into words, I earned their universal enmity. A glib chick indeed—by what right had I acquired the power of speech? The pain of social ostracism was more than I could endure, and, dimly sensing that verbalization was taboo, I then and there took a vow of silence. If a fluent tongue condemned me to be a pariah, never again, I swore, would I open my mouth.

It was at this crucial point that the catalyst appeared, the person who was to change my life—S. G. Prebleman. As he later confessed to me, he had no more prescience than I of the fateful meeting that impended; he and his wife had driven into Perkasie that forenoon for a new hammock and some onion sets, and the impulse to buy a few baby chicks was wholly spontaneous. The sound of his voice, before I even saw him, struck a deep, responsive chord in my being. "Fourteen cents apiece?" I overheard it exclaim incredulously. "Honey, they're a steal! We could stick a bunch of these in the barn, feed 'em table scraps—it'd cut our grocery bills in half!"

"Good grief, haven't we trouble enough already?" a weary contralto voice protested. "Next thing I know, you'll be raising chinchillas."

"Which it's a daffy idea, I suppose," the male voice rejoined. "Well, Bright Eyes, just for your information, there happens to be big money in chinchillas. I read an article the other day in the *American Boy*—"

"Senility, here we come," she interjected. "The *American Boy* collapsed ages ago. But don't mind me—you go on reading it if it gives you pleasure. Listen, I'll meet you at the parking lot."

As her footsteps receded, a florid face bisected by a piebald mustache loomed into view overhead. The eyes behind the tiny steel-rimmed lenses devoured us greedily for a moment; then our whole world went topsy-turvy again. Huddled in a basket on the floor of a station wagon, a dozen of us jounced into another and far more precarious phase of adolescence. Prebleman, whose bucolic knowledge derived in the main from *Walden*, knew nothing whatever about rearing domestic fowls. He constructed a sleazy coop out of several fly screens, and, in lieu of the traditional diet of mash and cracked corn, fed us potato chips, olives and soggy cashews, stale hors d'oeuvres, soufflés that had failed to rise, and similar leftovers. Odd as it may seem, I thrived on this regimen—the only one who did, I must admit, for my eleven comrades croaked almost at once—and developed into a fine, meaty bird. As sole survivor of the flock, I naturally attained a special niche in Prebleman's affections. Whenever he trundled a barrowful of empty bottles to the dump (a daily ritual, it seemed), he would stop by to gloat over my progress. I had no inkling of the future until, one spring day, he leaned over my run and blurted it out.

"Hi ya, gorgeous," he cooed, smacking his lips. "Mm-hmm, I can just see you in a platter of gravy next week, with those juicy dumplings swimming around you. Hot ziggety!"

Horrified at the doom in store, snatching at the only means I had to avert it, I groped for and recovered my faculty of speech. "You—you vampire!" I spat at him. "So this is why you coddled me—fattened me—"

"What did you say?" he quavered, turning deathly pale.

"Not half of what I'm going to!" I said distractedly. "Wait till I spill my story to *Confidential* and the tabloids. Wife beater! Lothario! Wineskin! I'll blow you higher than a kite!"

He stuffed his fingers into his ears and backed away. "Help! Help!" he screamed. "It spoke—I heard it! A talking chicken!" He stumbled off down the slope, and seconds later the household was rent by agitated babble. From what little I could glean, his recital was dismissed as just another attack of the fantods, but when he reappeared toward dusk with a peace offering of kasha steeped in milk, I instantly sensed a profound change. His manner was conciliatory, almost servile.

"Look, Miss, we're not cannibals," he began awkwardly. "That stuff about eating you was only bantam—I mean . . ."

One cannot but display magnanimity toward genuine contrition; I besought him to ignore the whole incident, and we soon established a healthy rapport. After satisfying himself with a few questions as to my verbal ability, he put forward a most arresting proposal—in essence, that we collaborate on the story of my life. Flattering though the offer sounded, I felt obliged to point out that I had never written anything. "*Ach*, you won't have to," he assured me. "I'll put it into prose. All you do is talk into a tape recorder, off the top of your head—er, excuse me, at random."

"But isn't a chicken's career rather stodgy?" I demurred. "I'm afraid people wouldn't find it very exciting."

"Honey, I'll make you a prediction," said Prebleman, producing a contract and a fountain pen. "Three days after this book of ours appears, it'll lead the best-seller list. You'll have guest shots on Paar, Sullivan, Como—you pick 'em. The magazine rights alone'll net us three hundred Gs. Add to that the movie sale, the dramatization, and, of course, the diary you keep meanwhile, which George Abbott turns into a musical so the whole shooting match starts all over again. No more white-washed roosts for you, girlie. You'll be sleeping between percale sheets!"

What with visions of myself sporting diamonds the size of hen's eggs, and his honeyed assurance that our agreement surpassed Zsa Zsa Gabor's with Gerold Frank, I was too dazzled to mull it carefully, and while I thought Prebleman's ninety-per-cent cut excessive, I signed. The project, we found, demanded readjustment of both our schedules. To avoid rousing his wife's suspicions, my collaborator proposed we work at night. I countered that, unlike him, I was generically unfitted for slumbering in the daytime. At last, we compromised by foregathering at 3 A.M., spurring ourselves on with black coffee and NoDoz. On occasion, our creative ardors did in fact awaken Mrs. Prebleman, but her spouse quick-wittedly clapped me under his dressing gown and feigned somnambulism.

To recount the tribulations we underwent once our task was finished would serve no useful purpose. Suffice it to say that my story everywhere met reactions ranging from skepticism to open hostility. Time and again, Prebleman offered in vain to transport me to Publishers' Row to prove the manuscript's legitimacy. Unfortunately, at the one audition he contrived—an address to the partners of Charnel House—I was stricken with laryngitis, and the meeting broke up amid catcalls. Finally, Arthur Pelf, a weasel who ordinarily published spurious sex counsel and curiosa on birching, consented to sponsor the book. The rest is literary history; overnight, *Vocal Yolkel* became a sensation, a veritable prairie fire. Five editions were exhausted in a fortnight, Sol Hurok pacted me to a speaking tour of fifty principal cities, and David Susskind announced a four-way telecast between the two of him, myself, and Julian Huxley on the topic "Which Came First?" The critical reception we evoked was quite as overwhelming. John Barkham and Virgilia Peterson coined enough superlatives to fill a book, which was immediately published by Bernard Geis Associates, converted into a musical by George Abbott, and closed in New Haven after one performance.

But my gratification was destined to be short-lived. Although astronomical revenue poured in from these and other sources as well, like records and mechanical toys, I saw none of it. Prebleman had tucked me away in a shabby theatrical hotel on New York's West Side, under the watchful eye of an ex-pugilist friend, the while he lolled in luxury at the Waldorf collecting the lion's share of our income. At my merest allusion to money or an accounting, he either clammed up or shrilly accused me of ingratitude and venality. Heartsick that success had disrupted us, but powerless to act, I prayed for any release from my intolerable plight. It came from an unexpected quarter. One afternoon, while my custodian was absent in the barbershop, a floor waiter entered stealthily, carrying a pillowcase. "Sh-h-h!" he warned. "Listen, fools rush in where Wiseman fears to tread."

"Wha—what do you mean?" I asked.

"That I adopted this guise to spring you," he whispered. "I'm Phil Wiseman of the Amalgamated Talent office, and we can break your contract with that muzzler."

"That's what all you agents say," I said distrustfully. "Supposing Prebleman drags me to court."

"He wouldn't dare," Wiseman asserted. "We could blackmail him for transporting a chicken across a state line. Here—slip into this bag."

While the idea of such Machiavellian tactics was abhorrent,

it was the only way out of my dilemma, and I reluctantly acceded. Wiseman sped me to a prepared hideout in Fordham Road, a kosher butcher shop where I remained incognito in a flock of other Leghorns until the litigation subsided. As I had prophesied, Prebleman did his utmost to discredit me, but was ultimately persuaded to accept a cash settlement. We never saw each other again; many months afterward, I heard he was haunting various obscure Pennsylvania hatcheries, pathetically mumbling to the crates of chicks as they emerged and hoping to duplicate his coup.

And here was I, I reflected as I gazed at the pigeons wheeling over Bergdorf Goodman, at once the luckiest and loneliest creature on earth. I had everything—my own television program, a syndicated newspaper column, reserved seats at every preem, jewels, cars, furs—but it was so much tinsel. I would gladly yield it all to nuzzle the man's dressing gown again, to caress that prognathous jaw and see those pinpoint eyes twinkle in the lamplight. For I realized ineluctably that, despite his avarice, treachery, and general swinishness, S. G. Prebleman was the most lovable galoot I had ever known.

No Autographs, Please— I'm Invisible

I WOKE UP with such a sense of jubilation on that Monday morning in London a few weeks ago, such a positive leap of the heart, that for a moment, paradoxically, my buoyancy frightened me and I wondered if I was ill. From where I lay, shrimplike, in my hotel bed, I could see rain pelting against the window and a leaden oblong of sky; it was the kind of mournful, oppressive day to instill the darkest of premonitions, and yet I felt an inexplicable urge to rejoice. Then it all came back to me in a rush: my mission was completed. Somehow—by what herculean effort I couldn't recall—I had wallowed through two guest shots on the B.B.C.'s newest television program, an enterprise I had undertaken as a lark and inflated into an ordeal. If anyone remembered the fatuities I had mouthed on the broadcasts, I reflected, it mattered not a tinker's damn. I had successfully resisted the impulse to scream or faint while the cameras were trained on me, I hadn't uttered any conscious obscenity or gross insult to the Crown, and I now had twenty-four hours of unclouded leisure before flying back to New York. What better way to inaugurate it than with a really hearty English breakfast of kippers, toast with marmalade, and tea? I was so jaunty as I reached for the phone that I all but dislocated my shoulder.

In the three-quarters of an hour it took to fill the order, my mood of elation wilted appreciably, and the food did little to compensate. The fish was leathery, the toast burned, and the tea pure gall, but I clung to a rosy, objective view of myself, dawdling in a dressing gown over the bizarreries in the London *Times*, and the thought of how much envy the scene would inspire in friends back home revived my spirits. To further hearten me, a whole slew of acquaintances who had seen the programs rang up with invitations to drink or dine. Dizzied by my unwonted popularity, I accepted all of them indiscriminately, and then, of course, spent thirty frantic minutes disentangling the skein and alienating the people I had to put off. By the time my social calendar was organized, I had whipped myself into a state of tension worthy of a ranking débutante. How obtuse of me, I thought, not to have foreseen the consequences of being a TV personality! In all likelihood, I would be pestered everywhere I went today—stared at in shops, besieged for autographs, embraced by normally reserved beauties with flawless English complexions whom I had captivated with my sparkle. I wondered whether I oughtn't provide myself with a pair of smoked glasses, but vetoed the idea on consideration; they would only make me even more conspicuous.

Surprisingly enough, the day wore away with a minimum of the turmoil I anticipated. An actor friend I encountered lunching at the Ivy, a chap usually well informed about the arts, never once mentioned television—though I deftly led the conversation around to it several times—and I was forced to conclude that he was too jealous of my impact to refer to it. The tobacconist in the Haymarket who sold me a pound of Turkish gave me a long, penetrating stare that plainly indicated he had seen me somewhere but couldn't quite place me. I hung over his showcase of pipes for a minute or so to refresh his memory, and at last his face cleared. Excusing himself, he asked if by any chance I was connected with a firm of exterminators in the outer suburb of Tooting Bec. At Marshall & Snelgrove's department store, where my wife had enjoined me to apply for a particular type of blouse, I was certain that a floorwalker recognized me, because I intercepted a wink he gave one of the salesgirls. When I raised my eyebrows inquir-

137

ingly, though, he turned pink and moved off, doubtless overcome by shyness. Nothing your average Englishman abhors
more than sentimental fuss.

By and large, my euphoria persisted all afternoon, until
about seven, when I was having a drink with a couple named
Brian and Lucy Mossmount at their flat in Eaton Square.
What impelled me there I can't for the life of me imagine; my
only link with Mossmount, a stockbroker and big-game hunter,
was that he had once offered to arrange a tiger shoot for me in
Cooch Behar, a project I never had the slightest intention of
pursuing. Present also were a vinous elderly peer called Lord
Harlequin (or so I gathered in the flurry of introductions) and
the latter's date, Miss Teddy Pangborn, a flashy American
blonde with an unmistakable aura of the theatre.

"We were discussing your TV show before you got here,"
Mrs. Mossmount was quick to enlighten me. "None of us saw it
but Brian, and he hated it—didn't you, darling?"

"Well, not altogether," said my host generously. "I thought
you scored once or twice, old man, but you missed all kinds of
opportunities. Mind if I particularize?"

I assured him that criticism, however niggling, was meat and
drink to me, and he embarked on a painstaking dissection of
the program, tinged with more than an implication that Scotland Yard was lax in permitting me to leave the country.
Luckily, His Lordship had meanwhile started a sulphurous
discourse in which he excoriated the Labour Government for
the scarcity of grouse, and Mossmount relinquished his hold on
me. In the conversational realignment that ensued, I found
myself tête-à-tête with Miss Pangborn. My supposition was
correct. She was a graduate of American musical comedy, it
emerged, and she had momentous news to impart of the local
entertainment scene.

"Listen, there's a night-club act you absolutely must see
before you go home," she said vehemently. "Juno the Magnificent—this *brilliant* transvestite at the Club Mephisto. Grumps
—Lord Harlequin, that is—and I are catching the one-thirty
show. Why don't you join us?"

138

I explained that I was on my way to a dinner party, that I proposed to be in bed as close to midnight as possible, and, finally, that wild horses could not persuade me to attend any such display. "I've seen all the female impersonators I want to," I said. "Julian Eltinge; Bert Savoy; Karyl Norman, the Creole Fashion Plate—"

"Now, it's no good sulking—I've made up my mind," she overrode me. "I'll pop around at eleven to fetch you wherever you're dining. What's the address?"

"Jeffrey Cracknell, 62 Kensington Place," I blurted, and the minute I did, could have bit my tongue off. The realization that I had deliberately jeopardized myself appalled me, but the party was dissolving and my entreaties to Miss Pangborn went unheard. In the cab that bore me to Kensington Place, I evolved a scheme to outwit her. I would feign a headache on reaching the Cracknells', perhaps even a slight temperature, and, toward the end of the meal, escape on the plea that I was *hors de combat* with some fearsome malady like blackwater fever. As it turned out, I never got the opportunity; the diners were already midway through their first course when I entered. Amid considerable raillery, the burden of which was that TV stars could hardly be expected to arrive on time, like ordinary mortals, I was wedged between an emaciated matron aglitter with diamonds and a bearded exquisite in an advanced state of disdain.

"So you're the television chap they were talking about earlier," my foppish neighbor remarked, studying me out of the corner of his eye.

"Oh?" I asked. "What was their reaction?"

"Well, I shouldn't press the point if I were you," he said. "Tell me, do they pay you pots of money for that sort of thing?"

"It varies. I usually get eighty to ninety thousand pounds for an appearance."

He blinked at me. "Fancy that," he said. "Are you sure you're not pulling my leg?"

"I wouldn't dream of it," I said. "You look so fragile it'd probably break off."

"My word," he said. "I say, you Americans do indulge in the most extraordinary flights of fancy."

The lady on my left, by contrast, presented no problem; I aroused so little curiosity in her that she ignored me altogether, even when I politely inquired whether her diamonds were genuine or paste. Since this was the one conversational ploy that occurred to me at the moment, I murmured, "Ish ka bibble," retired into my shell, and finished the meal in silence. As the evening progressed, however, and the hour of Miss Pangborn's arrival drew nigh, I became increasingly nervous. I visualized her, clad for some reason in a form-fitting gown of gold sequins, bursting in with the announcement that she was carting me off to see a transvestite, and I felt I could never survive the humiliation. It was too late for specious excuses about chills and fever. I must bolt, let the Cracknells think what they pleased. With a studied casualness born in youth of slavishly imitating Lowell Sherman, I rose, stifling a well-bred yawn, and drifted into the hallway. Then, whisking my hat and mackintosh from the coat tree, I slid noiselessly out the door, raced down three flights of stairs, and ran straight into the arms of Miss Pangborn on the sidewalk.

"My dear, what divine timing!" she chortled. "You remember Grumps—that's Lord Harlequin—of course? Well, the poor thing passed out at dinner. I had the most dreadful job getting him home. So-o-o," she went on coyly, "I guess you're elected to take me to the Club Mephisto, or do you find my company too odious?"

It was useless to cry out, to beat my fists against the inevitable; I was trapped, and there was no choice but to submit. I numbly followed Teddy, as she insisted I call her, into her miniature sedan, and we whizzed off to Soho. Thanks to her penchant for shortcuts through alleys, mewses, and arcades, we fluthered over the entire West End en route to our destination, but a really gratifying surprise, far beyond my wildest hopes, greeted us. The club was chockablock, its entrance ringed by two dozen would-be patrons voicing their frustration. In vain, Teddy pleaded for admission, asserting that I had come all the way from New York to see Juno the Magnificent; the management was adamant.

"A rotten shame," I commiserated as we crawled back into her car. "Ah, well, those are the breaks. And now, if you'd be kind enough to drop me at my hotel—"

"I'm *hungry*," Teddy whimpered. "Grumps keeled over before I had a single thing to eat. Let's go get a snack somewhere."

"In London? At this time of night?" I chuckled derisively. "Don't be absurd. There's no such place—take my word for it."

"Oh, but there is," she said brightly. "A marvellous new spot—the Club Oriflame, on Curzon Street. You'll adore it."

Short of wresting the gearshift from her hands, I used every conceivable form of suasion to make her ferry me home— wheedling, bullying, pathos verging on tears—but nothing availed. I knew for a certainty what awaited us at the Club Oriflame; I could have drawn a picture of the knifelike croupiers, the chemin-de-fer and blackjack layouts, the doctored roulette wheel. As though hypnotized, I heard myself being introduced to the sleek, villainous proprietors as a prominent Hollywood playboy, and, bleating like a sacrificial lamb, I followed Teddy to the crap table. She hadn't the slightest inclination to gamble, she protested, she merely wanted to watch until our steaks were ready, but when the brigand in charge of the dice signified that her turn had come she underwent a magical change of heart. I needed no coaching in the role expected of me. Even before she could exclaim in chagrin at having left her money in another bag, I had withdrawn a fistful of fivers and was pressing it on her. Contrary to my misgivings, however, Fortune smiled on my companion. She made four straight passes, amassing a hillock of chips I estimated as representing well over two hundred pounds. I earnestly besought her to quit before her luck ran out, and was rewarded with a glance that contained hardly a trace of recognition. Here was my chance to flounce out in pique, though, truth to tell, I was loath to flounce without recovering my grubstake. I decided to present Teddy with an ultimatum.

"All right for you, Miss Smartypants," I said. "I'm going into the dining room back there, and if you don't show up in ten minutes I start eating without you. Is that clear?"

"Like crystal, honey," she said, and scooped up the dice. "O.K., anyone; I've got fifty quid that says I can roll a six. Am I faded?"

She was, and so was I when the headwaiter shook me awake at three-fifteen; in fact, I scarcely knew where I was until his bill put me *au courant*. The two bottles of Veuve Clicquot it listed baffled me at first, but, after jogging his memory, he recalled that Miss Pangborn had charged them to me on her departure. As the man pocketed his tip, I noticed that he was regarding me fixedly. Suddenly a gleam lit up his features and he leaned toward me with a confidential smile. "I beg pardon, sir," he said. "You're American, aren't you?"

I nodded.

"And didn't I see you on the B.B.C. this weekend?"

I nodded again.

"Well, sir," he said. "You may think it presumptuous of me, but I'd like to offer you a suggestion or two on how to improve your act. First of all . . ."

Afternoon with a Pint-Sized Faun

Two lucky youngsters . . . are Michele Farr, 11 years of age, and Bruce Zahariades, 14, who created the roles of the evil children Flora and Miles in the New York City Opera Company's recent production of Benjamin Britten's "The Turn of the Screw." Offstage, however, they proved to be more enchanting than enchanted, at least on the morning when they sat in a City Center office and chatted about themselves. . . .

"If I had all the money I needed," he [Bruce] speculated, "I'd build a ranch, with about twenty horses and a big car and a chauffeur who always smiled. Most chauffeurs are sour. Then I'd build a restaurant with big old beams like an English pub, and I'd buy a year's supply of Dover sole. That's my favorite dish. I'd have a swimming pool big enough for a motor boat and a huge grand piano that I'd have tuned every week."—*The Times*.

I'VE DRIVEN them all in my time, brother, and I don't know which are worse—the ones that made it overnight or those that inherited it. You stay behind the wheel long enough and nothing surprises you. I once worked for an old battle-axe in Bala-Cynwyd, I won't say she was rich but every time a gas bill was paid in Philadelphia she siphoned off nineteen cents, and it kept two gardeners busy just shovelling the loot

143

out of the driveway. Twice a month like clockwork, she used to get blind on apricot cordial at the Rittenhouse Club while I froze my butt in her town car. So this perishing cold night I was gone five minutes, no longer, scrounging a cup of coffee, when her nibs staggered out. She started to rip into me—you never heard such language—but I fixed her. I shoved the old crock in a snowbank, threw the ignition key after her, and headed for Reading Terminal. My people come from Fox Point, Rhode Island, where George M. Cohan grew up. He never took any lip from anyone, and neither do I.

The exact same thing happened with Ben Kornflake, the head of Ben-Ko Teenfrocks. There wasn't a nicer, more considerate guy in the whole Garment Center till he fell for one of his models, an Oriental. Oriental, my eye, unless Newark suddenly became part of Asia behind my back. Anyhow, inside two months Ben divorces the woman he's lived with twenty-eight years, dyes his hair red, and marries the doll. Well, from that moment on, he was like Jekyll and Hyde, a changed man and no wonder, the fur coats and jewelry she racked up and mousing around the saloons every afternoon with a different Brazilian. By rights he should have blacked her eye, but instead he took it out on me. The chrome was rusty, I drove too slow, I was chiselling on the gas—nag, nag, nag. I finally got a snootful. "You know what's eating you, Pops?" I told him. "You're too chicken to face facts. Let me tell you about that tsotsky of yours."

Being as how there was no job hanging over my head the next morning, I slept late, did the crossword puzzle in the *News,* and went around to the chauffeurs' room at the garage to chew the fat. They said the Regency had just called, asking for someone to drive a guest of theirs, a prominent TV personality. The type individual they specified—a settled party with a calm, cheerful disposition—sounded like me, so I hustled over. When I get to the suite the bell captain told me to contact, a kid about twelve years old opens the door. He has on one of these fancy smoking jackets with watered-silk lapels and a meerschaum pipe hanging out of his face.

"Hello, bub," I said. "Is Mr. Claud Fragonard here?"

"You're looking at him," he said. "Didn't you ever see the Nailheads on TV?"

"No," I said. "I'd just as lief watch the garbage in the Jersey Meadows. Are you the one that needs a chauffeur?"

"I want somebody can smile, not an old crab," he said, starting in to shut the door.

"I guess I spoke out of turn, Mr. Fragonard," I said. "That pipe you're smoking kind of startled me."

"Oh, there's no tobacco in it," he said, warming up. "My doctor ordered me to cut down on cigars—I smoke maybe twenty a day when I'm working. Well, come in, come in," he said, twitching like a bullfrog. "I'll be with you in a minute. I'm on a long-distance call."

He went in the bedroom, and I had a gander at the joint. It sure was a lulu—a big concert grand, gold-colored, with a TV set and a tape recorder to match, and bookcases full of TV scripts bound in gilt with his initials stamped on the back. And everywhere you turned, dozens of photographs of babes, all with mushy inscriptions like "Hold me, tiger" and "To Claud, with a million kisses." It reminded me of those pictures of Lou Tellegen's den and Nat C. Goodwin that you used to see in Hearst's *American Weekly*. I was just checking on whether Lina Cavalieri was there, or Gaby Deslys in her milk bath, when I caught him studying me in the doorway.

"Not bad, eh?" he said, rocking back and forth on his heels. As I live and breathe, it was Rockcliffe Fellowes in his hunting lodge. "Those are only the show-biz characters and the swingers. I keep the débutantes inside."

"It must be a drag, that many heads pursuing you constantly," I said.

"Between you and I, it is," he said. "Still, you can't hardly blame them—my average income is more than Lucille Ball's."

"Yes, but how much does that leave you after taxes?" I said. I like to sympathize with rich people's problems; it gives me the feeling I belong.

"I do all right," he said. "My accountant invested in a couple of carpet stores and retail shoe outlets over in Paramus. We're making so much dough they sometimes have to burn the money at night. That's what causes your present smog conditions in Manhattan."

"It figures," I said. "Well, you certainly have everything here a red-blooded boy would want."

"Did you take note of the piano?" he said. "I had it specially built to my specifications, of solid gold. . . . You don't believe me, do you? You think I'm strictly full of hot air."

"Look, Fragonard," I said. "I'm only a workingman, just trying to make both ends meet. You say it's solid, that's O.K. by me."

Be damned if he doesn't whip out a gold Scout knife. "Don't take my word for it," he says. "Go ahead and gouge out a chunk. Stab it."

Well, it was the McCoy, all right, so now he's proved what an operator he is, he says will I begin pronto, on account of he has to inspect his holdings in Paramus. I did guess wrong on the car. I thought it'd be a zebra-striped Rolls or something flashy, but it was an ordinary Cadillac limo. I suppose with all those dames chasing him, he didn't want to be too conspicuous. Anyway, in a half an hour's run we're at this cockamamy shoe store wedged in between a diner and a plumbing supply, and he makes me go in with him. The guy in charge was one of these fat little fusspots with a purple nose like a grape that's always giving their hands a dry wash. Claud ticked him off toot sweet.

"Very well, Follister," he said. "On your way. Take five."

"Five what?" said the manager.

Claud gives me a disgusted look. "The kind of squares I'm up against, is it any wonder I have an ulcer? Listen, useless," he hollers at the guy, "vamoose—beat it!"

"I'm waiting on a lady—"

"I'll handle her," says Claud. "Go on, get lost!"

Follister took off, and Claud sits down beside the customer, a middle-aged woman twice his size wearing a pinkish derby hat trimmed with a veil. He asks if there's any particular style shoe she's after. Coming from a twelve-year-old kid, the question must have surprised her, because she just gawked at him.

"Oh, well, plenty of time for that later," says Claud, and takes her hand. "Let's go into orbit, baby. How's about a little kiss?"

The woman let out like a screech. "How dare you!" she says. "I ought to smack your face, you hoodlum!"

"Yeah?" says Claud. "Well, get this straight, picklepuss—I'm one of the top TV stars in the business. You lay a finger on me and I'll have you pinched for assault and battery."

The woman turned so red I thought for a minute she was going to explode. Then she grabbed up her pocketbook and ran out the door.

"Hey, we better clear out," I said. "She's liable to call a cop."

"A lot of good it'll do her," he said. "I got every shamus in Paramus on my payroll. But we wasted enough time here—there's more important stuff to do. Drive me to the Fulton Fish Market."

Shoe stores, fish markets—maybe I ought to keep a knotted towel handy in case this joker gets ugly. Still, I seen my share of eccentrics, like I said, so I held my tongue. On our way down Ninth Avenue, we had to stop several times to hand out autographs. I personally didn't hear anyone ask Claud for them, but it could be they used sign language. We trekked all over the blessed market until he found the salesman he wanted.

"Hoskings here is the only one that knows a scup from a flounder," he says. "Well, what's the news? Did my favorites arrive?"

"The pompano?" the fellow says. "Yes, sirree—absolute beauties. Nearly six hundred pounds, which they should last you well over a year."

"Great," says Claud. "My chauffeur'll give you an assist. Pile them up on the back seat of the car."

"Wait a second," I says. "You can't put raw fish in there, for God's sake. It'd ruin the upholstery."

"So what?" he says. "I was throwing the car away anyhow."

"Oh, boy," I said to myself, "if this was France in the olden days, they'd be carrying that head of yours on a pike," but what the hell, it wasn't my dough. By the time we finished loading, the back was almost full and he rode the jump seat uptown. I could see he was dying for me to ask questions, but I wouldn't give him the satisfaction.

Pretty soon he started in to fidget. "Aren't you curious what I intend to do with these fish?" he said.

"No," I said. "The type people I usually work for can afford to use them for fertilizer."

That stopped him, but not for long. "All right, wise guy, I'll tell you," he said. "I'm having a private seafood restaurant built, up on Third Avenue, with red leather benches like a French café. The idea is, I'll be sitting inside eating pompano and nobody else will be able to get in, because the place'll be locked." He let out a guffaw. "Can you imagine those yaps hammering on the door? I break up just thinking about it."

"You fracture a lot easier than I do, pal," I said. "To me it's as funny as a cry on the moors."

"I thought you had a sense of humor when I hired you," he said.

I was about to tell him I was a chauffeur, not a straight man, when suddenly, in the rearview mirror, I see him blow some kind of dust at me from the palm of his hand. In practically the next second, I'm sneezing so hard that before I could help it the car jumped the curb, missed a couple of pedestrians by inches, and landed smack up against a hydrant. I turn around with my eyes smarting, and this bloody loogan is doubled over laughing.

"Are you crazy?" I said. "What in God's name was that?"

"Sneeze powder," he says, hardly able to get the words out. "Isn't it the greatest? Listen, let's try it on the guy that brings the tow car."

I got out from behind the wheel and opened the rear door. I

crooked my index and middle finger, took the little crumb's nose between them, and twisted until he dropped down on his knees, whinnying in torment like the Three Stooges. Then I straightened my tie with that warm, cozy glow you get from a job well done and went down the subway.

Misty Behind the Curtain

LATE OF A SWELTERING July afternoon this past summer, the hundred-odd occupants of a streetcar clanging along the waterfront of Trieste were handed a delicious, un-expected treat—the spectacle of an American tourist, ever a favorite target for derision, making a bloody ass of himself. A balding presbyopic individual with a ragged handlebar mustache and a complexion the color of beetroot, about to embark on a tour of Yugoslavia honeycombed with such hazard and tribulation as to dwarf the *Anabasis* of Xenophon, he was vainly attempting to wedge three dozen tins of dog food into an already overburdened compact. Nearby, and cucumber-cool in her simple but expensive cottons, stood a statuesque *signora* resembling Jetta Goudal in her prime, holding the leash of another thoroughbred, a magnificent silver standard poodle, and proffering the kind of wifely advice that induces apoplexy. As the dog food tumbled out of the car windows, bounced off the pavement, and rolled helter-skelter across the tramway lines, a veritable paroxysm of joy shook the passengers; they guffawed, bellowed, cackled and pounded each other's scapulae in sheer pleasure. At last the overwrought American—who, by a breathtaking coincidence, bore the same passport and social security number as myself —could endure no more. Uttering a plaintive bleat like the paschal lamb, I sank down onto the curb and, burying my face in my hands, dissolved into sobs.

"I wish I were dead," I wailed. "I wish I was in Dixie, in Bali, in Fiji—anywhere but this godforsaken hole. Why didn't we leave well enough alone? I was so happy in Provence—*foie gras* at every meal, three bottles of Burgundy a day—"

"There, there," my wife comforted me. "Once we get to the Dalmatian coast, everything'll be peaches and cream. Don't you remember those lovely posters we saw in London—the sparkling blue Adriatic, the immaculate ships, the cheery, colorful peasants thronging to sell their handicrafts for a few dinars?"

Whether it was the catharsis of tears or the contact of her cool fingertips, my mood suddenly underwent a magical change. Energetically bundling her and Misty, the poodle, into the car, I presented the onlookers with a small token of Italo-American amity—to wit, the evil eye—and, springing behind the wheel ere they could reciprocate, made for the pier where the S.S. *Pascudnik*, our carrier to Dubrovnik, lay berthed. Word had apparently been flashed ahead from Interpol that a couple of society jewel thieves disguised as Judge Harold Medina and Jetta Goudal were Yugoslavia-bound, for a whole phalanx of customs officials collared us at dockside. After a microscopic scrutiny of our visas, *triptyque*, driving licenses, credit cards, and the poodle's ears, they discovered we lacked the most vital of all documents, a tourist gasoline permit—without which, they gloated, no motorist could quit the country. Luckily I had some fluency in the Italian vernacular, having at one time composed dialogue for Chico Marx, and finally convinced them that since we were half-wits who might become a public charge, we should be expelled posthaste. The ship's bosun, who had been dancing about in a fever of impatience meanwhile, thereupon signaled his crew to load the car. They flung nets over it at random, neatly entangling the dog and several spectators, and with a volcanic jerk hoisted the seine aloft, where it instantly fouled in the hawsers. I was strongly tempted to box the winchman's ears and show the dunderheads how the thing should be handled, but on looking around discovered that my wife had pinioned my arms. Ultimately the pandemonium simmered down to chaos; the car was snugly stowed on deck and the sun roof left open as a receptacle for orange peel, cigarette butts and trash, and amid a turmoil of whistles, bells and hysteria that outdid the annual fair at Nizhni Novgorod, the *Pascudnik* cast off.

As a climax to his celebrated escape act in vaudeville about 1921, the late Harry Houdini used to have himself entombed, upside down and lavishly manacled, in a forty-quart milk can—an exploit billed, for some mysterious reason, as the Chinese Water Torture. Compared to our situation aboard the *Pascudnik*, Houdini was in clover. Our cabin, approximately the size of Dr. Wilhelm Reich's renowned orgone box, faced the engine room, a location that guaranteed an unfailing supply of steam. It contained two grimy bunks, a sink encrusted with verdigris, and a strip of matting just broad enough for a band of roaches in Indian file. To further insure claustrophobia, someone had painstakingly screwed down the porthole and painted it fast. During the three nights we spent in this pressure cooker, the mercury never dipped below ninety-five. A devastating blanket of heat lay over the *Pascudnik* as it inched its way along the coast; stupefied from lack of sleep, leaden-footed and eyes red-rimmed, we tottered about like somnambulists. If we expected any stimulus from our fellow-passengers, we were soon disabused. Of the fifteen assorted *Mitteleuropans* glowering at us in the lounge, none spoke any recognizable tongue, nor were they disposed to fraternize. At the sight of the poodle, they gibbered with terror and crossed themselves as if exorcising a werewolf. The most harrowing feature of the journey, however, was the food. Even a goat would have rebelled at the unending parade of greasy soup, Wiener schnitzels tougher than blowout patches, and malodorous cabbage that issued from the galley. In desperation, we finally fell back on a box of dog biscuits exhumed from our luggage which, when steeped in hot water, gave us the illusion of nourishment. I hated to deprive Misty, but it was a case of *sauve qui peut*.

The three ports the *Pascudnik* called at en route—Rijeka, Zadar and Split—afforded some surcease, minor though it was, from our misery. In Rijeka, the onetime city of Fiume where that fiery *littérateur* Gabriele D'Annunzio had found an outlet for his military genius, I found two bars of mildewed chocolate and some stale Fig Newtons that partly allayed our hunger. Otherwise, it was a dispiriting spot reminiscent of Fall River, Massachusetts, made no more endearing by those ubiquitous portraits of Big Brother. Zadar was somewhat cheerier; here, at least, there was a seaside café whose slivovitz was potable and whose clientele had drunk enough of it to temper their scowls. Split was good value for the first time—a vital, turbulent community centered inside the magnificent palace Diocletian had built for his declining years. Thanks to a knowledgeable guide who took pains to communicate his enthusiasm, we whiled away a carefree hour among the antiquities and stored up sufficient moxie to face the remainder of the voyage.

To those unquenchable romantics on whom a walled city acts like adrenalin, who long to scale towers and sniff the mold of dungeons, I can unhesitatingly recommend Dubrovnik. It abounds in drawbridges, portcullises, casemates, barbicans, *chevaux-de-frise,* and similar remnants of the days when knighthood was in flower. It was my misfortune in youth, however, to be dragged through *Ivanhoe* and the Arthurian cycle by a singularly repulsive teacher, and in the process I contracted a lifelong allergy toward chivalry. Within a quarter of an hour I began sneezing so violently and broke out in such hives that my wife had to bathe my temples with Courvoisier and rush me back to the hotel.

The Venezuela-Riviera, as it was majestically named, was a pretentious fleabag of stucco and red tile on a promontory outside the town. During our tour of the sights, some nonpareil fathead had dumped a mountain of timber against the shed wherein our car was parked. Inasmuch as we were slated to take off at daybreak, this naturally set my foot tapping, but the manager smoothly assured us that we would be sprung. We were, in every sense. At ten that evening, a couple of Torquemadas in leather jerkins arrived with a gasoline-fed chain saw and, stationing it directly beneath our window, fell to work. The screech of the blade ripping through the green lumber must have been audible in Thessalonica. It exploded our eardrums, shook the plaster out of the walls and set Misty howling in anguish. For seven mortal hours the obscene rasp of the saw dominated the night, and when, at last, we shook the sawdust of Dubrovnik from our feet, I was so addled that I drove thirteen miles with the hand brake on before recovering my wits.

There are doubtless worse roads in the world than those in Montenegro, the constituent republic of Yugoslavia we were traversing, but if so, nobody thus far has bothered to map them. As we rocked along in low gear, skidding in and out of craters, crawling perilously over tree stumps and boulders, the trek southward became a nightmare out of *Pilgrim's Progress*. Time and again we lost our way and floundered into immense valleys of scree where the road dwindled into a mule track; for hours on end we crept across bottomless gorges, our wheels spinning on the edge of eternity. At Cetinje, in an outdoor *Stube* filled with desperadoes clearly plotting to waylay us, we snatched a morsel of sustenance, some Turkish coffee and a flavorful sausage embodying the flesh of a mastodon, and pressed on. Ultimately, and through what I can only believe was divine intercession, our plucky little vehicle found its way back to the coast, and, bone-weary, filthy and with catastrophic headaches, we fetched up at that highly publicized watering place, Sveti Stefan.

Though faintly reminiscent of a copywriter's dream or one of James Fitzpatrick's ineffable travelogues, this fishing village converted by governmental fiat into a sanctuary for rich divorcées and their *cicisbei* nevertheless furnished some surcease from our tribulations. All too soon, however, an incident that had occurred prior to our embarkation at Trieste began to effloresce. As I was transferring a handful of maps to the boot of the car at an AGIP station outside Venice, I had noticed among our impedimenta a mysterious brown parcel about twelve inches long, from the wrapping of which protruded the blade of a knife.

"What's the matter?" my wife queried as I resumed my seat and reached for the ignition key. "Is anything wrong with the car?"

"There's a bundle in the back I never noticed before," I said, frowning. "It's got a knife or something sticking out of it."

"Oh, *that*," she said, with the silvery chuckle her sex always employs to conceal underlying guilt. "Goodness, from your expression I thought Lord knows what had happened. Your face looked like Maurice Schwartz in the last act of *King Lear*."

"Never mind the character study," I said impatiently. "You bought something you shouldn't have and now you're trying to squirm out of it."

"All right then, so I did," she admitted. "It's only a few little steak knives I picked up the morning I went shopping in Milan. You're forever complaining how dull ours are, and these were such a bargain that I couldn't resist."

"Honeybunch . . . sugarplum," I groaned. "What are we, in heaven's name—a vaudeville act? It's a wonder you didn't buy a bullwhip while you were at it, so we could flick cigarettes out of each other's mouths."

"I wouldn't trust myself," she retorted. "I might be tempted to give you a lesson your parents should have taught you seventy years ago."

Had it not been for a couple of beefy Teutons alongside us in a Mercedes who were monitoring the exchange, I would have boxed the creature's ears, but, sensing that it might tarnish the American image, I had contained myself and driven on. I clean forgot the episode until an hour after our arrival at Sveti Stefan, when another fragment of the past revived it.

Staying at the hotel was a former show-biz acquaintance of mine, a Paramount starlet of the vintage of Toby Wing. Folly Lou Zuckerman, as she was now known, had just crossed Turkey and Greece in a white convertible, accompanied by a Pekinese and a miniature schnauzer. The three of us and the three dogs shared a meal that made welkins ring throughout

Montenegro, and Folly Lou retired early, pleading that she had to start for Zagreb at daybreak. At dawn the next morning, the hotel was awakened by lamentations and a tohubohu louder than that attending the destruction of the Portland vase. Folly Lou's entire wardrobe, furs, and jewelry, which she had packed in her car the night before, had vanished into thin air. In due course, a pair of sullen, unshaven Yugoslav detectives materialized. As they were pottering around the convertible and dusting it for fingerprints, I opened the rear of our compact, parked nearby, to ascertain whether our belongings were intact. All of a sudden, one of the gumshoes appeared beside me and peered intently into the boot.

"What's eating you, Charlie?" I demanded. (I believe in being forthright with shamuses, Communist or not.) "You don't think *I* had anything to do with this heist, do you?"

He mumbled some evasive reply in Serbo-Croatian and, plucking the bundle of steak knives from the interior, went into a whispered huddle with his colleague. Then, summoning the desk clerk to translate, the two subjected me to a catechism that left me sweating with fear. Not only did I lack a permit to import the cutlery but our admitted destination was Belgrade, the government seat, and my enthusiasm for Marshal Tito so tepid as to stamp me a potential assassin. At this critical juncture, Fate mercifully interceded to save our skins. A begrimed militiaman roared up on a motorcycle, bearing news that three Bosnians in a jeep had been apprehended in Ulcinj with the ex-starlet's effects. Instantly, the fog of suspicion enveloping us dissipated; the detectives, wreathed in smiles, returned the knives with abject apologies, everybody trooped off to the neighboring café to pledge one another's health in slivovitz, and the last we saw of Folly Lou she and the militiaman, blind drunk, were headed for Ulcinj at sixty miles per hour in the white convertible.

After another three days, thoroughly parboiled and rendered queasy by the twitter of the loose-wristed fraternity around the hotel, we mutually agreed it was imperative to vamoose, and pushed off. The route we chose northward to Belgrade, via

Titograd, wound across the great coastal range that parallels the sea and, while we were blessedly unaware of it, includes some of the most difficult terrain in eastern Europe. Armed with no more than a packet of sandwiches and a tankful of *benzina*, we set off one hot morning at eight, fatuously convinced that we could drive the four hundred and sixty kilometers to the capital by nightfall.

It must have been about dusk that day, as we were emerging from the ninth in a series of unlit mountain tunnels between two pinpricks on the map named Bijelo Polje and Prijepolje, that our self-confidence began to wilt. Misty, who hitherto had lain curled in a ball on the floor, suddenly stood up and emitted a long, melancholy yowl.

"What's eating that beast of yours?" I snapped, swerving to avoid a rock.

"Maybe she senses something," my wife ventured timidly. "We've had a couple of vultures circling over us the past half hour."

The words had hardly escaped her lips when we got proof incontestable that the animal was clairvoyant. Slithering around the next bend, we came face to face with a steamroller abandoned by its crew in the middle of the road. With a chasm on one side and a cliff on the other, I had no choice but to stamp convulsively on the brakes and, *mirabile dictu*, stopped short a bare inch from the juggernaut. Our sole alternative now was to try to back through the tunnel until we found some point wide enough to turn. Forty-five minutes later, thoroughly dehydrated and my hair snow-white, we started retracing our way to Bijelo Polje in pitch-darkness. This tiny contretemps, it developed, was merely a curtain raiser for the trials in store—the crevasses spanned by rickety wooden bridges, the rock slides, the dizzying hairpins and switchbacks, and the interminable detours that punctuated our serpentine route. Aeons passed without signs of another vehicle, let alone a habitation of any sort, and whenever an onrushing truck or jeep did appear, the encounter became a lunatic joust on the edge of kingdom come. By slow, agonizing stages we struggled at length into a hamlet called Nadir, whose food and sanitation were everything its name implied, and where we made an electrifying discovery: the luggage boot containing all our possessions was hopelessly jammed. Under the circumstances it was too arduous to attempt Belgrade, and we decided to break the trip at Titovo Užice, a provincial outpost hailed in the guidebook as a center of culture and rest. So asphyxiating was the stench of germicide in our room there, though, and so dubious the bed linen, that within three hours we were again in the saddle. Late that afternoon, grimy as chimney sweeps and nursing savage heartburn from the omnipresent Turkish coffee, we rolled under the porte-cochère of the Athénée-Popinjay, Belgrade's foremost hotel.

About five minutes afterward, as we rolled back out into the Bulevar Revolucije, I recovered the power of speech that had temporarily deserted me in the lobby. "What do they mean, they don't take dogs?" I shouted at my wife. "I'll show 'em, I'll show the bastards! I'll call the American Embassy—no, I'll call my lawyers, Rough & Trumbull—no, I'll call up Tito personally—"

"For God's sake, control yourself," the woman implored me. "You look like a pregnant Concord grape. Ask that swineherd over there, or whatever he is, if there's any hotel that does accept pets."

Helped by a score of bystanders who swarmed around, I managed to translate our problem into Serbo-Croatian, and inside the hour we were installed at the Villa Bedraglia, a ramshackle establishment harboring so many silverfish, earwigs and gnats that one more animal passed unnoticed. Our first requisite, obviously, was to undo the luggage boot, a task that defied the staff and the two locksmiths they produced. The real virtuoso in such matters, they confessed shortly, was one of the bellhops at the Athénée-Popinjay, and cringing with humiliation, I had to creep back there to enlist his aid. He fashioned an impromptu jimmy from a coat hanger and, with dexterity born of long practice in rifling foreigners' baggage, maneuvered open the catch. Perhaps, as my wife contended, the twenty-five-cent piece I tipped him was niggardly, but since he glommed my wrist watch while we were exchanging handshakes, I felt the incident promoted a closer rapport between our two ideologies.

I daresay that when nostalgia overtakes a Yugoslav songwriter, he yearns to be carried back to old Belgrade, but whatever the charm of that metropolis may be, it utterly eluded us. The gloomy Parisian-style tenements and the offices sheltering the bureaucracy, the myriad noisy streetcars and the shops filled with shoddy merchandise, cast a pall on spirits already sorely laden. As for the vaunted artifacts—the embroidered blouses, the basketwork and ceramics, and the icons—the preponderance was purest *schlock* off the Atlantic City boardwalk. I reached the saturation point—and I regard myself as a patient man—the fifth evening of our stay, just as a gypsy violinist resembling Jan Peerce was fiddling airs from *Countess Maritza* into my wife's ear. Midway through his recital I swept my Serbian salad to the floor and arose.

"O.K., that tears it," I said decisively. "We can get this, without dysentery, at Moskowitz and Lupowitz, on Second Avenue. We're heading for the Rumanian frontier first thing tomorrow morning."

"Rumania?" my wife exclaimed, aghast. "Are you crazy? There's nothing there but a lot of Seltzer drinkers and chicken thieves!"

"I know it," I said, "but it's the quickest way out of here. Bring us the check, comrade waiter."

Eighty kilometers onward and nineteen hours later, we chugged up to the frontier checkpoint at Vršac, a hut of stuccoed cement amid illimitable wheat fields, presided over by a lady commissar who, while she bore a striking resemblance to Mildred Natwick, possessed none of the latter's charm. As she scanned our passports, unable to detect any irregularity, her features puckered as though she had bitten into a quince. They brightened appreciably when one of her subordinates, emitting a series of clicks like a mechanical doll, stalked in and dropped our package of knives on her desk with a clatter.

"Aha!" she burst out. "Contraband goods—a clear violation."

"Of what?" I said, bristling.

"The law of March 27, 1953, protecting the public welfare," she snapped. "It is expressly forbidden, under pain of imprisonment, to introduce any weapons into the Rumanian People's Republic. Confiscate them," she barked at her aide. "And as for you, my dear sir—"

"Hold on there a moment," I interposed. "Is this your vaunted Socialist democracy? By what right do you deprive a person of his livelihood?"

It took her a moment to comprehend the sense of my words. "You mean you employ these knives in your business?"

"We most certainly do," I said. "Madame here is a professional freak—a sword swallower. She engulfs the blades while I dance on my hands and our dog plays the harmonica. Would you like us to give you a demonstration?"

"No, no," she said hastily. "We never interfere with strolling players. Here, take your—ah—tools, and a prosperous engagement to the three of you in Rumania."

The Novy Moscovy, the hotel in Bucharest where we finally managed to wheedle a room after a fruitless circuit of the capital, was a dingy edifice on the main thoroughfare, all red plush and peeling gilt. Our second-floor windows commanded an unobstructed view of three rows of trolley tracks, and the noise was cataclysmic, but, even so, it was preferable to the rear, which overlooked a swimming pool with an artificial-wave machine and a gypsy orchestra that performed until dawn. Within twenty-four hours, the illusion instilled in us by folk like Eric Ambler and Sacheverell Sitwell that Bucharest was the Paris of the Balkans went glimmering. The cuisine, the omnipresent Wiener schnitzel washed down by draughts of red wine adulterated with Seltzer, was disheartening, the populace either cowed or downright insolent, and the architecture third-rate Second Empire gone hopelessly to seed. To add to our disenchantment, I shortly began to be oppressed by a conviction that we were under surveillance. Whenever I took the dog out, there was invariably some faceless character in a grubby trench coat dawdling about the lobby, pretending to be absorbed in a newspaper, and twice when we unexpectedly cut short a day's sightseeing the concierge stalled us on the flimsiest of pretexts, obviously warning off someone engaged in searching our room. An episode I ordinarily would have dismissed as trifling confirmed my suspicions. We were seated at dinner one evening in a mosquito-ridden open-air restaurant, doggedly chewing our schnitzels and wincing at an accordion rendition of Liszt's "Fourth Hungarian Rhapsody" throbbing from a microphone apparently concealed in our dish of pickles. One of the waiters, brushing past with a heavily loaded tray, twitched the tablecloth and sent my knife spinning into the gravel. As I automatically craned around to see where it had gone, a chap at the next table tapped me on the arm. "Permit me, sir," he said, graciously extending a knife. "Please use this—although," he hazarded, with an unmistakable wink, "I'm sure you would prefer your own, *n'est-ce pas?*"

My immediate impulse, of course, was to demand what the devil he implied, but in the same instant I clearly perceived his design. The man was an *agent provocateur* trying to unnerve me, to elicit where I had secreted the steak knives, to goad me into an admission that we had sneaked them into Rumania for political mayhem. I threw him a glacial smile that told him I was not to be drawn, and turned my back.

Knowing that the occurrence was bound to agitate my wife, I glossed it over, but the following morning I lost no time getting to the garage and checking the contents of the compact. My premonition was correct; the boot was visibly disordered, though the knives, surprisingly, were still there. Careful to insure that I was unobserved, I whisked them under my jacket and sped back to the hotel.

"Now, listen, dear," I said to my wife, having established to my satisfaction that nobody was crouched at the keyhole. "Don't get hysterical or anything, but we're in a peck of trouble. I've got every reason to believe that the Securitate's been messing around in our machine. It's all topsy-turvy."

"Stuff and nonsense," she said, calmly buffing her nails. "That's the way you left it, and you've got the only key. How would anyone else get into it?"

I repressed a sigh of exasperation. "You talk like a sausage," I said. "Why, the Rumanians practically invented espionage—they're past masters at it. We've been tailed ever since that dame at the frontier spotted these knives. But never mind that now—where can we hide them until we take off?"

While her attitude plainly betrayed that she thought me stiff with paranoia, the woman could not dodge responsibility for causing our dilemma, and she reluctantly stashed the package in a handbag—one of several she kept in a suitcase for dress wear. The next couple of days were relatively free of care; as far as I could tell, our luggage was unmolested, and the operative in the trench coat seemed to have disappeared from the lobby. Then, the afternoon preceding our scheduled departure, an untoward incident awakened all my trepidation. Several days prior, we had attended a cocktail party given by some embassy personnel, at which, made expansive by the local plum brandy, I expressed a longing to visit the castle in Transylvania associated with Count Dracula. At once, the whole complex mechanism of diplomacy started whirring. Calls flew out to the Foreign Office, ponderous formalities were exchanged, and an appointment was set up for us to confer with the Commissar for Folklore, a Mr. Bulgic. It was on the afternoon in question, as we were trudging into the Folklore Institute with laggard feet, that my wife made a disconcerting revelation. "Oh, my God!" she exclaimed, her jaw dropping. "You know what I've gone and done? I took along the wrong pocketbook—the one that we hid the knives in."

"Well, of all the bonehead—" I sputtered, and quickly checked myself. "Look, we haven't time to go back to the hotel, and we daren't leave 'em in the car. Just dummy up, and whatever happens, don't let that bag out of your hands—do you hear?"

Mr. Bulgic was a squat, bullnecked individual with the pale, cold eyes of a Malemute, and the icy flipper he held out plainly indicated that we were impinging on his studies. Behind him stood a trio of assistants summoned to furnish moral support—a fattish young woman whose Tartar features sported a thick coat of rice powder; a cadaverous youth with a fixed, supercilious smile; and a dwarflike spinster on the order of Edna May Oliver. The oval table around which we grouped ourselves was dimly lit by a suspended lamp of Tiffany glass, and, from the shadowy walls beyond, steel engravings of Lenin, Gorki, Tolstoi, and a number of other Russian notables eyed us accusingly. Excusing himself and his colleagues in rapid, heavily accented French for their inability to speak our language, Mr. Bulgic crisply inquired what service the Institute could render.

"Well, to tell you the truth, Mr. Bulgic," I confessed awkwardly, "I'm afraid our quest is really a very minor one. Would you by any chance happen to know where Dracula's castle is located?"

"Dracula?" he repeated blankly. "Who in the world is that? Some mythical figure in one of your Western fairy tales?"

"No, no—the vampire," I said. "You know, the infamous nobleman in Bram Stoker's novel, who ran around Transylvania drinking people's blood. Surely"—my voice seemed to acquire a shrill, piping quality in the half-darkened room— "surely you must have heard of *him?*"

Mr. Bulgic shrugged and, turning to his assistants, shot a question in Rumanian at each of them. They all shook their heads. Perhaps, he suggested, I could give some inkling of the story—in fact, a précis of the plot. A rivulet of perspiration began coursing down my spine; it was forty years since I had read the book, and at least thirty since Bela Lugosi had held me spellbound with the movie version. Suddenly, as I sat there tongue-tied under the unwinking gaze of the quartet, I was overcome by the vast iniquity of my position. Why should I

163

have been tricked into this predicament, compelled to undergo an oral exam like a quivering schoolboy, just because some busybody at a cocktail party had misconstrued a casual remark of mine? It was outrageous, insupportable. I sprang to my feet. "O.K., knock it off," I said roughly. "If that's how you feel, you can keep your old castle, and I hope a turret falls on you. Come on, honey."

I reached around, without looking, for my wife's arm, and then it happened—the disclosure most shameful, the humiliation supreme. The strap of her handbag entwined itself around my wrist, and as I shook it off I projected the package of knives outward onto the middle of the table. There was no mistaking its contents; the sleazy paper had parted, and every blade, gleaming wickedly, lay exposed. The four Rumanians leaned forward as one man, their eyes distended in horror, and for all I know are seated there yet, turned to stone. We didn't tarry for their conclusion. We flew straight back to the Novy Moscovy, collected the poodle, and drove like the wind through the Carpathians to the border. I suppose we passed Count Dracula's lair somewhere en route, but it never occurred to us to stop. Pretty tame stuff. After all, when you've tasted the Balkan intrigue we have, you don't frighten as easy as you used to.

Flatten Your Wallet—
High Style Ahead

ABOUT FORTY-FIVE YEARS AGO, when vaudeville was in its heyday and I clung like a steeplejack to the second balcony of the Keith-Albee in Providence worshipping such demigods as Willie Howard, Grace LaRue, Tom Patricola, and Lieut. Gitz-Rice, there was a celebrated contortionist whose act never failed to captivate the audience. Billed as "Desiretta, the Man Who Wrestles with Himself," he would appear in parti-colored tights with contrasting rosettes, limber up with a few stately gyrations to the strains of the "Hesitation Waltz," and then, grunting and panting fiercely, so manipulate his torso as to create the illusion of two opponents locked in combat. Several decades later, a colleague of mine, a former monologist and juggler who had know Desiretta professionally, told me an anecdote about him that has remained verdant in my memory. En route between two engagements in the Middle West, Desiretta chanced to be seated in a railroad car containing a group of mildly addled folk from a local institution bound for a picnic. He was dozing over the latest issue of *Zit's Theatrical Weekly,* quite unaware that his fellow-passengers were out of the ordinary, when their guardian entered and began counting the flock to make sure none of the members had strayed off. "Twenty-two, twenty-four, twenty-five," he mumbled, spanning the passengers with his hands. He paused doubtfully as he came abreast of Desiretta. "Pardon me, friend," he apologized, "but who are you?"

The acrobat blinked up at him. "Me?" he said. "I'm Desiretta, the Man Who Wrestles with Himself."

"Of course, of course," the other said quickly. "Twenty-six, and the two behind you make twenty-eight. . . ."

As one who has been grappling with himself in an effort to comprehend a wholly new trend in merchandising, I have lately felt a certain kinship with Desiretta, not unmixed with apprehension that everybody involved in the sales process—seller and buyer alike—may be a trifle balmy. My doubts originated early in December, soon after Neiman-Marcus, the Texas outfitters, announced an especially posh line of apparel in *The New Yorker*. The clothes illustrated in their advertisement, a gentleman's kimono and a hostess gown, were tailored from a fibre the text identified as "Shahtoosh—most precious fibre in the world from the throat hairs of the wild, elusive Himalayan ibex." Just how wild and elusive ibexes are and how reluctant to yield up their throat hairs became apparent when one read the prices of the togs—$1,500 and $1,795, respectively. At that particular point, though, I urgently needed a few stocking presents to embellish the cornucopia I was preparing for Christmas, so, snapping my fingers at the expense, I ordered half a dozen gowns and kimonos. The response they evoked was hardly what I anticipated. Without exception, the recipients bristled, whether as a reflex action to the throat hairs or because they assumed I was trying to overawe them with my munificence. The gesture cost me a cool ten thou, but I didn't begrudge it. It taught me to distinguish my real friends from the phonies.

In dangling before me a product so recherché and costly that ownership would enhance my status, Neiman-Marcus was, of course, employing an altogether traditional sales technique —one familiar to me from infancy. Little more than a week later, however, another department store, Ohrbach's, confounded me by adopting a diametrically opposite approach. Under a photograph of two hollow-eyed starvelings in the New York *Post*'s "The World of Women," there appeared this singular caption: "Top of the list among the sweaters girls want most this year: At left, the spare little shell everyone's mad about for its fashionable new 'poor' look and its comfort under jackets. An Italian import in turquoise mohair bordered with matching color beads, it is $17." The revelation that henceforth it was smart to be stony, that indigence was synonymous with elegance, fair took my breath away. Here was a *bouleversement* indeed, an up-to-the-minute transposition of Lazarus and Dives. By pressing my ear to the women's page, I could almost detect the sound of an angelic choir.

How the poverty ploy will affect the equilibrium between retailer and consumer as it gains momentum is anybody's guess. Mine—my guess, that is, not my equilibrium, which is a bit chaotic from wrestling—is that it may well wreak havoc. I embody it in a handy, easily digestible dramatic capsule, to be taken with a grain of salt:

SCENE: *The salon of Le Ginz & Popkin, a firm of exclusive couturiers in the East Fifties. No effort has been spared to avoid ostentation in the decorative scheme. The floor is uncarpeted, the furniture consists of half a dozen orange crates and a seedy Morris chair, and a naked electric bulb swung from the ceiling provides the only illumination. As the curtain rises, Cosmo Le Ginz, a sallow tomboy with a severe bang bisecting his forehead, in an Edwardian sack suit and effulgent waistcoat, superintends a workman engaged in chiselling a small area from the wall to expose the lath.*

LE GINZ (*backing off to examine the effect*): There, that's fine—hold it! It just cried out for that one little accent.
WORKMAN: Whatever you say, Mac. You got a broom, so I can sweep up the plaster?
LE GINZ: No, no, leave it, by all means. It's essential to the composition.
WORKMAN (*his creative instinct kindled*): You know what I'd like to see, maybe? A nice rathole on the baseboard there, covered with a piece of tin.
LE GINZ: Well, perhaps when we launch our spring collection. There's no room in the budget right now for fripperies.

WORKMAN: You're the doctor. (*He shoulders tools, exits as Nate Popkin, the other partner and a perpetual dyspeptic, enters.*)

POPKIN: Look, Cosmo, what have you got against Mrs. Virgil Floodgates?

LE GINZ: Now, don't start needling me about that woman, Popkin—

POPKIN: Here's a dame socially prominent, which her husband has a finger in every financial pie—a person worth conservatively two hundred million bucks—that's begging us on her bended knees to see the line, and you won't even let her in the store. Sweetheart—baby—what sense does it make?

LE GINZ: Nate, listen to me. When you and I founded this concern, we had nothing but a dream, a concept that money is the enemy of chic. We've worked and we've slaved, and today we've got possibly the smartest, most insolvent clientele in New York. Do you want to destroy an accomplishment like that for the sake of a few lousy dollars?

POPKIN (*humbly*): You're right, kid—I'm so oriented pelfwise that I keep losing sight of our initial objective. Only I don't think it's fair to keep the both of them in suspense.

LE GINZ: Who?

POPKIN: She and her daughter—they've been cooling their heels in the foyer over three days now. Couldn't you just spare five minutes to settle their hash in a tactful fashion?

LE GINZ: Well, O.K., but sneak them in the back way. If word got around we were catering to people like that, it'd raise hell with our corporate image. (*Popkin exits, leaving Le Ginz alone onstage without a telephone or soliloquy—an oversight he surmounts by extracting a bouquet of paper flowers from his pocket and arranging it. Mrs. Virgil Floodgates and her daughter, Botticella, enter. They wear tailleurs the fabric of which is Ahchoo, woven from the buckram found in the spines of Gutenberg Bibles.*)

BOTTICELLA: Oh, Mummy, what a heavenly showroom! It has

that divine grubby quality Italian directors always capture
in their films.

MRS. FLOODGATES: Yes, so uncompromising and free of rococo,
like its guiding spirit, who I descry standing there. Mr. Le
Ginz, I'm Drusilla Floodgates. Botticella here is shortly
making her plunge into the social swim.

LE GINZ: And you crave a gown befitting the occasion, of
course. May I ask you an impertinent question?

MRS. FLOODGATES: A wizard of the shears don't have to apologize to us mere groundlings.

LE GINZ: You are too kind. Mrs. Floodgates, what makes you
think you're poor enough to afford my clothes?

MRS. FLOODGATES: Well, I certainly have no intention of
paying for them, if that's what you mean. My husband
and I sometimes let ten years elapse before settling our
bills.

LE GINZ: But you imply that you do, eventually.

MRS. FLOODGATES: Only when we've exhausted every legal
loophole, every ounce of pettifoggery and deceit. No, Mr.
Le Ginz, you can rest easy on that score. Once I buy
anything from you, you'll whistle for your money.

LE GINZ (surveying Botticella critically): Well, even if I did
make an exception, it's a major technical problem. The
girl's a mess—shining hair, erect posture, not a single tic.
She'd have to be transformed completely to harmonize
with one of my creations.

BOTTICELLA: Oh, please, sir, if you'd only allow me to try on
something—

MRS. FLOODGATES: Just so she could brag to her friends. They
absolutely venerate you, adore you—

LE GINZ: We-e-ll, it violates our entire policy, but I'll waive
the rules this once. Slip off your dress. (As Botticella
hastens to comply, he opens a closet door revealing a
garment rack, rummages through a number of frocks and
selects one.) Here, this texture should offset your color-
ing. . . . Hold still while I zip you up. . . . There.

169

BOTTICELLA: It's enchanting—too precious for words. Look at the way it droops, Mummy.

LE GINZ: That's the new slovenly line—very high style. And so is the material. It's a sleazy jersey like bouclé, made out of old peat bags.

MRS. FLOODGATES: Yes, I see the name in the selvage—"Genuine Michigan Moss." But frankly, Mr. Le Ginz, do you think it's—well, lacklustre enough for a début?

LE GINZ: Oh, this isn't the finished model by a long shot. We'd have to rip the hems, add a smudge or two of chicken fat—really give the dress some character.

MRS. FLOODGATES: What do you think, darling?

BOTTICELLA: It's yummy. I absolutely dote on it.

MRS. FLOODGATES: Grand. Then we're all in agreement—

LE GINZ (abruptly): On the contrary, Madam, we couldn't differ more. I'm sorry, but now that I see her in it, your daughter's not becoming to that dress. I'm afraid you'll have to try somewhere else.

MRS. FLOODGATES: Wh-why, how dare you! Are you suggesting that my Botticella is incapable of looking like a scarecrow?

LE GINZ: You can't make a sow's ear out of a silk purse, Mrs. Floodgates. She can't be truly chic as long as she's got so much loot, and she can't conceal it. There's nothing as phony as a false waif.

MRS. FLOODGATES (wringing her hands): But what ever are we to do? The social event of the year—the picture magazines promised to feature Botticella in your gown—

LE GINZ: I wish I could lower our standards to oblige you, but it's out of the question. Excuse me. (He starts to exit, but stops as Virgil Floodgates, an archetypal plutocrat, plummets in, his wattles quivering uncontrollably.)

FLOODGATES: Drusilla! Where are you?

MRS. FLOODGATES (agitato): What is it, Virgil? What's wrong?

FLOODGATES: Disaster—stark, unrelieved calamity! You know our thirty-six-room mansion on Hobe Sound with eleven baths, extensive grounds, and marina in which our private yacht, a veritable floating palace panelled in mahogany and rosewood, is moored? The whole shooting match has

been swept away by a hurricane. But wait—worse is yet
to follow. Whilst Spaulding, our butler, was down at the
cobbler's this morning, some member of the light-fingered
gentry rifled our Park Avenue premises, copping all your
jewels and finery, a collection of Easter eggs designed by
Fabergé for the late Czar of Russia, and bibelots of value
inestimable.

MRS. FLOODGATES: Oh, Virgil, the accumulations of a lifetime
erased as if by a gigantic sponge.

FLOODGATES: Yes, and unless my intuition deceives me, this
telegram I stuffed into my pocket without opening heralds
a fresh catastrophe. (*He opens it, reels.*) Good grief!

MRS. FLOODGATES: More bad news, dear?

FLOODGATES: The worst. Passaic Playthings, Inc., in whose
stock I invested every penny of our fortune on a tip that
Diabolos were returning to favor, has gone bankrupt.
(*Heavily*) This is the coup de grâce, folks. I foresee
myself, blue with cold, hawking hot chestnuts outside the
Public Library.

BOTTICELLA (*joyfully*): Daddy darling, you've just made me
the happiest girl in the world!

FLOODGATES: Eh? What's that? What did you say?

BOTTICELLA: Now I can have the dress, can't I, Mummy? Can't
I, Mr. Le Ginz?

LE GINZ: Of course, my dear. Under the circumstances, I can't
think of anyone who'd lend it more distinction. Take it,
and after it's rained on, bring it back so we can make a
few adjustments.

MRS. FLOODGATES: My stars, despite all our misfortunes, there
certainly is a silver lining. I'll never be able to repay you,
Mr. Le Ginz.

LE GINZ: I sincerely hope so. (*As Mrs. Floodgates and Botticella exit with Floodgates, explaining what has happened,
—and God knows it must tax them to the utmost—
Le Ginz rubs his hands and bustles off to report the sale to
Popkin.*)

CURTAIN

Caveat Emptor, Fortissimo
ex Philadelphia

I MUST ADMIT that I was fit to be tied when three-quarters of an hour had elapsed without any sign of Barney Bienstock. After all, I had cancelled a dentist's appointment at his insistence, traversed the city to lunch with him at a restaurant I abhorred, and here I sat, frozen, elbowed by busboys, and malevolently eyed by a headwaiter grudging me the cubic footage I displaced. The gabble of the Broadway crowd around me—agents, box-office treasurers, and movie exhibitors—was earsplitting, and the reek of their cigars, imprisoned by the low milk-glass ceiling, made my eyes water. Just as I was girding to leave, Bienstock, modish in a duffel coat and a tiny plaid cap that perched on his head like a baked apple, wriggled his way feverishly through the press of diners, hugging a dispatch case. "Swinish of me—unforgivable!" he panted. "But it wasn't my fault, word of honor. They yanked me back for retakes on this commercial I did. A dog's life—that's what a TV actor leads." He tapped my glass. "Come on, have another of these while I unwind."

I accepted, in deference to his obvious tension, and, exhaling deeply, he conjugated the rigors of his calling. It appeared that the Cosmonut Corporation, packager of a leading assortment of nutmeats, had established in surveys that partygoers relished the walnuts, almonds, filberts, and pecans in its selection but invariably left the cashews untouched. To offset this, it had commissioned a film in which Bienstock, introduced as a world-famous authority on nutrition, hailed a milestone in medical research—i.e., the finding that cashews were loaded with Plectrin C, a vitamin essential to life. "When they saw it, they decided it didn't have enough scientific pizzazz," he recounted. "So I shot it over wearing a surgeon's tunic and a goatee, with a mirror on my forehead. Then they threw out the whole business and made me a carnival pitchman, in a derby hat and sleeve garters. Oh, well, what the hell," he said shamefacedly. "It's a living, and the residuals'll keep the wolf away until a part turns up. However, that isn't why I called you. Could you spare an hour this afternoon to help out a friend?"

As Bienstock outlined it over our blueplates, the favor he sought sounded less than monumental. The apartment he and his wife occupied was so noisy that, to retain their sanity, the pair had decided to move. After a protracted search, Hedwig had narrowed things down to a possibility at the Casa Modigliani, a new dwelling on First Avenue in the Seventies. Its location, conveniences, and rent appealed to her, and Barney had acceded to the move without seeing the place when Hedwig's mother, in Philadelphia, sent them a newspaper article that gave them pause. The gist of it, said Bienstock, was that it was folly of apartment hunters not to check a prospective rental beforehand for noises that might prove distracting. "Here, I brought it along," he said, extending a clipping from the Philadelphia *Inquirer*. "Don't bother to read it all—just what I marked."

The underscored portions of text implemented the theme. An individual named D. W. Ladd, Jr., vice-president of the Owens-Corning Fiberglas Corporation, described at length a number of tests whereby one could ascertain the noise potential in whatever apartment one was considering. These included an examination of the thickness of the walls, operation of the bathroom fixtures and kitchen appliances, a scrutiny of electrical switches and outlets, an investigation of the incinerator's function—in short, an exhaustive catalogue of every detail that might eventually plague the occupants.

"Oh, come off it," I objected. "Nobody's going to go to all that trouble. A certain amount of noise is inevitable."

"Sure, sure," Bienstock agreed. "But I think the guy has a point here where he says, 'Take along a portable radio and a friend. Have your companion, in the bedroom with door closed, play the radio at different volume levels while you listen from other rooms.' Or this suggestion: 'Have a companion pound on the wall in one room while you listen from an adjacent room.' That's what I figured we'd do this afternoon—hop over to the joint in a cab, make sure it hasn't any glaring defects, and you'll be on your way inside an hour. How's about it?"

To say that the idea quickened my pulse would be inexact, but I couldn't think of any polite means of extricating myself, and fifty minutes later the two of us stood in the lobby of the Casa Modigliani awaiting the arrival of the renting agent. The décor was standard and uninspiring—an Art Nouveau fountain devoid of a trace of moisture, banked by half a dozen equally dusty liriodendrons, and, in homage to the patron saint of the premises, three or four reproductions of his work, visibly curling on the fake Carrara walls. After an aeon, a porcine young man in a hacking coat and chukka boots strolled in, chewing a toothpick, and identified himself as Burton Nougat, the owner's nephew. He surveyed us under drooping, supercilious lids as Bienstock—a bit incautiously, I felt—revealed the precise nature of our errand. Apparently concluding that we were building inspectors on the prowl for violations, he frostily announced that he was not empowered to admit any casual passersby or Nosy Parkers to the apartment, and that he was busy.

"Doing what?" retorted Bienstock, nettled. "From the clothes you've got on, you must have been steeplechasing. Where do you stable your hunters—on the roof?"

Nougat reddened, compressed his lips—an action partly negated by the toothpick—and stalked out.

Bienstock, in some frustration, had just begun to apologize for dragging me on a wild-goose chase when a plump, bald-headed party in sharkskin hurried in. He proved to be Mr. Kaywoodie, the owner, and by a coincidence a cousin of Bienstock's present landlord, Max Toplitz, who, he informed us pridefully, had built the Toplitz Towers of Ilium, New Jersey. He begged us to overlook his nephew's rudeness. "A college boy, a know-nothing," he said with contempt. "Five years he worked for a diploma so he could antagonize possible tenants —go figure. Anyhow, this isn't your problem. You want to glance over the unit I showed your wife—correct? Well, sir, coöperation is my middle name. Follow me, gentlemen."

As we rode upward with him in the elevator, Bienstock evidently judged it best to take the bull by the horns. He exhumed the clipping that contained Ladd's advice, notified our escort that he planned to use it for guidance, and, opening his dispatch case, disclosed a transistor radio, a hammer, and a packet of fruit peels and coffee grounds he had laid in to test the garbage grinder.

"Great," Kaywoodie approved heartily. "You've got a real head on your shoulders, Mr. Bienstock. If every prospect had your foresight, it'd save us plenty of grief. Well, here we are at 7-W, and any flaws you find, you can bet your bottom dollar they'll be rectified one-two-three. Your happiness is my first consideration."

From what one could discern in a brief circuit of the apartment, it was a pleasant, if unremarkable, affair—a modest living room, two adequate bedrooms and baths, and a cheerful kitchen, all facing a court that seemingly insured privacy. My friend, though, wasted no time rhapsodizing over its advantages. He loped through the rooms like a bloodhound on the scent, slammed the doors experimentally and flung up the windows to peer at the flat opposite, ran the faucets with maximum force, and shook the refrigerator, now and again pausing to consult the newspaper cutting and mutter inaudibly to himself.

"*Nu*, how does it strike you offhand?" asked Kaywoodie anxiously.

Bienstock frowned. "It doesn't," he replied. "For one thing,

175

those windows across the court are too close to these. Here's what Ladd says: 'Windows should be far enough apart so that cross-talk will not carry from an open window into one in the next room or apartment.'"

"He's absolutely, one hundred per cent right," said Kaywoodie. "As a matter of fact, I meant to call this error to your attention myself. Don't worry, though. I know how to deal with it. I'll have the windows over there bricked up."

"But the people who live there," I demurred. "They won't have any light or air."

"That's their headache," he returned stonily. "I repeat what I said—Bienstock must be satisfied, come what may."

"The next drawback," Bienstock resumed, "is more serious. I noticed that the outside doors in the hallway face each other. Ladd is against that, Mr. Kaywoodie. 'Check to see that doors are staggered along the corridor,' he advises, 'so that noise from one area will not pass directly across into another area.'"

"How do you like that?" Kaywoodie exclaimed ruefully. "I told the architect to stagger them, I told the contractor stagger, and the minute my back is turned they louse me up. Well, it'll just have to be done over, that's all."

"It's going to involve quite a structural alteration," I hazarded.

"Yes, and a small fortune," he said. "Still, if it's a question of this man's peace of mind, who am I to pinch pennies?"

"Very gracefully put," Bienstock acknowledged. "I appreciate that. Now, then, let's try the radio test they recommend." He picked up the transistor. "You two listen closely while I play this outside. Ladd claims that if there's proper noise suppression in the hall, you won't be disturbed."

Kaywoodie, smiling benignly, watched him go. "A lovely person," he commented. "What business is he in? . . . A TV actor?" An indulgent chuckle escaped him. "I love actors—they're such gypsies. They sleep all day, drink and holler all night—real live wires. And you're never sure whether they're going to pay the rent, either. It makes kind of a game for we landlords."

A dissonance of music, news, weather reports, and commercials blasted through the door, as audible as if the set were in the room, and when Bienstock rejoined us I saw that he anticipated our verdict.

"This place is a whispering gallery," he declared. "I could hear every word you said, Mr. Kaywoodie. Watch." He knelt by the front door and dealt it several sharp blows with his hammer that splintered its surface. "Hollow-core doors," he said. "The very kind Ladd warns against. Let me read you what he says—"

"It ain't necessary," Kaywoodie broke in. "I can see with my own eyes. I'm installing a new heavy-gauge steel door for you, and while I'm at it I may as well replace all the others on the floor. Now, is there anything else?"

Bienstock studied the clipping. "Not much, except this note on the utilities," he said. " 'Run the shower, flush the toilet, and operate the garbage-disposal unit and other kitchen appliances. . . . Whistling noises indicate pipes too small to carry their water load, while vibrating and clattering pipes usually point to unsatisfactory insulation from the apartment walls.' "

"Look, my boy," said the owner. "With you I don't beat around the bush. The plumbing in here is the worst that money can buy. It's noisy, it leaks, and half the time it doesn't work at all. So if it's O.K. by you, I'm prepared to tear the whole thing out and substitute a good, expensive grade of pipes and fixtures like they have in the Waldorf-Astoria." He held up his hand. "Now, wait a minute—I know what you're thinking. You're thinking, 'How much will all this cost, to stagger the doors, to seal the windows, et cetera? Conservatively, fifty, a hundred thousand dollars. How is Kaywoodie going to persuade the corporation to spend so much, just in order to noiseproof a two-bedroom flat for Bienstock?' Well, baby," he said, jabbing his forefinger at him, "don't give it a second thought. I am the corporation, and what I say goes."

"I'm sure it does," said Barney. "The fact is, though—"

"One other thing," Kaywoodie interrupted. "I'd advise you to insert a noise amendment in your lease, so that even after I make the changes you can cancel if you find the place unlivable. I realize I'm talking contrary to my own benefit, but I always try to look at it from the tenant's point of view."

"Thank you," said Bienstock, "but I've decided not to take the apartment in any case. It's too noisy."

"I can't say I blame you," admitted Kaywoodie. "I guess it *is* a lemon. Still and all, I certainly am obliged to you for giving up your valuable time to point out our mistakes. . . . Could I use your bag for a minute to write on?"

Mystified, my companion handed it over. Kaywoodie extracted a check from his billfold, filled it in, and presented it to him with a flourish.

"Hey," Barney protested. "What's this for?"

"Why, to express my gratitude to you," said Kaywoodie. "It's the very least I can do. And furthermore," he continued, ushering us out to the elevator, "I want you to know that I envy any landlord you finally decide to rent from. He's going to get a topflight, Grade A noise expert and a wonderful human being. Well, this is where I leave you fellows, and God bless you both."

I thought Bienstock's haste in covering the three blocks to the bank in a dead run somewhat unseemly, but since I'd stuck with him thus far, I ran along. The effort proved worthwhile, because a truly gratifying surprise awaited us there. Instead of twenty dollars, as we'd at first supposed, the check was made out for twenty thousand. My friend was so overcome by the munificence of the gesture that he subsequently changed his name to Kaywoodie Ladd Bienstock and bought a coöperative, where, I regret to say, he and his wife are thoroughly miserable. The quiet is such, they complain, that you can hear a pin drop.

Presto Change-o—Bunco?

With the simplest of props, Anne [Bancroft] can make people see what isn't there. One day on the film set of *Miracle Worker*, she prowled around examining the furniture, much of it authentic antiques. . . . Now she spied a crib that bewitched her. The stage carpenters told her it had had a few broken slats, which they had repaired, so it had cost only five dollars.

"I'll give you six," she said instantly.

"What do you want with it?" they asked. "You haven't got a baby to go in it."

"I'll find one," she said. "Somebody in my family is always having a baby. Six-fifty?"

"It's impractical," insisted one stagehand, who was a father. "Too low. You'd break your back."

"Nonsense," Anne retorted. She seized a folded pink blanket, cuddled it, crooned to it, and lowered it gently into the crib—and for a hushed moment, everyone stood still, caught in the age-old wonder of woman and child. One man breathed, "Jeepers," and the actress looked up, wrinkled her nose, and said, "See?" triumphantly. . . .

She would like very much to do a musical soon. One day, between matinee and evening performances, she and a friend went to a health-food store and took dinner back to the theatre. Suddenly, Anne began singing, and her friend looked up, astonished. "I didn't know you could do that," she said. "It's great." To which Anne replied gently, "I know," not in boast but simply as she might acknowledge that the sea is salt. It is a fact, one more thing to live with.—*From an article in* McCall's.

THE DIESEL-POWERED railroad car that had borne me up along the Delaware River lurched into Glover's Grange, deposited the sole other passenger, a vinous brakeman who had been intoning gems from *Rio Rita* without surcease for the past hour, and wallowed on. I reopened the timetable and, laboriously deciphering the asterisks and double daggers, estimated that we had less than a five-minute run to my destination, No Sparrow Falls. If Basil Woolwine met me there, as his agent had faithfully promised, I had a full afternoon to devote to our interview and, with luck, could be back in New York for dinner. Everything was working out just as planned. I settled down into the gritty plush and, chin cupped in hand, gave myself up to pleasant reflection.

Yes, I thought, I really had scored a coup; this project of mine, if fruitful, might very well turn into a ringing journalistic triumph for the *Proscenium Review*. That a neophyte like me, a young associate editor fresh from an obscure Midwestern faculty, should presume to seek an audience with an actor of Woolwine's eminence was incredible enough; no member of the press, let alone an avant-garde periodical such as ours, had ever been able to pierce his isolation. The man abhorred publicity, I was told—immured himself in his country retreat to escape it. But when, after Machiavellian intrigue and pleas this side of tears, word came that Woolwine had consented to receive me, what a change my colleagues underwent, how unconcealed their adulation. Even Mr. Urquhart, my chief—a person so immersed in dramatic theory that he never attends the theatre—deigned to compliment me. "Good work, Schmidlapp," he said, and then hesitated anxiously. "You *will* be careful not to make this too lucid, won't you? I mean, don't write anything *hoi polloi* will understand." I assured him that I would be turgid to the point of unintelligibility, and he positively beamed.

A montage of decaying brick warehouses, lumberyards, and

used cars flicked past my window, and a second later the diesel slowed to a halt beside a mouse-colored depot writhing with Victorian curlicues. Except for a telegrapher languidly draped over a sheaf of waybills, the platform was deserted. I explored the adjacent parking area, but there was no sign of Woolwine or anybody resembling an emissary. Oh, well, I decided, perching myself on a baggage truck, one didn't expect actors to be punctual, especially a star of his lustre. Obviously, the prospect of appearing in a highbrow publication piqued his vanity or he wouldn't have asked me down, so it behooved me to be stoical. . . . Then, as the minutes ticked away, I began to feel a tide of irritation welling up inside me. The least you deserved for a tedious three-hour journey to the hinterland was to be met promptly. It was hardly good manners—in fact, it was a rotten imposition—to maroon me out in the middle of nowhere and I proposed to tell Woolwine so. Needless to say, my resentment evaporated the instant he hurried up to the platform, contrition writ large on his features. The man's charm was overwhelming; his personality—driving, restless, magnetic—engulfed one as turbulently as Niagara does a straw.

"Schmidlapp?" he inquired breathlessly. "I say, forgive me, will you? Such a morning—everything topsy-turvy. Have a good trip down?"

"Excellent—" I started to say.

"Tommyrot," he interrupted. "It was a tedious three-hour journey to the hinterland, and you felt the least you deserved was to be met promptly. A rotten imposition to maroon you out in the middle of nowhere, you were thinking, and you proposed to tell me so. Am I right?"

"Jiminy fishhooks, Mr. Woolwine!" I exclaimed, flummoxed at the accuracy with which he had divined my thoughts.

"Yes, I happen to be psychic," he admitted. He said it without arrogance—almost wistfully, as if beseeching your friendship even though he was a paladin. "However, enough of this tawdry *ambiente*—shall we get along to my place? I hope you don't mind riding over in this old crate."

"Which one?" I asked uncertainly.

"Here," he said, tapping the baggage truck. "My own car's in the shop at the moment, but, given a simple little prop, Thespian guile can ofttimes create a startling illusion." He withdrew a sports-car cap from his pocket and, tilting it over his eyes at a rakish angle, swung up on the truck. "Come on, shake a leg," he said impatiently, as I clambered up beside him. "All set? Watch out for the gearshift. . . . Roger—away we go!"

That theatrical witchery can perform miracles we know; the most insensitive among us has felt his spirit liberated, his soul take wing, at the magic of stagecraft and sensuous language. But to be completely whisked out of reality in broad daylight, to feel oneself swept at dizzying speed along a rural highway, deafened but exhilarated by the throb of horsepower incalculable—that demands a histrionic gift verging on the hypnotic. So cunningly did Woolwine reproduce the sound of hammering cylinders and the screech of gravel under our wheels, indeed, that time and again I cringed in terror lest we hurtle into the ditch. Nor was I the only one to succumb to his legerdemain; as my pilot struggled to hold our vehicle to the road, the telegrapher, carried away by the verisimilitude of the scene, shouted above the roar of the exhaust, "Consarn ye for scorchin' around the countryside! You've just slaughtered half my chickens, durn ye!"

With a squeal of brakes, Woolwine pulled up sharply, leaped down, and, extending his hand, helped me back onto terra firma. While awe-struck at his virtuosity, I could not help noticing that we were precisely where we had started—a reaction that must have communicated itself to him, because he clucked sympathetically. "A bit shaky, are you?" he queried. "You'll be tiptop by the time we get home. It's a stone's throw from here—hardly four miles."

Considering that he had disrupted his schedule to see me, it would have been uncouth to demur, so I smiled assent and we struck out. The vivid green of early summer mantling the Pennsylvania hills, the sleepy canal threading the meadows, and the quaint covered bridges evoked some deep strain of poetry in my host, and as we wended our way he recited bucolics he had composed that bore comparison with those of Wordsworth, Coleridge, and Gray. I was about to compare them when some deep strain of tact warned me not to, and instead I sought his opinion of various acting techniques—the Method, the Stanislavski system, and the like. To my chagrin, he was averse to any exegesis whatever on the subject.

"Look, Clyde," he said. "I'm just an instinctual mummer—a genius, if you will—but I don't know from formulas. I'm sort of a brilliant alchemist—I transmute the basest metals into gold through the wizardry of my temperament. Rules and schools I don't abide by."

"You draw your raw material from life itself," I said understandingly. "From the harsh interplay of passions—from greed, lust, avarice—"

"Also from the Shuberts, Bloomgarden, and David Merrick," he specified. "With me on the marquee and those birds on the adding machine, we've got it made."

My conjecture was accurate; like all major artists, Woolwine scorned easy recipes for success, deriving sorcery from no ingredient but his God-given power to inflame the imagination. How prodigious this was I realized a few minutes thence, when we stopped off at a crossroads store to buy the wherewithal for lunch. Despite my fervent protest that a salad or cold cuts would be adequate, Woolwine strove to force a Lucullan repast on me.

"Let's have a real gourmet spread!" he urged, with a mischievous glint reminiscent of one of Murillo's urchins. "What about a tureen of rich, golden fettuccine laden with butter and Parmesan, accompanied by a bottle of chill Soave and followed by heaps of tiny wild strawberries? Or, better still, a delicately crisp veal scallopine, flanked by tender new asparagus and toothsome home-fries? Whichever way, we must have an antipasto—tasty minuscule shrimp, pepperoni, chick-peas that melt in the mouth—"

So graphic an image did he summon up by word and

gesture (and I flatter myself that I am not impressionable) that, for an instant, all our paltry surroundings—the shelves piled with detergents and tinned goods, the anarchy of pretzels, shoe polish, and hardware—receded into thin air, and we were in some chic *ristorante* in Ischia or Capri, a pair of hedonists lapped in sybaritic luxury. Around us swirled the wealth and fashion of Roman society, creating and destroying reputations with a witty phrase. The illusion was enhanced by the storekeeper, who, visibly kindled by Woolwine's rhetoric, whipped a mandolin from underneath the counter and burst into a full-throated rendition of "O Sole Mio." The final plangent chords, of course, brusquely recalled me to earth, yet with such a conviction of having dined to satiety that I lacked only a toothpick for complete bliss. Woolwine generously purchased a whole box of them—largely, I thought, to mollify the storekeeper, whose imagination he had perhaps overinflamed—and we proceeded on our way.

It was doubtless youthful naïveté, but, in view of Woolwine's professional stature, I had preconceived his home as a typical country gentleman's estate—a palatial fieldstone residence amid a complex of neat outbuildings, a cathedral-like barn adorned with hex signs, and an opulent swimming pool. I was, therefore, somewhat chapfallen to behold the actuality, a squat oblong structure of cement block, the bleak façade of which strikingly resembled that of a wayside liquor shop. Its situation, halfway up an eroded gully under a frowning cliff, combined the precarious and the sinister, and it was landscaped with a series of swollen concrete rock gardens full of chlorotic vegetation.

"Not quite what you foresaw, is it?" Woolwine chuckled, his clairvoyance quick to perceive my dismay. "I don't blame you for being taken aback—it's an abomination. But, you see, to anybody who lives in a world of utter make-believe, externals are meaningless. I'm anesthetic to this suburban monstrosity; I create my own background and characters as the need arises. For example—"

He dove into his pocket, extracted a set of muttonchop

whiskers, and in a trice was transformed into the simulacrum of a dignified English butler. With naught but a few cents' worth of crêpe hair, he had become the embodiment of generations of servitors obsequious yet haughty—a portrayal so richly evocative that I stood rooted to the spot in enchantment. As if by the wave of a necromancer's wand, the mean little dwelling vanished and we were in the hall of some fabled baronial castle. Fascinated, I marvelled at the rows of ancestral armor, the battle pennons, the massive fireplace on whose spit an ox slowly roasted. . . . I abruptly became aware of a hand twitching my sleeve, and awoke with a start to find myself back in vernal Pennsylvania. Woolwine, who, it appeared, had taken advantage of my daydream to procure several bottles of beer, smiled indulgently as he uncapped one for me.

"When you sink into a reverie, bud, you sure submerge," he commented. "Now then, as my guest, you're free to do as you please, naturally, but I'm going to make a suggestion. Instead of rubbering through the interior of this house, which is ugliness personified, why don't you crouch down right there on your hams while I limn it for you in winged words?"

Gratified that my presence seemingly inspired him, and eager to see how his conception differed from mine, I complied, and was rewarded with a truly protean performance. In a series of lightning characterizations that included a humorous old coachman named Uncle Cudgo, a courtly Southern planter, and the latter's dissolute, willful granddaughter, a creature that was purest Tennessee Williams, Woolwine recreated the very essence of an ante-bellum mansion. Hand in hand with them, I roved among the spacious rooms, lingering over the daguerreotypes in the faded albums, the family portraits and silver, even testing the keys of a lovely rosewood spinet. What did it matter that the music was simulated, that Woolwine was merely humming through tissue paper stretched over a comb? The fantasy was all that mattered, and it held me spellbound.

The afternoon shadows were lengthening, and perhaps I

was a trifle unsteady from too much beer and fantasy, when my host escorted me to the border of his demesne and, at my insistence, cast a horoscope for the theatre of tomorrow. "I see an entirely fresh new concept of drama knocking at the door," he said, a faraway look in his eyes. "A theatre without plays in the conventional sense, devoid of scenery and untrammelled by actors. I would strip away all the fakery and abracadabra that clutter up the modern show shop—the lights, the costumes, maybe the audience itself—"

"But, suffering catfish, Mr. Woolwine," I protested. "You can't do that! What would be left?"

"Just me," he returned calmly. "Face facts, Schmidlapp—the day I donned greasepaint, a whole profession became obsolete. When the historians of the future compile their record, who do you think will be remembered—all those ineffectual, no-talent bastards in Actors' Equity beating out their brains, or one lone genius with a pocketful of props?"

There was no possible answer, and I attempted none. Instead, I wrung the hand he proffered me, shouldered my coat, and set out to retrace the four miles to the station. It was a more hazardous journey this time, in that I knew I dared not stumble, for I bore a burden infinitely fragile, infinitely precious—a chalice filled with wisdom. But, of course, that too may have been illusion.

Nobody Knows the Rubble I've Seen/Nobody Knows but Croesus

You meet them wherever you roam, in Helsinki or Hong Kong, Patchogue or Perugia, Moscow or Martha's Vineyard—those aromatic, imperious, gravel-voiced characters with unlit Coronas embedded in mahogany faces, clad in Italian silk suits tailored by Sy Devore. Their fashionably haggard wives flaunt Buccellati's latest brooch or Gucci's shiniest handbag and sprinkle their speech with melting allusion to Billy (Wilder), Irving (Lazar), Harry (Kurnitz), Irwin (Shaw), and all the other gods of Leonard Lyons' daily pantheon. They drive Aston-Martins as a matter of status but secretly prefer Cadillacs, maintain a *dacha* in Palm Springs but yearn for one at Klosters, and frenziedly collect the more abstract Expressionists, disdaining any upstart who owns less than two Rothkos and a Rauschenberg or, in exceptional cases, two Rauschenbergs and a Rothko. Whether in Nyack or Nairobi, Bessarabia or Bonwit Teller, "21" or Timbuktu, they are as unique, unmistakable and easily identified as the water moccasin, and just as lovable. Though they migrate widely and mate wildly, they always return in due course to their native habitat, six square miles of reclaimed desert in southern California called Beverly Hills.

For economic reasons too painful to enlarge on here—my father was euchred out of his share of the Iraq oil fields by

Calouste Gulbenkian, and, lacking the adroitness to pick pockets, I was forced to become a screenwriter—I dwelt among these high rollers for more than a decade, from 1931 to 1942. But for the sunny benevolence that was my sole heritage from Dad, I might well have been scarred for life. So awesome was the display of ostentation around Beverly in the thirties, so reminiscent of Maggie and Jiggs the lordly swagger and mincing condescension, that it made one's toes curl. In the words of a friend of mine characterizing a movie mogul, a member of the community, it was a case of "from Poland to polo in one generation." Like that fabled satrap, most of the residents were picture folk—producers, actors and directors— and they strove to outdo each other socially, sartorially, and, above all, architecturally. The broad, palm-fringed streets of the compound were lined with *estancias* worthy of Porfirio Díaz, ante-bellum Southern mansions that put Natchez to shame, Renaissance *palazzos*, Japanese pagodas, and turreted Norman châteaux with catapults designed to hurl boiling schmaltz onto the invader. Over the immaculately barbered lawns and the exotic shrubbery lay a vast cathedral hush like that of an expensive insane asylum. No bee droned in the greenery unless his credentials were checked; the whole district, from Coldwater Canyon to the La Brea tar pits, was off limits to the commoner, and anybody chancing into it on foot was promptly lagged on suspicion of vagrancy. The late Mr. William Faulkner, taking a quiet constitutional along Alta Placenta of a Sunday morning, was whisked off to the jug to languish five hours, plaintively protesting, in his hominy-grits accent, that he was a harmless scribbler. The desk sergeant finally sprung him, though not without an admonition that Faulkner looked like a cat burglar and had better hire himself a Thunderbird PDQ if he wanted to stay out of the pokey.

If a Nobel Prize winner could stub his toe so unwittingly, it was no wonder that my wife and I were wide-eyed greenhorns at our first sight of the Promised Land. Never had we beheld anything as paradisiacal as Hollywood: the benign sunshine, the vast open-air markets bursting with produce, the friendly passersby lithe and tanned in their sportswear, the cunning boutiques full of bronze baby shoes, miniature turtles, Mexican saddles worked in silver, and photos of real-life movie stars. Oranges six dozen for a quarter! Hillocks of succulent figs and dates for a dime! Totally forgetting our hatred of citrus in any form save lime rickeys and old-fashioneds, we raced around amassing bushels of tangelos, grapefruits, lemons and nectarines. Inside three days, our hotel swarmed with flies and we had generated enough acid to charge every storage battery at River Rouge. Meanwhile, the scales had begun to fall from our eyes and we were acquiring some perspective on the inhabitants of this Arcadia. Every mother's son was on the muscle, trying to sell us an authentic Vermeer exhumed from a Pasadena hock shop, to trace our genealogy, to get a studio audition for a gifted ten-year-old who played the musical saw like Heifetz or to bury us in an exclusive cemetery guaranteed free of seepage. Their buoyant health, needless to say, was pure illusion; hypochondriacs all, they subsisted on cracked sawdust and parsnip juice, and daily shrank their brains on the analytic couch to purge themselves of devils. In between obeisances to Freud, they banded into a hundred weird sects; the town boiled with Swedenborgians, fire worshippers, Gnostics, Anabaptists, students of Bahaism, Penitentes, Vedantists, Puseyites. When I returned from the studio one afternoon and found my wife, two joss sticks protruding from her ears, recumbent before a statue of Ishtar, I knew it was Curtainsville. What we needed was a little white cottage as far away from Hollywood as possible, where my angel could bake salt-rising bread and I could potter around with a pair of shears, snipping *Mammalia ponderosa* from the girlie magazines. I sprang to the Yellow Pages and began combing them for a reliable real-estate agent.

Mrs. Pandora was an angular harpy in a set of cashmere sweaters and three strands of pearls, with alabaster choppers gleaming in a face clearly inherited from a praying mantis. In purest Santa Barbara labials, she apprised us instanter that she was a blue blood reared at Sneden's Landing and that she dealt only in Beverly Hills rentals. To shoehorn a couple of plebeians into the preserve would demand all her guile, but she regarded it as a challenge. Cringing and knuckling our forelocks, we besought Mrs. Pandora to open her box. The first place she showed us was a Louis XVI *gentilhommière* of thirty-six rooms and nine baths on a bluff overlooking Sunset Boulevard. It had a boxwood maze in which the original owner, an Osage Indian lush, had lost his way and perished of thirst. Prior to his demise—or perhaps afterward, Mrs. Pandora was not quite sure—he had shot the bulbs out of all the candelabra, which made the house a difficult one to entertain in.

"What's that clanking sound I hear?" my wife inquired of the caretaker, peering into the murk.

"Oh, that's just the oil rig, ma'am," he replied. "Mr. Wildgoose had it installed in the basement to pump his bourbon upstairs. I leave it run to remind me of him like."

A steal though the house was at twelve hundred a month, the noise revived memories of my lost patrimony, and we mushed on. In rapid succession, Mrs. Pandora unveiled a Moorish mosque which, to provide adequate muezzins for its minarets, would have bankrupted us; an all-glass dwelling, whose rooms were demarcated by curtains of toilet chains; and a swank bootery opposite the Beverly-Wilshire that she felt would convert into a home at trifling cost. The profusion of footstools made it an ideal setting for bingo parties or a minstrel show, but Madame, with typical feminine capriciousness, insisted on a more conventional abode. At last we hit on the perfect solution, a modest Cape Cod Colonial of primrose stucco flanked by a pool. Depositing fifteen hundred dollars and three gills of blood as security, we moved in, hired a maladroit Estonian cook, and prepared to live graciously. At seven the next morning, I was aroused by a deafening tattoo at the front door. I stumbled downstairs and found a woolly mammoth on the order of Andy Devine, garbed in a seersucker robe and swim trunks.

"Whassamatter, stupid, you got sleeping sickness?" he bawled. "I been half an hour here waiting for my dip!"

Before I could marshal my wits, he elbowed me aside and, bursting open the French doors with a crash that showered the patio with glass, flung himself into the pool. As he wallowed about, spitting and snorting through his blowholes, I rushed to inspect the terms of our lease under an infrared lamp. Sure enough, there it was—a sneaky codicil entitling any chum of the landlord to use the premises whenever the whim overtook him. The ensuing two months were purgatory. Hordes of loafers trooped through the house filching cold chicken from the icebox, phoning friends in Marrakesh and Tasmania and scrawling graffiti on the bathroom walls. The coup de grâce was a wienie roast staged in the garage by a couple of the *vitelloni* employing an armful of first editions and a jerrican of gas. When the insurance adjuster finished assaying the remnants of our Auburn coupé and handed me a settlement of $3.17, I threw in the towel and sent out an SOS for Mrs. Pandora.

A rigid diet of dandelions and spaghetti over the next two years, plus the pittance my wife earned demonstrating potato graters at the Farmers' Market, enabled us to meet the rent on a cavernous bungalow of California redwood off Benedict Canyon. Its Stygian interior was full of black widows, but since we could afford only wood alcohol and were blinded much of the time, the darkness scarcely mattered. To redeem matters somewhat, I was doing well at the studios; a movie I had written, in which two people find love after their sexes are transposed by a mad scientist, was being hailed by the critics and my salary had tripled. This determined us to move into a residence befitting our new prestige in the community. Mrs. Pandora was radiant at the news.

"I've got just the spot for you!" she exulted. "A teensy jewel box over on Salpiglossis Drive, authentic Queen Anne and furnished with the most adorable antiques. Of course Mrs. Pinchpfennig would never accept your social references—her people practically founded Altoona, you know—but let's offer her an extra hundred a month to overlook your background."

The bribe was effective and the stash everything she had

claimed—a decorator's dream, all Chippendale and rare Chinese wallpaper, carpeted in Aubusson and upholstered in *toile de Jouy*. My wife's bliss as she fussed over the tea service was touching, but I felt unfulfilled; the house lacked warmth— ideally a majestic, wrinkled bloodhound snoozing on the hearth. From earliest youth, I ululated, all through my bachelorhood, I had craved one of these noble creatures. I conjugated my longing so persistently that at length the poor woman gave way. Within minutes, I was onto a kennel in Sherman Oaks, where a litter of outstanding pups was visible. An hour later, eleven velvety little rascals with soulful eyes were tumbling over me in their pen, gnawing my ears and kissing me. From their number I chose, after long deliberation, a ravishing female, a Barbara La Marr of the dog world, and christened her Liza. Since we paused frequently on the homeward journey to neck, the trip was a long one and Liza ravenous on arrival. As my wife watched her gulp down three pounds of hamburger, a box of charcoal biscuits, half a dozen raw eggs, and a slab of jack cheese, her face paled in apprehension.

"Listen," she said nervously. "This cannibal queen you came up with—do you think we can support her?"

Conscious of what an impulsive ass I had been, I took refuge in bluster. "O.K., that tears it!" I shouted. "Begrudge me the one thing I've ever wanted—a homeless little puppy! What if she does eat a few scraps? Why, the dough you squander on shoes alone—"

"In heaven's name, stop screaming," she broke in. "No wonder your birthstone's the amethyst—your face is the very same color. I'm sure the dog'll find something to eat."

Her words were prophetic; during the night, Liza managed to extricate a crown rib roast and a pecan pie from the kitchen, and for good measure ate the legs off a fiddleback chair. Chained to a jardiniere the following night, she freed herself with a mere headshake and consumed several petit point cushions and a George III shaving stand. Toward dawn, she was stricken by the memory of our necking party and began baying, a doleful, unending howl that echoed from Laurel Canyon to the shores of Malibu. Word that a manhunt was in progress spread like wildfire, and pandemonium reigned supreme. Lying abed with my teeth clenched, I reached the only possible conclusion. I threw on a coat over my pajamas, slung Liza into the car, and broke every speed limit back to the kennel. Nobody stirred to witness the prodigal's return; I deftly inserted her into the cage among her kinsmen and vamoosed, leaving the owner a puzzle that probably triggered a nervous breakdown. As for Mrs. Pinchpfennig, she magnanimously agreed to a compromise of $2,200 in court, which, added to my legal fees of $1,750, got us neatly off the hook, and we moved into a motel.

When the swallows returning to Capistrano deposited a small pink-and-white bundle on our doorstep, a gypsy existence was no longer feasible, and Mrs. Pandora reappeared with her Aladdin's lamp. This time, she produced a Spanish hacienda the size of the Alcázar, its massive walls embossed with bulls' heads squirting water into fountains. The property was particularly favored by writers, she confided as she led us on a tour of inspection; in fact it was currently occupied by some novelist named Aldous Hochspiel or the like, said to be terribly famous, who was writing a musical for George Raft at M-G-M. I had never met Huxley, toward whom I was idolatrous, and my disappointment grew as we traversed the rooms without even a glimpse of him. Just as we were leaving, Mrs. Pandora smote her forehead.

"Gracious, what a ninny I am!" she squealed. "I forgot to show you the upstairs powder room!" Useless our protest that we could imagine it; she refused to listen. "No, no, you've got to," she insisted, herding us back. "It's simply delightful, an absolute dream!"

Up we trudged through an endless circuit of corridors, and eventually, with a triumphant bleat, she threw open a door. There, in the middle of a hexagonal room lined with mirrors, crouched my hero, myopically pecking at a Hermes portable. As he caught sight of us, he sprang upright, defensively clutching the machine to his breast in a flutter of yellow second sheets that swirled about him like leaves. For an aeon, the three of us hung there confronting genius at bay reflected from every known angle. Then Mrs. Pandora broke the spell.

"Thank you, Mr. Hochspiel," she chirruped. "Well, that's the upstairs powder room."

Why we ever rented the place, except that I fatuously hoped to absorb Huxley's gift by osmosis, I cannot remember; but two months afterward, we had cause to regret it. One evening, as the maladroit Estonian was serving dinner, she idly informed us that a man had called that morning about the rats in the trees.

"The wh-which in the trees?" my wife stammered, dropping her fork.

"The rats," said Narishka impatiently. "You know, that palm tree in the patio where the baby naps. He stuck on some kind of a collar to keep 'em from jumping down."

I chuckled at the improbable tale and, overturning a plate of soup to reassure the child's mother, strolled out to investigate. To my consternation, there was indeed a baffle on the tree trunk, of the sort used on ship's hawsers in port. With the smoothness of a well-oiled mechanism (which I was at the moment), I leaped into action. I flew back into the house, dabbed ammonia on my spouse to revive her, and phoned the police that an outbreak of cholera was imminent. Then, wrapping our infant in an Andalusian shawl, I fled with it to Schwab's drugstore and instructed Sidney Skolsky to put the story on the A.P. wire.

Back at the *ranchería*, meanwhile, my wife had hastily thrown together a few necessities like her Buccellati brooch and Gucci handbag, and in less than an eyeblink we caught the midnight choochoo back to Alabam'. Months later, in the Swiss Alps, I received a note from the authorities explaining the mystery. Our next-door neighbor, an elderly Gorgon afflicted with insomnia, had neurotically convinced herself that the dry clashing of the palm fronds was caused by rodents and had so complained to the Board of Health. Hailing my vigilant public spirit, the note extended a warm invitation to revisit Beverly Hills and the promise of a lively welcome on our return. I may very well, if nothing better turns up, but frankly, I've always considered tar and feathers so unbecoming to a chap. Don't you?

Muddler on the Roof

EDITOR, *Country Life*,
Tavistock Street, Covent Garden,
London, England.

DEAR SIR,

I assume, never having seen anything to the contrary, that the correspondence columns of your tiptop periodical are open to all, and by "all," I mean it quite literally. In your many years of publication, you have doubtless attracted mail from every imaginable type of reader, but I daresay this is the first time you have received a communication from anyone like me. Nevertheless, I am impelled to write because I recently chanced to witness certain events touching upon some letters you published in the past; and if you will be good enough to bear with me for a moment, I shall endeavor to narrate them in their proper chronological sequence.

First, as to my identity. I am a member of the order *Marmota monax,* which is to say a ground hog—or woodchuck if you prefer; the names are interchangeable here in North America—and I reside in rural Pennsylvania, approximately two miles west of the Delaware River. The hillside in which my burrow is located technically belongs to a party named S. G. Pebbleman, who also owns the surrounding ninety acres. (In actual fact, his bank owns them and my forebears lived here ten thousand years before Pebbleman ever set foot on it, but I shan't demean myself by harping on petty details.) As to the man's vocation, I am unable to pinpoint it; it is apparently of a sedentary nature, since he sits cooped up in an outbuilding for days on end, crumpling sheets of paper. I guess there must be a demand for this type of handicraft, though I have yet to see him ship any of it off to market.

At any rate, to get on with my account, I was sashsaying around the woodshed one morning not long ago when I came across a stack of old magazines discarded by the household. Among them were several issues of *Country Life*, and in browsing through these, I noticed a couple of letters from readers dealing with the behavior of hedgehogs. Now, I have never laid eyes on a hedgehog to the best of my knowledge and belief, and I'm not sure we even belong to the same genus, but the surface similarity of our names intrigued me, so I read said epistles carefully. Here was the first:

"A Hedgehog on the Stairs. Sir—With reference to Brigadier Blest's letter of October 29, I can vouch that hedgehogs certainly climb stairs. During the last war my wife and children were living in Owestrey in Shropshire, and one weekend when I was home on leave, my wife and I woke in the night to hear a scuffling noise with an occasional thud. We naturally thought someone was moving about in the house and I went out on to the landing but did not turn on the light so as not to attract attention. There was then another thud just at the top of the stairs, and when I turned on the light I found that a hedgehog had very nearly reached the top, but had just missed his hold, which accounted for the thud.—R. C. Yates, Viceroy Close, Bristol Road, Edgbaston, Birmingham."

Well, thought I to myself, hedgehogs must be a pretty gifted lot if they can work their way up a staircase, and what's more, in the dark. The second letter spoke of their agility with almost superstitious awe. Captioned "Hedgehog up the Ivy?," it said: "Sir—With reference to recent letters on climbing hedgehogs, my experience of hedgehogs is that they do climb far too well, and have escaped from any walled or wired enclosure that they have been put into by me. I think an enterprising hedgehog would have no difficulty in clinging to the ivy on a house wall sufficiently well to climb to an upstairs window.— V. M. Burn (Miss), Farnham, Surrey."

The idea of a hedgehog, whatever its conformation, behaving like a human fly was so preposterous that I nearly laughed out loud. I had a strong suspicion that the lady's plaudits were tinged with girlhood memories of Douglas Fairbanks or that immortal cracksman, Raffles. Anyway, as I said above, I had occasion shortly thereafter to witness an episode somewhat akin to the experiences of your readers, except for one important difference. The dramatis personae were reversed; Pebbleman was the central figure, I merely a fascinated observer.

Let me confess at the outset that my own foolhardiness involved me in the affair. I never venture into the yard enclosing the house, but that particular day I happened to spot some succulent young herbs inside that sent me, and I figured I could pull off a fast foray. Halfway to my prize, I heard voices so close that I practically somersaulted getting behind a spiraea bush. When I peered out, there they were on the back porch—Mrs. Pebbleman smartly turned out as usual, and he— well, in those work pants of his.

"I may not be back until four," she was saying. "We'll probably lunch in Allentown, and then Shirley wants to look at some antiques over near Applebachsville. What were you planning to do today?"

"Oh, outdoor stuff mainly," he said in what immediately struck me as an evasive manner. "You know, trim around the roses, patch the screen door, that sort of thing."

"Right," she said. "You need a little exercise." She paused as if weighing her words. "But look, dear, you *will* remember, won't you?"

"What?"

"To stay out of the cellar."

"For God's sake!" he exclaimed, bristling. "Are you starting that all over again? Just because four years ago I once got stuck in the crawl space under our bedroom—"

"I didn't mean that specifically," she stopped him. "It's the humiliation of calling the fire company to get you out of these jams. Promise you won't tackle anything that requires rescue work."

From the shade of pink he turned, I guess Pebbleman was

about to make a pretty withering reply, but she was out of the gate before he could marshal the words. He idled around thoughtfully chewing a blade of grass as her car cleared the lane and vanished up the county road. Then he procured an old kitchen chair, braced it against the porch, and, standing on tiptoe, tried to reach the gutters. The altitude, however, appeared to dizzy him and he descended shakily. I had a moment of panic when he wheeled and advanced directly toward the bush where I was hiding, but he was just looking for a vantage point from which to inspect the roof. After contemplating it fixedly for a few moments, he came to some sort of decision and hurried indoors.

Well, you may ask, why did I linger now that the coast was clear? It was only a matter of twenty feet or so to the fence, and once there, I could have slipped through the rails into the deep grass beyond. The answer is that I had a premonition, a hunch that something special was brewing. These portents of mine always work out, and this one was no exception. All of a sudden, the lower sash of a second-floor window overlooking the porch was raised, and through it I saw Pebbleman laboring to remove the screen. He won out after a smart tussle, and presently thrust a broom and a burlap sack onto the slate roof. Then, very gingerly, he projected himself forward and outward, and finally ended in a simian crouch.

I was spellbound watching all this, of course, though I couldn't for the life of me imagine what his purpose was. He revealed it straightaway when, slowly creeping toward the gutters, he extended the broom and began poking out the winter's accumulation of leaves and twigs. Senseless though the whole procedure seemed, you had to admire the fellow's pluck. It was a feat a gymnast would have prided himself on, and while Pebbleman's strength was no doubt formidable from having crumpled so much paper, most of it was concentrated in his fingers. Yet it was those, sadly enough, that caused his debacle. In lunging at the farthermost gutter, he lost his grip on the broom and it tumbled off the roof, rebounding from the flagstones below. With a sigh of impatience, he turned in the direction of the window through which he had come. Simultaneously, the sash dropped with a crack like a pistol shot, and Pebbleman was marooned.

And right then and there I beheld an extraordinary spectacle. Many in his predicament would have given way to hysteria. They would have broken down, sobbed, beaten their clenched fists on the slate in frustration. Not so Pebbleman. Coolly and methodically, he set to work to effect his escape. He first sought to raise the sash by an upward pressure of his palms against the windowpane, but to no avail. Next he tried the adjacent windows, using the same technique and whimpering to maintain his courage. Then, clearly disheartened, he inched his way to the edge of the roof and craned over it. As far as I could deduce, he was estimating the probable damage to his ankles if he clung to the brink and dropped the intervening four feet. Evidently the risk dismayed him, for he recoiled and mopped his brow. Was it the sight of the pocket handkerchief that suggested a possible means of succor? It must have generated some hope; as quickly as the precarious footing allowed, he tottered to the angle of the porch visible from the county road and waved frantically to the infrequent cars that passed. None even slowed down, but the majority of the drivers whipped out their handkerchiefs and waved a cordial response.

The sun was high in the heavens by now, and the slates so hot that Pebbleman was forced to take refuge in a wedge-shaped bit of shade hardly wider than a knife blade. At long last, he appeared to have evolved a solution. He removed his shirt, twisted it and the burlap bag into the rough semblance of a rope, and, tying one end to the gutter, prepared to lower himself. He would almost certainly have plummeted to destruction had divine providence not interceded. Around the corner of the house came a couple of twelve-year-old boys wheeling bikes. They froze when they saw the figure on the roof.

"Hey, Mister, what are you doing up there?" one of them called out.

"That's for me to know and you to find out," said Pebbleman tartly. "What are you doing down there?"

"Selling subscriptions. Would you be interested in our combination offer? The *Paris Review* plus *Crocheting World* and the *Canadian Mink Raiser,* two years for only $9.95."

Pebbleman deliberated. "Well, I might spring for part of that," he said. "Tell you what. Fetch down the ladder you'll find in that tool house and I'll try the *Paris Review* for three months."

"We can't sell less than a year."

"O.K., O.K.," said Pebbleman impatiently. "Get going on that ladder. . . . What are you two whispering about?"

"Maybe it's better if you sign up before we bring the ladder," the youth said. "We could pass the application up to you on a cleft stick."

"Why, you little measle," said Pebbleman. "Are you trying to blackmail me?"

"That's such an ugly word, Mister. Call it rather a *quid pro quo.*"

"You're pretty mature for your age, aren't you? You sound like the heavy in one of those old vaudeville sketches."

"Yup, we youngsters grow up real fast nowadays," said the lad. "So how's about it, Dad? It's just a simple horse-trade."

Well, they argued back and forth for a while, but the boys had the whip hand and Pebbleman knew it. They finally reached a compromise whereby he was to sign the application when he got halfway down the ladder. I vamoosed right after they went to fetch it, not wishing to crowd my luck, so I can't say whether he kept his word. The last I saw, however, he was chasing the two off the place with his broom, like the Inspector used to with Hans and Fritz. All in all, it was an absorbing experience, and if any other ground hogs have encountered similar climbers, I sure would appreciate reading about them in your columns. With profound thanks for allowing me to use them, I am, sir, your obedient servant,

MORRIS J. MONAX

Great Oafs from Little Monsters Grow

Loathe it, condemn it, resist it if you will, but you can't ignore it: every day, in every way, youth is becoming more precocious. A friend of mine, just back from a year's residence in Italy, stoutly avers that of all the wonders he saw none compared with his *portiere's* baby, an infant less than fifteen months old. "He's a holy terror—a real *feroce*," he declared. "Hangs around the kitchen all day swilling Orvieto and smoking cheroots by the bundle, and if you so much as look at him he rips out a string of Neapolitan cuss words that'd curl your hair. You know those fat little jowls a baby has? Well, his are already blue from shaving, and twice during our stay there we caught him tickling the maid, a peasant girl from Calabria. I've got a hunch he's mixed up in the drug traffic."

To say, as will chauvinists, that the foregoing is an example of certain isolated cases confined to Mediterranean climes, whose cycle of growth is speedier than our own, is equivocation; in whatever field, whether politics, science, or the arts, the voice of the stripling is heard in the land, rising with cicadalike insistence. Only a few months ago, it penetrated to the book page of the *Times*, as follows: "Talent blooms ever earlier and earlier. A novel by Caroline Glyn, fifteen, called 'Don't Knock the Corners Off,' about a nine-year-old girl, will be published by Coward McCann on Jan. 3rd. The young British author is a great-granddaughter of Elinor Glyn. Mrs.

Glyn wrote her first novel at the age of thirty-five and the romantic 'Three Weeks,' which was about a grown-up girl, when she was forty." In the theatre, where prodigies have always been a dime a dozen, the advent of a *Wunderkind* is naturally less momentous, but one exemplar a while back was so feisty that Frances Herridge, of the New York *Post*, judged him worthy of interview: "Producers don't come any younger than Peter Bogdanovich, who at twenty has spearheaded the $15,000 production of Clifford Odets' 'The Big Knife' at the Seven Arts Playhouse. . . . Peter made up his mind about theatre, he said, when he was fifteen and in Collegiate School. 'The dramatics club was putting on "The Rainmaker" and I had the title role. I worked so hard on it I did almost no schoolwork. Hadn't even cracked my chemistry book when we suddenly had an exam. I had to fake it. The upshot was I was accused of cheating and taken out of the play. I was so mad I wouldn't go to school for three weeks. . . . I've been able to learn more on my own,' he said—adding that in his spare time he was a drama and movie critic for *Ivy Magazine,* which goes to the Ivy League colleges. 'I'm a great finagler,' he said. 'That gets me in to the plays and movies for nothing.' "

Thanks to a sixth sense that warns me of the proximity of budding genius, I had always avoided exposure to it by nimble footwork until last week, when the machinations of a Broadway agent brought me to grief. Over the luncheon table and caught up in an ecstasy of Martinis, this busybody represented to a young producer, named, by a coincidence, Nimble Footwork, that I was an ideal choice to adapt some property of his for the stage. Inasmuch as a play had exploded in my face the past season, leaving contusions that were still purple, the idea filled me with repugnance, but in a moment of aberration I stopped by the office of the agent, Moe Joost, to discuss the matter.

"What have you got against the kid?" Joost was demanding heatedly. "He's wide awake, dynamic, a fireball! And, what's more, he's loaded—his old man manufactures those nose drops which they sell millions of gallons on television."

"I know, Moe, but he's a child," I protested. "Seventeen years old, for God's sake."

"Fourteen, to be exact," he corrected. "But that's beside the point. How old was Red Harris when he started in?"

"Do you mean Red Lewis or Jed Harris?" I asked, confused.

"Lewis, Harris—what difference does it make?" Joost snapped. "He was a mere squirt, and so was Mervyn Thalberg and Irving LeRoy. This lad is a real showman, I tell you." He energetically unfolded a copy of *Variety*. "Look at his schedule for next fall. A musical version of Nat Hawthorne's *House of Seven Gables*, with Vera Hruba Ralston as Hester Prynne. Bulfinch's *Age of Fable*, with an all-colored cast, directed by Mickey Rooney. *Potash and Perlmutter* in modern dress, starring Laurence Olivier, with incidental music by John Cage. And, lastly, Ibsen's *John Gabriel Borkman*, done entirely with puppets. Anybody has versatility like that, brother, you better latch on to him but fast."

"Well," I said reluctantly, "I *could* listen to what he's got in mind—"

"Sure, go over and intuit each other," Joost approved, clapping me on the shoulder. "Now, hustle along—I'll phone him you're coming." He paused, a trifle uncertainly. "Oh, by the way, one thing. Stay off the subject of nose drops—he's a little sensitive about the family scratch. Not that he's a snob, mind you—not at all. He's a very simple person, just like you or I—do you know what I mean?"

I promised to commit no *gaffes*, nasal or financial, and headed for Footwork's office, on Broadway in the lower Fifties. The directory in his building listed a profusion of fly-by-night enterprises—song pluggers, importers of banjo heads, jobbers of transvestite clothing—but nothing indicative of the individual I sought. After laboriously unscrambling the legend "Krowtoof Productions," I realized that he was disguising himself in traditional fashion from creditors and revenue agents, and found my way to his cubicle. My arrival coincided with that of a wing-footed messenger from Lindy's delivering a packet of sandwiches, and together we beat a prolonged tattoo on the door before evoking an answer. A sallow, dishevelled youth resembling Aubrey Beardsley in decline, with eyes that glittered like patent leather in a triangular face, greeted me breathlessly. "I'm on a long-distance call," he panted, and grasped my hand wetly. "Pay off this guy for me, will you? I'll straighten it out with you later."

I complied, and as Footwork sprang back to the phone, fumbling open the sandwiches, I took discreet inventory of the premises. The usual theatrical office décor—the saccharine portraits of Harry Richman and the rump-sprung leather divan —was nowhere in evidence; instead, a neo-Calder mobile danced spastically overhead, and dotted among the Art Nouveau posters on the wall were half a dozen photographs of Gelber, Jack Richardson, and similar Delphic talents, their burning devotion to Footwork inscribed in the same suspiciously childlike scrawl. The young impresario, phone receiver wedged against his clavicle, was meanwhile dictating into it, between mouthfuls, an acid critique of *After the Fall*, the chief shortcoming of which, in his view, was a superfluity of polysyllabic words. Somewhere in his career, Footwork observed tauntingly, Arthur Miller had swallowed a dictionary, and his play, unintelligible to anyone under fifty, was destined to enrage and discomfit every adolescent.

"You probably wonder what that was all about, don't you?" he said, chuckling, as he hung up and revolved toward me. I shook my head to signify a complete lack of interest. "So I gathered. Well, I cover the Broadway scene for *Coolsville*, the hippest high-school organ in the Buffalo area. I'm on the cuff at every box office, night spot, and eatery in town."

"Except Lindy's," I qualified, clearing my throat. "Look, those sandwiches of yours came to two eighty-five, without the tip."

"No kidding!" he marvelled. "Man, where could you get a meal like this under four bucks? But never mind—we'll be bathing in champagne and caviar when our show hits the street, this I promise you. O.K., let's get down to business, but first some background—"

A sudden crash of piano chords echoed through the wall separating us from the adjacent office. "Who on earth is that?" I demanded.

"Only the greatest, Dads," he replied. "It's the Duke—he's writing the score for my new musical, *The Woodcarver of 'Lympus*. And what a headache I had clearing *that* property, yuk-yuk. I saw it one night on the *Late Show* and *boi-n-n-ng*, I get the inspiration—why not do this as a musical with the Duke and Lena and Walter Pidgeon, and, whammy, we zing in a couple of great production numbers with lots of pizzazz and dese and dose"—his hands molded voluptuous corsages from thin air—"and we're home, man; I mean they're naming banks after me, and the ice—oh, my God, it's like Labrador. . . . Well, I spent a fortune in dimes phoning all those TV execs for the rights, and they wouldn't budge, the bastards, so I told the Duke to go ahead anyway. What the hell, he needs an outlet for his energy—right?"

"This—ah—idea you wanted to discuss with me," I reminded him.

"Oh, yes," he said. He scratched his chin reflectively, then looked around at me with a winning smile. "I had my first shave day before yesterday," he confided. "You're probably too old to remember, but man, what a gas it was—the steaming hot towels and the pull of the razor and the bay rum afterward. There's a wonderful theme for a kookie comedy there, like *Ah, Wilderness!*—you know, all the nostalgia of putting on your first pair of longies and like that—" He broke off and stood up. "How do you like these, by the way?" he asked anxiously. "They're acrid and Orlon, and the man at Barney's says they'll wear like iron."

"Scrumptious," I said, consulting my watch. "But listen, I'm afraid—"

"O.K., O.K.," he said hastily. "Well, here's the *drehdel*, the gist of my thinking. I was remembering back to those biographical plays on Roosevelt and Helen Keller and Freud, and it suddenly occurred to me there ought to be one dealing with peak incidents in the life of your various creative greats, such as Jonathan Swift, say, or Wagner or Alexandre Dumas." He gulped down a sour tomato in its entirety. "Now, take Swift, for instance. I see him pacing up and down his study in torment, with sheets of foolscap and a feather pen and musty volumes all over the joint. He's Despairsville, see, on account of he's got Vanessa and Stella Dallas on his back, and he's fed up with humanity, but good. Then, all at once, *voom!*—he stops and smites his forehead. 'I got it, I got it!' he hollers. 'I'll vent my spleen on the crumbs with a bitter parallel about a sailor! I'll have him captured by these teensy little midgets, and then by these kind horses, and then by these foolish philosophers in outer space. And I'll call the result . . . I'll call the result . . . "Gulliver's Travels"!' "

"A most original idea," I commented. "How about Wagner?"

"Well, with him you go for a big musical climax," said Footwork, plainly heartened by my encouragement. "At the beginning, he's also in his study, toiling over one of his compositions and marking down sharps and flats on a sheet of music. He tries this, tries that, but it's frustration time— Blocksville. Then, at his darkest hour, in comes his sweetheart—I forget her name."

"Wesendonk—Mathilde Wesendonk, I believe," I ventured.

"Check," he confirmed. "Wagner jumps up from the bench, grabs her in his arms, and they exchange a long kiss. 'Oh, Richard, hold me close,' she whispers. 'Your kisses are like wine.' So they smooch some more, and then he dives back to the piano and begins belting out this whole grandiose passage. 'What are you playing there, Rich?' she says. He looks up unseeingly. 'The rapture music from *Tristan and Isolde*,' he hollers. 'And I'm going to call it . . . I'm going to call it . . . the "*Liebestod*"!' "

"I see the general drift," I said. "Dumas—is he in his studio, too?"

"No, that's the twisteroo," said Footwork. "He's in a sidewalk café, sipping a cognac. This waiter's telling him a story about a prisoner confined in a dungeon called the Château d'If, that he escapes by sewing himself up in a priest's shroud and then goes around revenging himself on his enemies. When the waiter finishes, Dumas flings down a coin and embraces him on both cheeks. 'Pierre,' he hollers. 'I'm going to write that chronicle, and I'm going to call it . . . I'm going to call it . . . "The Count of Monte Cristo"!' "

"Well," I ruminated. "Your three elements are dramatic enough, I suppose, but how are you going to combine them?"

"That's your job, Pappy," said Footwork insouciantly. "You're the writer."

"Oh, no, I'm not," I disclaimed. "Not unless I hear that magic golden lubricant gurgling into my account."

Footwork tapped a pencil thoughtfully against his teeth. "How much does it cost to get your thoughts on paper?" he asked at length.

"Well, fifty thousand pries the cover off the typewriter," I said. "For another fifty, I might negotiate a rough draft—just a working script, of course."

"That's pretty steep," he complained. "I had in mind a two-hundred-and-fifty-buck advance against a small royalty."

"Would you mind speaking a bit louder?" I requested. "My ears must be stopped up—I'll have to get me some of those what-you-McCall-'em nose drops."

Footwork turned a slow lacquer red—the color of a Burmese plate—and arose, jiggling the mobile above him into a state of unbearable agitation. Five minutes later, I was southward bound on Broadway, whistling as I walked. The next morning, I received a call from Moe Joost, the burden of which was that I had created a very unfavorable impression. In his client's considered opinion, the project called for a much younger man, as I, for all my facile charm, was far too hidebound in my thinking. O.K.—I probably am. I just can't get over the fact that I never recovered the gelt for those sandwiches. Well, what the hell. Maybe I can worm it out of the Internal Revenue Service.

Hey, What's Wriggling
Around That Caduceus?

For anybody who, like me, has always regarded the medical profession with a mixture of awe and mistrust —engendered, I suspect, by harassment of one's tonsils in youth and overexposure to Sir Luke Fildes's gloomy masterpiece, *The Doctor*—there was more than a grain of vindication in the *Times* of London the other day. A group of the surgical élite, it appears, held a conference at the Royal College of Nursing to discuss an ordinarily hush-hush topic, the question of patients operated on for the wrong complaint. One of the participants was a Mr. F. P. Raper, consultant surgeon of the United Leeds Hospital, and whatever his effect on the audience, he wrung a hoarse shout of approval from yours truly. Said the account, "[Mr. Raper] emphasized the importance of the surgeon seeing the patient before the operation in the anaesthetist's room to make sure that he was the right patient and to check on the operation he was to have. This might also reassure the patient himself that the right surgeon was operating on him." The speaker was obviously dwelling on the ideal rather than the attainable, for another member of the symposium, Dr. Brooke Barnett of the Medical Defence Union, said that "they were now dealing with the case of a private patient who not only had the wrong operation but the wrong surgeon operated on her." I trust Dr. Barnett pleaded in extenuation that the plaintiff was also the wrong patient, thus restoring a cozy semblance of logic to the proceedings.

To be quite candid, the deeper one delves into the British physician, the more his confidence in materia medica tends to waver. Not long ago, the New York *Times* carried a dispatch from England about some twelve-foot pythons that a bank at Amersham was using to discourage potential cracksmen. The idea had been evolved by a seventy-two-year-old big-game hunter of Slough, Buckinghamshire, named Bill Farquhar Moody, who was extending it to safeguard automobiles as well. "For car protection I recommend a nice 6-foot boa constrictor or python," he was quoted as saying. "Four Slough doctors have snakes in their cars. They leave them on the front seat to deter thieves. It is very effective seeing a rock python coiled around the gear lever."

Now, goodness knows someone on an errand of mercy has every right to defend his property from molestation, and indeed the choice of a constrictor rather than a cobra or Russell's viper bespeaks a humane and enlightened spirit. I do feel, notwithstanding, that the practitioner who employs a reptile as watchdog invites situations that may easily get out of hand. One such, for example, emerges from the pages of a sporadic journal kept by a young American doctor, Lindsay Woolsey, during a belated vacation in England.

PRINCES RISBOROUGH, BUCKINGHAMSHIRE, OCTOBER 7

What a hugely satisfying week this has been, and so fortuitous—all because of an impulse, the day after I arrived in London, to wander into a Curzon Street snack bar, which in turn led to a chat with an elderly lady in a tweed cape, practically a dead ringer for Margaret Rutherford, who persuaded me to scrap my whole itinerary. Whether it was the American accent that intrigued her or my camera equipment, I couldn't make out, but within minutes, she had taken complete charge of me and was insisting I hire a car and see some of the English countryside. I wasn't too keen about the notion at first, for I still had Paris, Brussels, and nine other capitals to get through on the eighteen-day tour the travel agency had sold me. On reconsidering, though, I realized how absurd it was for a man half-dead from exhaustion and overwork, snatching his first holiday in four years, to tie himself down to a backbreaking schedule. Ninety minutes later, I walked out of a carrental establishment in the Strand with the key of a bright-red MG, a fistful of road maps, and a membership in the RAC, and the very next day at eight, I was on my way.

Well, once I got out of London, which consumed most of the morning, everything was sheer delight. I headed northwest, in the general direction of Whipsnade, dodging main roads wherever I could and investigating every byway that took my fancy. The stone farmhouses nestling in the wellordered fields, the sleepy churchyards with their ancient oaks and elms, the colorful pubs at which I drank my pint of bitter—it was all just one continuous delight, and the place names, of course, were out of this world—The Pheasantries, Leighton Buzzard, Terrier's End, Wardrobes, Dodd's Charity, and a pinpoint on the outskirts of Tring called, believe it or not, The Twist. The truly heartwarming aspect of the trip thus far, though, has been the civility and spontaneous kindness of people along the way. Everyone extends himself to the utmost, performing the smallest service so amiably you wonder how the English ever earned the reputation of being cold and reserved. Their food, frankly, doesn't fill me with quite such enthusiasm, and if I never again taste brown Windsor soup, bubble and squeak, or the custard dessert called Spotted Dog, I shan't repine. Still, this is mere faultfinding. Thanks to my elderly benefactress in the tweed cape, I feel all the tensions and anxieties of practice diminishing with each mile I travel. Tomorrow I turn southeast through the Chilterns toward High Wycombe, Amersham, and Slough. I must say I can't recall a single period in my life so tranquil and carefree, nor can I foresee how anything could possibly mar it.

CHALFONT ST. GILES, OCTOBER 12

Day in, day out, my motor ramble continues to afford unalloyed pleasure, but I should mention a curious experience

I had at Amersham yesterday. Inasmuch as my English currency was dwindling, I stopped off at a bank there to cash some travellers' checks. The cashier was apparently unfamiliar with these particular checks, and excused himself to consult a facsimile kept in the rear, near the vaults. Well, I was leaning on the counter, waiting for him to return, when a snake reared up in the wicket less than a yard from my elbow. Not a garter snake or anything that small—a gigantic creature with great glittering eyes and a body, thick around as my arm, that must have been a good twelve feet long. It was one of those characteristic visitations—purely hallucinatory, of course, and induced by fatigue or eyestrain—that patients are always reporting, and my diagnostic training should have enabled me to recognize it as such. Unfortunately, I reacted emotionally and, I am ashamed to confess, emitted a piercing scream. For a moment, everybody stood transfixed; then the entire staff came running to ascertain the cause, but meanwhile I'd regained my composure sufficiently to dismiss the incident with a laugh. Afterward, I thanked my lucky stars I hadn't succumbed to hysteria and blurted out a description of what I'd seen. We Americans are considered eccentric enough as it is without resorting to such whoppers.

OAKESHOTT ARMS HOTEL, SLOUGH, OCTOBER 17

Arrived here last night by way of Gerrard's Cross and Stoke Poges, and have decided to pause here a day or two to rest up. To tell the truth, I'm a little tense, and I can't quite figure out why. Have I seen too many cathedral closes, or is it this unending English courtesy, or what? In any case, my nerves are on edge, as I realized in the course of a stroll I took this morning in the High Street. Among the cars parked along the curb was an Armstrong-Siddeley saloon, a model I'd seen fleetingly but never had had a chance to inspect. Just as I was peering into the interior, shading my eyes with my hand, I suddenly had the most extraordinary sensation of being watched—from the inside. Since the car was empty, I knew I must be mistaken, yet all at once, a sinuous reptilian shape unwound itself from the gearshift, slithered across the front seat, and struck at me through the window. And now comes the shameful part, the detail I can hardly bring myself to put down. Totally forgetting my Amersham seizure, which should have taught me the phenomenon was psychic in origin, I let forth a paralyzing screech and raced back to the hotel in lunatic fashion, bowling over passersby like ninepins. In the five hours elapsed since then, happily, I've grown somewhat calmer and have been able to ingest a little bouillon and two slices of Holland rusk. Someone has been pounding on my door at intervals throughout the afternoon, calling my name with great urgency, but I don't propose to answer until I feel my normal self.

SLOUGH, OCTOBER 18

It begins to look as if my holiday, peaceful except for the two jarring incidents previously noted, may be shortened by professional demands. The person knocking so insistently was the manageress, whose brother-in-law, a gamekeeper named Sholto, lodges on the premises. This worthy, evidently, has been stricken with repeated attacks of delirium in the past twenty-four hours, and as I had thoughtlessly divulged my identity on arrival, Mrs. Grindge importuned me to have a look at him. In vain I protested that I was not licensed to practice in Europe; tears mingled with prayers until I finally relented. On examination the patient showed manifest signs of excitement aggravated by fear. His pulse was rapid, the facial region flushed, and the breathing shallow. For the most part, he was tremulous and disinclined to reply to questioning, but from time to time he uttered strangled cries of "Look out!" and clawed at his wrists as if attempting to disentangle something. According to Mrs. Grindge, he had twice made anguished references to a doctor's satchel as harboring a python. While all evidence pointed to a classic delirium tremens, his relative stated emphatically that he took no more than an occasional glass of port. I prescribed a sedative and an ice pack, lavaged the patient to rule out the possibility of poison, and instructed Mrs. Grindge to jot down any further ramblings that might furnish causative clues.

How puzzling that the serpentine element should arise again, and so soon after my own misadventures. I wish I could rid myself of the nagging thought that there is some connection. It may be childish of me, and pure coincidence only, but it troubles me, damn it.

SLOUGH, OCTOBER 20

This affair is proving more complex than I had supposed. Sholto continues to be restless, exhibiting unabated symptoms of snake trauma. After sustained appeals to search her memory, Mrs. Grindge disclosed that prior to my entrance into the case, a local physician by the name of Grimsditch had in fact treated the patient for a trifling stomach upset. Hoping to derive a hypothesis at least, I rang the man, identified myself, and arranged to visit him this afternoon. There then ensued a most exasperating delay; Grimsditch promptly forgot my existence and, when he did materialize at his office, a full two hours later, displayed no recollection of our appointment. On the whole, he struck me as unprepossessing—a sallow, fretful individual with a permanent sniffle and the aggrieved manner of one constantly imposed upon. I again presented my credentials and was about to narrate the relevant circumstances when he suddenly arose and administered his medical bag, which reposed beside the desk, a savage kick.

"Settle down there!" he snapped. "I've had enough trouble from you, you bastard. Now then," he said, resuming his seat, "what were you saying?"

Sensing myself in the presence of an individual who was, so to speak, a shade out of the ordinary, I decided to use a more roundabout approach than I had planned, and asked with seeming carelessness whether there were many rodents in the district. Practically none, he answered; he supposed the majority had been devoured by snakes.

"Oh?" I said quickly. "Do you have many of those?"

"As many as we need," he said, with a cryptic smile. "And good fat fellows, moreover. Squeeze the breath out of a chap before you can say knife, they will."

Hardly had he spoken the words than the bag by the desk gave an unmistakable twitch. Grimsditch observed me staring fixedly at it and queried what was amiss. I could feel cold sweat trickling down my spine, but I was resolved not to panic.

"I hope you won't consider it pertinacious of me," I said, enunciating with difficulty, "but surely you don't carry a snake on your rounds?"

"What would you suggest instead—a gun?" he sneered. "Let me tell you something, my dear sir—every blessed man, woman, and child in the Chiltern Hundreds is a barefaced, unabashed thief. Why, only the other day, a patient I attended at the local hotel, a gamekeeper, stole this very bag—instruments, snake, and all. I didn't miss it straight off, being a bit absent-minded, but when I retrieved it and checked the contents, there wasn't a trace of the boa." A harsh cackle escaped him. "Probably writhing around this moment in the bleeder's bedroom, and serve him jolly well right."

The Deodars, Bexhill-on-Sea, October 27

As nursing homes go, this is a model of efficiency and quiet comfort, set in the most pleasant surroundings imaginable. Now that my period of bed rest has terminated, I have been taking short walks in the grounds and along the shingle without any supervision, and am confident that by the weekend I shall feel well enough to leave. The matron's assurance that nothing of an organic nature was found in my baggage, and a similar guarantee from the garage, which, pursuant to my orders, has kept the car in isolation, has aided my recovery materially. As yet, I haven't reached a decision on whether I want to resume medical practice in the States, but I refuse to worry about it. After all, I'm still young, even though my hair is snow-white. I wonder if that tweedy old lady in the snack bar would recognize me now. I'd know *her* anywhere—blast her.

If It Please Your Honor

Hollywood book dealer Bradley Smith last night was found guilty of violating state obscenity laws by selling a copy of Henry Miller's novel "Tropic of Cancer."

The verdict returned by the jury of three men and nine women ended the six-week Municipal Court trial that followed the arrest of the 31-year-old book dealer last October. . . .

Judge Kenneth A. Holaday, who presided over the lengthy trial, told the jurors he would like to give each of them "a medal for public service well and faithfully performed."

At that point, one of the jurors, Mrs. Lillian M. Lake, stood up and told the judge the jury had a gift for him, commenting, "We could not have stood through this for six weeks without your smile."

They presented the jurist with a tie clasp and then gave bailiff Jerome Shapiro and court clerk Richard Key a box of imported chocolate candy, which Mrs. Lake described as her "favorite pep pills."—*Hollywood Citizen-News.*

SCENE: *A jury room in the Hall of Justice, in Los Diablos, California. At stage center, a conference table flanked by chairs and littered with scratch pads. Beside door at left stands a coat tree festooned with variegated plastic rainwear. A wall clock bearing an advertisement for a prominent cut-rate mortuary proclaims the time as shortly past two. The stage is deserted at rise. Then door opens to admit a bailiff—whose name, by an extraordinary coincidence, happens to be Morris Bailiff—shepherding a panel of jurors, the majority of them female. While the individual members differ somewhat in age and weight, they are all typical Californians, leathery and exuberant yet plainly moribund. They straggle into place around the table as Bailiff withdraws.*

MRS. PFLAUM (*aggrievedly*): That piece of soup meat they gave me was like rubber. If I served it to my husband, he'd throw it in my face.

MISS FABRICI: All the food there is terrible. Did you see the cottage pie Mr. Robinette ordered? It was nothing but cornstarch—wasn't it, Mr. Robinette?

ROBINETTE (*sepulchrally*): Gastritis. I'd just as soon pour cement in my stomach.

MRS. TONKONOGY: Well, it's your own fault. I told you to try their special plate, the Yucatán-style chicken.

ROBINETTE: What's the name of it again?

MRS. TONKONOGY: Chicken-Itza. They fry it on hot stones, according to a lost Aztec recipe.

SHUBKIN: Ah, why don't you people stop kidding yourselves? It's one big racket, the restaurants in this neighborhood.

MISS PALMQUIST: There he goes again.

SHUBKIN: I know what I'm talking about—I've been on plenty of juries! No matter where they take you to eat, the judge always gets a rakeoff.

MRS. LATIGO: Not Judge Faulhaber. Judge Faulhaber wouldn't stoop to a petty stunt like that.

MISS FABRICI: No, he certainly would not. He's a very superior type person, and you ought to be ashamed, casting such aspersions. (*All the ladies attest loudly to the Judge's incorruptibility. Robinette pounds the table for order.*)

ROBINETTE: Now, let's not fritter away the afternoon, for God's sake. We have to reach a decision on this case.

MISS PALMQUIST: What's there to decide? We heard the evidence—the man's guilty.

SHUBKIN: Says you. I happen to think he's innocent.

ROBINETTE: Please, folks—will you kindly stop squabbling so I can review the highlights once more? . . . All right, here's the background. On January 14th last, the plaintiff, Virgil Chubb, of Pellagra Springs, Colorado, entered a souvenir shop on Hollydew Boulevard belonging to Sam Bronislaw, the defendant. Bronislaw sold him a postcard that showed a young woman buried up to her neck in oranges spilling out of a cornucopia, with the caption "Lotsa goodies out here in the Southland."

SHUBKIN: One minor detail before you proceed. This, er, babe on the postcard—was it established that she was naked under the oranges?

ROBINETTE: What's that got to do with it?

SHUBKIN: I was just trying to clarify the scene in my mind's eye.

ROBINETTE: Well, the prosecution didn't stress the point other than to say that the card had an adverse effect on Chubb. It inspired him with lustful thoughts, causing him to visit a massage parlor on South Hermosa Avenue, where he was rolled. Bronislaw, when taken into custody, denied he was the instigator of the affair. In hundreds of similar sales, he asserted, no customer had ever had their libido aroused nor their wallet glommed. He contended that besides being visibly ginned up on entering the store, Chubb wore an unmistakable leer. As for criminal responsibility, Bronislaw added, he himself was merely a retailer; if there was any onus, it rested on the manufacturer of the cards, the Thomas Peeping Corporation, of Chicago.

MRS. PFLAUM (*with a snort*): Excuses—he's trying to wriggle out of it.

MISS FABRICI: What are we shilly-shallying around for? Judge Faulhaber as much as told us to bring in a guilty verdict.

MRS. TONKONOGY: A fair-minded man like he couldn't do anything else. I hope he gives that smut merchant a good stiff sentence. At least twenty years.

Mrs. Latigo: He should get life, the no-good.

Shubkin: Hold on a minute, everybody. I've got a right to my opinion, and I still say the Court is prejudiced.

Robinette: Why? Simply because His Honor owns a shoe store next to the defendant's place of business?

Shubkin (*doggedly*): Well, you heard Bronislaw's testimony. He claimed that the Judge was using pressure to squeeze him out so he could expand. He tried to cancel his lease, he engaged hoodlums to throw acid on the stock, he even came in personally and threatened to break Bronislaw's arm.

Miss Fabrici: So what? You want to prevent someone from using up-to-date methods on account of he's a jurist?

Miss Palmquist: Look, Shubkin, you're in California now, not back East.

Mrs. Latigo: Mr. Foreman, I move that Mr. Shubkin's remark be stricken from the record and that we hear a report from the Gift Committee.

Robinette: I agree. All in favor? (*Resounding approbation*) Very well—I call on Mrs. Tonkonogy.

Mrs. Tonkonogy (*reading from notebook*): A total of $24.70 was collected from the panel to buy presents for Judge Faulhaber and the court attendants. Everybody contributed but Mr. Shubkin. (*All heads swivel toward the malcontent, who reddens in embarrassment.*) Our chief problem, though, was to select appropriate gifts.

Miss Palmquist: I thought we decided on a briefcase and handkerchiefs.

Mrs. Tonkonogy: So you did, but the Committee felt we needed something with more verve—something to fit the personalities of the recipients. Well, we finally found a perfect remembrance for the Judge at a rummage sale in Altadena. A genuine, handmade Russian knout.

Miss Fabrici: That'll make a lovely ornament for his chambers.

Mrs. Tonkonogy: Yes, and practical, too—he can use it on witnesses with sluggish memories. Now, for the clerk and

219

bailiff we chose a more traditional gift, but also full of pep and spice. We bought them each a box of those imported licorice chewies, Afro-Dizzies.

MRS. LATIGO: Well, then, I guess we're about ready to bring in our verdict. How do we stand?

ROBINETTE: Unanimous for conviction, all but Shubkin.

MRS. PFLAUM: Who cares what he thinks? A tightwad that begrudges two dollars shouldn't be allowed a vote.

MISS PALMQUIST: No, that's unfair. After all, he is a juryman, even if he *is* a louse.

ROBINETTE: All right, let's have a show of hands. Those for guilty? (*A dozen hands are raised.*) Twelve. Those opposed? (*Shubkin timidly signifies his dissent.*)

MISS FABRICI: Wait a minute—something's wrong. Isn't there an extra person in our midst? (*Sensation. Suddenly, as the panel members gape at each other, Robinette peels off a putty nose and false whiskers, revealing the lineaments of Judge Faulhaber.*)

MRS. TONKONOGY: Why, Judge Faulhaber, whatever are you doing here?

FAULHABER: Your astonishment is understandable, dear lady. I owe you all a profound apology for my little masquerade. Had it not been for certain special circumstances of this case, I should never have interfered in your deliberations.

MRS. PFLAUM: You mean you possess evidence which you dared not disclose it from the bench?

FAULHABER: Precisely. Being as how my shoe store was contiguous to Sam Bronislaw's mart, I naturally sought to bust up his traffic in lascivious postals, but that was only a tithe of the chap's infamy. He was an inveterate wife-beater. (*The ladies buzz indignantly.*) Yes, many was the sound drubbing I overheard him administer on occasion through the walls. It took iron self-control not to rush in there and cane the ruffian.

MISS FABRICI: Small wonder you strove to abrogate his lease.

FAULHABER: In vain, as you know, so that I was forced to resort to subterfuge. Being as how I have a modest talent for makeup, I assumed the guise of Virgil Chubb, a putative Coloradan, and framed Bronislaw on a bum rap. I think that if you take the trouble to visit South Hermosa Avenue, you will find no massage parlor at that address.

MRS. TONKONOGY: Well, this *has* been a day packed with surprises, and judging from his nonplussed expression, to nobody more than our colleague Shubkin.

SHUBKIN (*sheepishly*): Your Honor, I'm not very good at flowery speeches, but if there were more people like you, this community would be a better place to live in.

FAULHABER (*rounding on him*): What's wrong with this community?

SHUBKIN: Uh—nothing, nothing. My last shred of recalcitrance is gone. I find Bronislaw guilty as charged, and here's the two dollars I owe the kitty.

FAULHABER: That's more like it. O.K., gang—got those presents you spoke of?

MRS. TONKONOGY: All wrapped up and ready to go, Judge.

FAULHABER: Then let's file in and hand 'em to the old buzzard.

MRS. TONKONOGY: But, er, pardon me, sir—aren't *you* the old buzzard?

MISS FABRICI: You're practically the whole works around here, outside of the defendant.

FAULHABER: Damn tooting I am. Just give me a second to don my judicial robes and I'll show you. (*He exits, as the jurors fall into step and march after him to the strains of "For He's a Jolly Good Fellow."*)

CURTAIN

The Great Stone Face

IF YOU HAD HAPPENED to be a travelling man in New England in the spring of 1921, loafing around the Union Station in Providence of a bright May morning, munching Necco Wafers and waiting to change trains to Woonsocket, and if you had bothered to look up from your copy of Chic Sale's *The Specialist*, you would have observed a youth embarked on a momentous escapade. About seventeen, he was arrayed like the lilies of the field in a cardigan sweater and gunpowder-blue trousers with twenty-two-inch bottoms that swept the floor, and bore himself with a mixture of bravado and stealth. His furtiveness was justified, for at any moment a stray truant officer might have collared him and secured his utter humiliation. Now that three decades and the statute of limitations have intervened, his identity can be safely disclosed. The lamister was a senior at the Classical High School, director of its monthly student publication, *The Accolade*. Displaying a precocity that was to flower in years to come, he had looted the circulation proceeds and was headed for a day's spree in Boston, the Athens of America. A forerunner of Charles Ponzi, Samuel Insull, and a host of similar geniuses, the poetic, sensitive chap with finely chiselled resources was myself.

To describe conscientiously the debauch that followed would require Honoré de Balzac working in tandem with Henry Miller; I ranged from Norumbega Park to Scollay Square like a drunken hospodar, leaving a mulch of greenbacks in my wake. Loaded with Harvard pennants, hand-lasted English brogues, first editions of Arthur Machen, Edgar

Saltus and George Gissing and duodecimo copies of the Ru-
báiyát, Sasieni bruyere pipes and tobacco jars made of human
skulls, I fetched up toward eventide at Durgin-Park's superla-
tive Market Dining Room in the produce district. I was
demolishing a hillock of hot corn bread after my third tureen
of chowder and debating the advantages of Indian pudding
over strawberry shortcake when I overheard a customer
nearby airing a grievance.

"Judas Priest!" he was rasping in tones of purest sand-
paper. "What's holding up my fried cods' cheeks? I have to be
back in my dressing room in twenty minutes—I follow Pallen-
berg's Bears!"

Dazzled by the proximity of a live actor, I rubbered around
at the speaker. He was a well-set-up fellow in the late twenties,
with a granitic face in which the eyes were underscored by
pouches rivalling those of kangaroos. Discreet inquiry and a
princely tip to the waitress revealed him to be a monologist
and juggler at the Majestic, a house consecrated at the time to
Shubert vaudeville. It followed as the night the day, having
seen the man, that one see his work, and at eight-fifteen I was
ensconced in a box at the theatre, whiling away the tedium
with a sack of Jordan almonds, nougats, and fondant creams. I
have a foggy recollection of Herb Williams, of the incompar-
able duo of Williams & Wolfus, belaboring the orchestra leader
with a baseball bat and screaming "Spotlight!," of Lowell
Sherman in a skit wherein a veiled lady invaded his rooms on
his wedding night and attempted to blackmail him, and of
Miss Patricola, majestic in salmon beads, executing a soft-shoe
dance as she rendered "The Rosary" on her violin, but these
are merely mosaic fragments. It was my irascible fellow-diner,
programmed as Fred Allen, the World's Worst Juggler, whose
saucy tomfoolery stole my heart. So unbridled was my laughter, so resonant my applause, that the head usher twice
appeared to threaten me with expulsion. No comedian, I
gaspingly told myself, had ever equalled him. Even that
primordial wheeze about the illiterate cop, who, finding a dead
horse on Commonwealth Avenue, ordered him to be moved

over to Milk Street, made me split my sides. Idolatry could go no further. Had it not been for my Puritanical surroundings, I believe I would have pelted the man with roses.

After the curtain, on the glib pretext of interviewing Allen for the Yale *Daily News*, I gained admittance backstage and tracked him through a labyrinth of steam pipes and electric cable. He was seated in a noisome lazaret with a copy of John Maynard Keynes's *The Economic Consequences of the Peace* in his lap, with which, he told me, he had just killed a roach. A young woman from whose opera-length hose I had some difficulty detaching my gaze was perched on a wardrobe trunk, idly swinging her legs. I accepted without cavil Allen's statement that she was his mother, and proceeded to quiz him about his favorite flower, birthstone, hobbies, preference in pets, and the like.

"Tell me," he said dubiously when I had concluded. "Aren't you a little young for a Yalie?"

With the blandness of a confidence man, I responded that I was a prodigy, an exchange student from the Transvaal. Sensing that I was on the brink, I made my adieux. In the course of the return journey to Providence, I consumed three pounds of salt-water taffy, boisterously regaling the smoker with quotations from Allen's routine. By the next morning, the fearful mishmash of food I had eaten began to interact. I was bedfast for two days and, under pressure, sang. The whole sordid episode was revealed, there were anguished conferences between my parents, and eventually, by pawning everyone's possessions, the scandal was averted. I still carry a welt on my crupper engraved there by my father's belt buckle.

All of the foregoing (in Seidlitz form, naturally) bubbled through my mind one afternoon three decades later at Schrafft's on West Fifty-seventh Street. I was sipping a peanut-butter milk shake, so thoroughly immersed in reverie that the dialogue between my neighbor and the soda dispenser did not immediately register. Then, as I caught the celebrated nasal rasp and recognized Allen, memory ran amok. Except for a bulge in the exchequer, his waist and his patience were as slim as they had been thirty years before in the Hub City chophouse.

"Drop that scoop!" he was hissing at the clerk in a low, choked voice. "Don't move! Forget you ever made a chocolate float—just follow my directions!"

"But I've been making floats nineteen years, Mr. Allen!" the clerk quavered. "Out in Los Angeles—"

"Precisely," snapped Allen. "You thought you were going to foist off one of those jukebox specials on me, those umbrella jars full of foam and wind all mushed up with sherbet and a green cherry on top. Well, guess again, Nostradamus. Now, first draw your syrup—no, no, twice that much. Next, the coarse stream—" His face blanched. "Man alive! What are you doing? You're vaporizing it! *Coarse stream!*" Ultimately, with more *Sturm und Drang* than Boulestin ever expended on a blue trout, the beverage was decanted and Allen buried his nose in it. I waited a decent interval, introduced myself, and reminded him of our original meeting. As he shook my hand, a suspicious drop of carbonated water trickled down his cheek. "Yes, those were the salad days," he said nostalgically. "The bread pudding in the cafeterias, the Chinaman holding one's laundry in escrow, the thrill of being cancelled out in Sandusky just before the overture. What a fool I was to give up all that glamor and security for a measly seven hundred weeks of radio."

"Still, you achieved quite a following," I consoled him. "If you could have learned to bray like an ass and worn women's hats, you could be right up there today with Berle and Skelton."

"No, they're real artists," he said. "Have you ever seen Red imitate a baby? You can practically smell the Pablum. Look," he said abruptly, "I've got to get over to the post office before it closes; they're auctioning off some unclaimed bicarbonate of soda, and I want to lay in my winter supply. When can you come up to the house for a real home-cooked meal?"

"Of fried cods' cheeks?" I asked warily.

"Anything you say," he proposed. "Let's leave it to Portland. She makes a wonderful soufflé out of skimmed milk and leftovers; it's nourishing and cheap, and we can have New England broken cookies for dessert." A date was fixed, we tendered farewells, and he departed ere we could grapple for the check.

At six o'clock several nights later, Fred ushered me into the foyer of his West Side apartment, tossed my rubbers into a closet, and steered me toward the living room. He was wearing a monogrammed blue moiré robe that still retained its Sulka price tag, and he fanned himself with a sample card dotted with swatches of tweed.

"I've been on the go all day," he confided wanly. "Just let me straighten out my tailor here—I'll be with you in a jiffy." He turned to a wasp-waisted elegant who was buckling a distended briefcase. "Now remember, Finsbury, the fawn cashmere with the leather piping, and I want three vents in the jacket."

"That's pretty conservative, Mr. Allen," demurred Finsbury. "I wish you wouldn't veto the luminescent lapels."

"None of that Nutsy Fagan stuff for me, friend," said Allen. "You're talking to a Boston man. Up there we dress in quiet good taste."

"O.K., we'll give you the real banker's drape," said Finsbury. "By the way, I stupidly forgot to inquire in regards to your rainwear needs."

"Thanks," said Fred graciously, "but Aquascutum sends a man over yearly to attend to those. I might be in the market for some white piqué leggings before the next dog show, though; I plan to exhibit some basset hounds."

As he escorted the young man to the door, I became aware of another, in a brown alpaca duster, blending snuff in a corner. Tins of Copenhagen, Rappee, Checkerberry, Göteborg, and Lorillard's Maccoboy littered the floor about his feet, and he hung over his portable scales with the fierce concentration of a medieval alchemist. Fred, intercepting my glance, explained that although he himself rarely dipped, he often summoned experts to compound special mixtures for him. "It's smart to have your private blend lying around in case friends care to indulge," he went on. "The same with vintage wines. I made a deal with a vineyard up in Fresno, recently, whereby I get their very first pressing, the one they usually throw away. It's frightfully good with rat cheese, and most of the donkeys who come up here don't know the difference."

"Mr. *Al*-len!" a soprano voice called from the kitchen. "The murphies are almost done. Did you offer your friend a drink?"

"No, he's loaded; I don't think he ought to have any more," Fred called back thriftily. "You don't mind, do you, old man? It mounts up, the ice and the wear and tear on the glasses, to say nothing of the cost of the liquor itself. Here, have a pretzel while you're waiting." The plate he handed me contained salt for the most part, but I was attacking it with gusto when Portland, a slender and attractive figure in her bungalow apron, entered. Fred's sombre prediction that their hospitality would soon reduce him to beggary proved to be hyperbole; within the half-hour, insulated by several Martinis, we were sitting down to a capital dinner. Waving aside my compliments on her culinary skill, Portland assured me that her sisters were far more gifted cooks.

"There are three," she said. "Lebanon, Doctor Frederica, and Lastone." Doctor Frederica, she divulged, had been named after their father, Dr. Frederick Hoffa, and Lastone, who vaguely suggested some sort of antifreeze, was so dubbed because she was the youngest. "I was lucky, though," she said. "If Fred had kept his first stage name, I would have been Portland Huckle."

"Huckle was the way I was billed when I broke into show business," Fred said. "Paul Huckle, the Celebrated European Entertainer. I huggled as Juckle—sorry, I mean I juggled as Huckle—at those amateur nights up around Massachusetts, and then some booker renamed me Fred St. James after a theatrical fleabag he lived at in Bowdoin Square. Once I started playing the vaudeville circuits and went out to Australia, I worked under the name of Freddy James."

227

"How did you happen to go out there?"

"A whim," he replied. "I wanted to go on eating. An Australian theatre magnate caught my act in 1916, and I jumped from Birmingham, Alabama, to Sydney. Man, I went through things Marco Polo never dreamed of. The train to the Coast was one of those tourist affairs where the passengers cooked in a potbelly stove and hung their laundry in the aisles. We were derailed in West Texas, and I wound up naked in a chinaberry tree with a railroad headlight shining on me. The voyage across the Pacific was a nightmare. I was sick the whole time, and the old geezer in the berth under mine kept his false teeth in a glass of water so that they opened and closed with every roll of the ship."

"Did you see much of Australia?"

"All of it, and New Zealand too," he said. "I put in three years there—played every waterhole and whistle stop you could mention. Some of the places were so primitive that they paid me off in cassowaries. In many of them I was the only act on the bill, along with some old movie pageant like *Intolerance* or *Way Down East*. I had to shift my own scenery, operate the switchboard backstage, and tie off the curtain myself. In 1920, I came back to the States and toured the Shubert time until I drifted into revue—the *Greenwich Village Follies*, *The Passing Show*, *The Little Show*, and finally, *Three's a Crowd*."

"There's one phase of your career I've never understood," I said. "You were always pretty coy about Hollywood. What happened?"

"Well, I had a couple of unsettling experiences," he returned. "Every time I made a picture, gypsy moths or something got into it, because it would turn up in those grind houses in Skid Row along with attractions called *Daughters in Jeopardy* or *Marijuana, Weed with Roots in Hell*. To tell you the truth, if anybody came along with the right kind of vehicle—"

"I beg pardon, Mr. Allen." A diffident voice from the doorway heralded the entrance of the tobacconist in his brown alpaca duster. His face wore a look of suppressed excitement.

"Oh, hello, Hornbostel," Fred greeted him. "All finished snuffling? Here, give my guest a pinch. Now, you press this up against your gums—"

"Excuse me, sir," the young man blurted, "but I couldn't help overhearing what you said about a Hollywood vehicle. I'm working on a movie original."

"Yes, yes, so's everybody," said Fred hastily. "Listen, leave the bill on the sideboard. I'll send you a check in the morn—"

"Please, Mr. Allen, just let me sketch it in briefly for you," pleaded Hornbostel. "It's got humor, pathos, the works. Did you ever read *Little Lord Fauntleroy?*"

"Not since I was a stack boy in the Boston Public Library," my host confessed. "Look, Hornbostel, mail me a synopsis—"

"It wouldn't convey the flavor, the juice," interrupted Hornbostel, flattening him like a juggernaut. "You see, the trouble with the book, it was namby-pamby—all about a little pest with long blond curls who pokes his snoot into everybody's business and softens up his crusty old grandfather, a British earl. Strictly for the birds. Now I've brought it up to date, made real down-to-earth characters out of them. I call it *The Fauntleroy Story.* I see the hero as a kind of a psychopathic killer, a younger Richard Widmark. He's mixed up in a hot-car racket—"

"Wait a minute," said Fred faintly. "In the book he's supposed to be seven years old."

"He can still be," said Hornbostel with an impatient shrug. "He doesn't steal the heaps personally; he fingers the caper for the rest of the mob. Well, one day they glom a Rolls-Royce town car, and the irony of the setup is that it belongs to the kid's own grandfather, who's in New York trying to trace his heir. The earl—that's you—recognizes the little chap in the police lineup from this rose tattoo on his arm, forgives him, and takes him back to the castle in England. You follow?"

"Haltingly," said Allen. "And then his pals come over and blackmail him?"

"No, this is the switch!" Hornbostel chortled. "On the eve of the Grand National, the jockey that—we establish—is to ride the Fauntleroy entry pulls a tendon in his nose or something. The kid dons the silks instead, wins the race in a sensation-fraught climax, and we end on a big production scene at court where Queen Elizabeth draws Fauntleroy on her knee and says it was Yankee know-how that saved the day."

"Yep, that's what the exhibitors are crying for," agreed Fred. "A picture without an iota of sex."

"Well, frankly, that bothered me too," admitted the other. "Why couldn't we plant an older sister like Shelley Winters, maybe a high-class trampoline artist? She falls in love with the guy in charge of the portcullis, a handsome Robert Taylor type—"

"It's foolproof," broke in Fred. "It's the biggest thing since *Clarissa Harlowe*. Well, so long for now, Hornbostel," he said, rising. "You'll hear from me, I promise you."

"There's only one thing worries me, Mr. Allen," the tobacconist declared, standing his ground. "I can't decide whether the central character should be a boy after all."

"Well, neither could the author," said Allen. "She left it pretty flexible."

"I know, but suppose he was a girl," said Hornbostel eagerly. "A tomboy type, a cute little trick about nineteen years old. And suppose, just for the sake of argument, that the earl is a jaunty young man about town, a Ray Milland or Fred MacMurray."

"Why not Jan Kiepura, the Phantom of the Operetta?" suggested Fred.

"He'd be good too." Hornbostel nodded. "Well, anyway, he's been hunting high and low for her to announce she's come into the title of Lady Fauntleroy, but all the time she's like working in a five-and-ten-cent store as a song plugger and rooming in a brownstone. Well, due to the housing shortage, he can't find a place to stay, until by accident he stumbles into the very same spot. The landlady, figuring that a night owl only needs to sleep in the daytime, rents him Lady Fauntleroy's room, and there you have the delicious boffo of the lovers not realizing how close they are and yet so far. The audience'll yell!"

"Hold on," said Fred, confused. "What do you mean, 'lovers'? They haven't even met yet."

"Just a technicality." Hornbostel waved him aside. "He sees her lingerie on the fire escape and stuff like bobby pins scattered around, and she's always running into his shaving brush or suspenders."

"The way Ginger Rogers did in *Rafter Romance*, eh?" mused Fred. "Well, it ought to be sure-fire a second time."

"Check," said Hornbostel brazenly. "The rest of the story's simple algebra. Neither can marry the other on account of he's seemingly her grandfather, except he finds a mildewed document in the castle proving he's not a blood relative at all but just an ordinary peasant. Only, by then, she's run away to nurse her heartbreak on the Isle of Capri. He follows her there, and you close on the two smooching in a Hemingway-type gondola."

"Forgive me for intruding, folks." It was Finsbury, Allen's tailor, speaking discreetly from the threshold. "I came back for my briefcase, and I couldn't help overhearing. That last sequence of yours"—he turned to Hornbostel—"that really should take place in a charm school."

"A charm school?" repeated Hornbostel, slowly revolving toward him with fascinated attention. "You mean a lot of shapely dolls parading around in swimsuits with books on their heads?" The tailor nodded, his face aglow with creative pride. Hornbostel threw up his hands in ecstasy. "Mammy!" he exulted. "What a climaxeroo!" Portland, Fred, and I were jammed in the doorway like the Laocoön group, clawing for egress, before I heard the sudden note of uncertainty in the tobacconist's voice. "I wonder, though—do you think it's believable?"

"No," said Finsbury excitedly, "but I'll tell you how it *could* be. First off, you establish Fauntleroy as a midget. . . ."

Pastiche of the Author in Sweet Disarray

I had not seen Saul Bellow for four or five years, and meeting him again after all that time was a distinct shock, just as reading *Herzog* after not having read him since 1959 came as a real revelation. He is now 49 years old and he has grown almost alarmingly handsome. . . . His features—eyes, nose, mouth—are all large and full. . . . I said I thought *Herzog* was his best book, and Bellow said he thought so, too.

"Which makes it," I said, "better than everything else."

He smiled and ducked his head down. . . . Saul Bellow takes a compliment better than any writer I know. And if you don't think that takes talent, just try complimenting a writer sometime. . . .

He is certainly interested in other writers and their writing, and talked about . . . several young writers we both knew. I mentioned one who'd been having a hard time, and Bellow said, "That reminds me of what Samuel Butler once said. I've been having a lot of fun reading old Sam. Young people, I believe he said, should be careful about their aspirations. They might live to achieve them."

—*Robert Gutwillig in the* Times Book Review.

Mr. Angus Fenisong! Paging Mr. Fenisong, of the *Daily Blade!*"

The bellhop's insistent chant throbbed across the crowded

lobby of the Stilton, New York's most exclusive hotel, abruptly halting my contemplation of the fashionable noonday throng about me. As I rose to acknowledge it, I was conscious of not a few admiring glances, for, though I'm still a cub reporter, my exposés of the kosher poultry racket and the citywide recruitment of white slaves in laundromats had boosted circulation and made me a newspaperman to be watched. That I was earmarked for promotion was clearly evident from my city editor's greeting when he summoned me to his office that morning.

"Well, Scoop, how's our ace newshawk today?" he joshed me. "I've got a crackerjack assignment lined up for you. I daresay you've heard of Solita Blather?"

"Not the author of *Naked in the Hay, Hey, Naked Lady!*, and *Lady into Mink*?" I asked.

"Nobody else," he confirmed. "We just had a flash that she checked into the Stilton last night with the manuscript of her new novel, *The Lady Is a Mink*, the first book in history to be published in a genuine mink jacket, and that's a page-one feature. Think you can handle it?"

I naturally promised to do my best, albeit the task soon proved to be far from simple. Arresting and provocative as she was on the printed page, Solita Blather had never revealed herself to the public. In the few meagre clippings I unearthed from the morgue, she emerged as a drab, diffident personality whose mousiness suggested the rural schoolmarm rather than a best-selling novelist. I did, however, manage to glean several crumbs that I hoped would win me an audience: both of us were Virginians born under the sign of Virgo, and both our names had thirteen letters. It was a flimsy enough pretext for requesting an interview, to be sure, and yet it succeeded. Her voice on the phone, surprisingly, had none of the spinsterish quality I anticipated. Its warm, vibrant undertones bespoke a readiness to coöperate that I found heartening, and now that I had been kept waiting in the lobby for three-quarters of an hour, I was agog with curiosity as I ascended to her suite.

So unlike my preconception was the woman who answered

the door that I stood transfixed for a moment. Tall and radiantly blond, a dazzling smile dimpling her exquisite features, she was clad in a housecoat of some diaphanous material that accentuated a voluptuous figure. The heady scent of a French perfume I could not identify enveloped me as she extended her hands in welcome and drew me inside.

"To think that we've finally, actually met, Mr. Fenisong," she said breathlessly. "I wonder if you realize what this moment means to me. I read every word of those marvellous articles you wrote on the—the—what was it again?"

"The kosher chicken traffic?" I said. "You really liked them, Miss Blather?"

"*Liked* them?" she repeated. "They were masterly. They sent a cold, clean draft of air surging through the pages of—er—what paper did you say you were on?"

"The *Blade*," I said. "Well, I certainly appreciate that, and I want you to know that if anybody's responsible it's you. Ever since I first ran across your work, I've tried to model my style on yours."

"Why, how utterly darling of you!" she exclaimed. "That deserves a kiss." With a sudden, impulsive movement, she encircled my waist and crushed her lips against mine. Then, like a child overcome by remorse, she backed away. "Oh dear, what an impulsive goose I am," she said contritely. "Do forgive me, won't you, Mr. Fenisong? I get so few compliments from people I respect that I lose my head."

My fervent protestation that I attached no ulterior motive to the gesture stilled her qualms, and, entwining her arm through mine in sisterly fashion, she conducted me into the living room. It was a pleasant chamber for a tête-à-tête, dominated by a long, low divan backed by masses of flowers, with a profusion of books and magazines scattered about, and a bottle of champagne—a token of good will from Miss Blather's publishers—reposing in a bucket on the coffee table.

"Here, sit down beside me," she invited, hospitably patting the divan. "You know, Mr. Fenisong, I really owe you an apology for receiving you in such informal attire, but I can't bear the heat in these New York hotels. This negligee's as sheer as can be, and yet I'm practically stifling. Why don't you slip off your coat?"

"I'm O.K. as I am, thanks," I replied. "I don't want to get too relaxed."

"Of course," she said. "You've got to be constantly on the *qui vive*, absorbing impressions, evaluating and winnowing the raw material for your copy. But see here—why don't we have a sip of this wine while you decide what questions you're going to ask me?"

"I'd love to, but I never drink when I'm working," I said. "It tends to dull my faculties."

"Heavens, you *are* a disciplined person," she said. "Still, that shouldn't surprise one. It's reflected in all your work." She poured herself a glass of champagne, drank deeply of it, and leaned back. "All right, fire away."

"Well," I began. "First of all, where do you derive the inspiration for your plots, mainly?"

She toyed with the stem of her glass before answering, a mischievous gleam in her great violet eyes. "Isn't it weird?" she commented. "There must be some kind of telepathy between us—I knew instinctively you'd bring that up. Well, maybe you'll scoff, but most of them come to me in the bathtub. You see, Mr. Fenisong," she explained, "I don't know whether you noticed, but I happen to have a divine body. Not just a normal, run-of-the-mill physique but a superb, a breathtaking one. Does that sound horribly egotistical of me?"

"No, no indeed," I hastened to assure her. "If you're a particular type individual, why deny it? I mean, it's hypocrisy to pretend otherwise, isn't it? At least, that's how I interpret your thought."

"Precisely," she agreed, and helped herself to another glassful of champagne. "Well, to return to your question. Having a glorious figure, as I say, I naturally strive to keep it well groomed, so I sometimes loll in my bubble bath hours on end and mull over situations for my stories."

"And all that spadework pays off, believe me," I said sincerely. "The great thing about your characters, Miss Blather, is that they ring so true to life—you can practically reach out and touch them."

"Aren't you sweet?" she said gratefully. "Speaking of that, you look so unhappy slumped down there at the end of the divan. There's loads of room."

I got up and fetched a folding chair. "I think I'd prefer this, if you don't mind. It's easier on my back."

"You poor thing—you've a strained sacroiliac," she said, instantly sympathetic. "How inconsiderate of me. Have you had it massaged?"

"It's only a cramp, truly," I protested. "Tell me, Miss Blath—"

"I simply won't allow you to neglect it," she persisted. "Come and show me where it hurts, stubborn."

I repeated, as earnestly as I was able, that there were no grounds for her concern, and at last she forbore. Resuming the theme I had started, I asked whether her novels demanded a substantial amount of research.

"Scads, my dear—I'm an absolute perfectionist," she replied. "For instance, in *Follow That Bikini*, you may remember that Libertina, my heroine, takes refuge in a Miami Beach firehouse during the hurricane. Well, of course, I wanted the background to be as authentic as possible, so I flew down there, bought myself a white poncho and a pair of great rubber boots, and hung around this lunchroom on Lincoln Road where the smoke-eaters used to drop in for coffee. At first they were kind of shy, but after a day or two they accepted me as one of their own and invited me to their quarters. And do you know something, Mr. Fenisong?" she added triumphantly. "In the three whole weeks I lived and ate and played checkers with them, they never once suspected my real identity. When the book was published, to be sure, they made a huge fuss about the orgies and the drinking I described, but then you can't please everyone, can you?"

I said that she had a large, loyal body of readers who adored her work, especially university students, and that she would have made an inspiring teacher.

"Oh, I tried that for a while—not very successfully, though," she confessed. "I taught out at Wyoming U. a couple of semesters, and for a time I found it terribly exciting—all those lean, rangy chaps without a spare ounce of fat on them—but within a month or so, do you know, I made the strangest discovery. They weren't a bit interested in dating or smooching or any of the normal adolescent pursuits; they were just preoccupied with their musty old tomes, and was Kierkegaard a bigger influence than Sartre, and that kind of bilge. It reminded me of those immortal lines of Abraham Cowley, the poet (1618–67). I've had such a ball lately reading old Abe."

"I don't recall the passage you mean offhand," I said, racking my memory.

"Well, you should," she said. "It's right there on page 260 of Bartlett's *Familiar Quotations:* 'We spent them not in toys, in lusts, or wine, / But search of deep philosophy.' " She refilled her glass, emptied two-thirds of it, and shook her finger playfully at me. "That's the trouble with your generation, Fenisong. You're overintellectualized. You've become a bunch of thinking machines—cold, logical, devoid of tenderness—a lot of computers without a heart."

"Oh, come, Miss Blather," I protested. "It isn't fair to generalize. Maybe we just express ourselves differently."

"In what way?" she asked, leaning forward. "I'd love to hear your views on sex, to take a random example."

"Well," I deliberated. "I think it's a very important drive, mind you, but I feel we've put too much stress on it the last four or five years. There are so many other meaningful avenues in life."

"Yes, yes, like art and literature," she said impatiently. "Is that what you're trying to say?"

"Not necessarily. Simple, homely ways of fulfilling oneself, such as—well, I know you'll laugh at me, but whenever I'm tense or frustrated I turn to some humdrum occupation. Woodworking, for instance."

"You *do?*" she exclaimed, obviously impressed. "Oh, but how I envy anyone with coördination, with manual skills! I'm

CHICKEN INSPECTOR NO. 23

completely sunk if something breaks down or refuses to function. You should have seen me struggling with my electric curler this morning."

"Yes, inanimate objects can be pretty pesky on occasion," I agreed. "Getting back to your books, Miss Blather, the mink jacket your publishers announced—"

"My dear, it was a regular holocaust," she overrode me. "There were these enormous sparks shooting all over the place, and the cord was so twisted that I couldn't unplug it." She looked apprehensively over her shoulder at the bedroom door. "I just know it'll go up in flames if someone doesn't attend to it."

"I wish you'd told me earlier," I said, springing to my feet. "You should have reported it to the engineer at once. Where's the phone?"

"That's on the fritz, too," she said helplessly. "Isn't it awful? We're as isolated as though we were alone on a desert island."

"Now, now, there's no need to panic," I quieted her. "I'll run downstairs and notify the desk."

An expression of vast relief flooded her face. "But of course," she said. "How idiotic of me not to think of it." She uncoiled herself sinuously from the divan and arose. "And look, please don't bother to come way back upstairs. I'd never forgive myself if I made you miss your deadline."

I started to thank her for her thoughtfulness, but before I could finish she had guided me through the foyer and I was out in the corridor, my hat and coat piled in my arms. As the elevator bore me earthward, I dimly began to perceive the true essence of her spirit, the Blather nobody had ever been able to define. She was a chameleon, a restless, untrammelled creature dappled with sunlight and shadow. Could one capture her bright turbulence in words? Could one invest her with the same immediacy I had given to broilers and hookers? I did not know, but I squared my shoulders to the challenge.

Be a Television Writer!
Earn No Money!

ONE TURBULENT winter's evening several years ago, an oddly assorted party of four lay down to a Mexican dinner in an apartment on New York's upper East Side. What witchery our hostess employed besides tequila to make us sprawl on the floor as we dallied with her tacos and tamales, I can't remember, but there we were, two sultry beauties and David Susskind and I—neither of whom, by the wildest stretch of the imagination, could be deemed sultry or beautiful. As the frijoles loosened our tongues, Susskind and I began exchanging war experiences, and in all modesty, my account of how, against overwhelming odds, I had collected peach pits and tin foil for gas masks in 1918 excited the open admiration of the ladies. Susskind, of course, crimsoned with jealousy, and he promptly launched into a tale of some inconsequential action he had seen in the South Pacific.

"I was the deck officer of a corvette in the Marianas," he recalled, "and believe you me, those gol-durned Nips ran us ragged. But our chaps never lost their morale—they were splendid chaps, and if I say so myself, I worked hard to establish a relationship—an empathy, a dichotomy, I mean a dichotic empathosis—with those chaps under my command. The thing is, I like a happy ship."

I daresay that every man Jack of us there that night, and every woman Jill, never forgot that salty phrase, and I often feel that my career in television—which, by a curious coincidence, had nothing whatever to do with Susskind—might well be summed up as "a happy ship." It began some eight years back with a couple of *Omnibus* programs I wrote—"The Big Wheel," a nostalgic tribute to burlesque starring Bert Lahr, and "Malice in Wonderland," a vinegary fable about the adventures of a psychiatrist in Hollywood, with Keenan Wynn and Julie Newmar. So dazzled was I by the privilege of working with these performers that I refused any fee for my services, and so overcome by the gesture was Robert Saudek, the producer, that he momentarily lost the power of speech. In the next moment, however, he recovered it and said quickly, "O.K." Buoyant that the shows were not hissed, Saudek manifested his gratitude in princely fashion, with a water-soaked copy of the Farmers' Almanac for 1913 and a basket of Northern Spies. Most of the apples were wormy, but my wife—whose middle name, interestingly enough, happens to be Frugality—salvaged enough to make a strudel, on which we existed for several weeks.

One afternoon a year later, I was quietly proceeding along Madison Avenue when two individuals in tab collars so high that they almost obscured their low villainous foreheads emerged from a doorway, flung a burlap bag over me, and bore me struggling to the offices of CBS. Its executive producer, seated on a pile of telephone books to give himself majesty, was squinting through a book of fairy tales, his lips compressed. Before I could protest at the cavalier conduct of his minions—whose names, interestingly enough, happened to be Fred and Irving Minion—he informed me that I had been chosen to write a spectacular based on the legend of Aladdin. I confess that I was reluctant at first, but when he added that Sal Mineo and Anna Maria Alberghetti, a team often characterized as the Lunt and Fontanne of song, were to fill the principal roles, my last scruple vanished. But anxious as I was to fall to work, there was still one hurdle—the question of money. CBS was horrified at my refusal to accept any; I was equally resolved to take none; and the result was a deadlock. Finally, however, we reached a compromise. I was to have my choice of the executive's castoff clothing, and it was thus that I acquired the spiffy "tux" I wear to this day. What if the pants are a bit baggy or if the silk facings are dappled with schmaltz? I can still boast that they once belonged to Hubbell Robinson, often characterized as the Fu Manchu of the networks.

As for "Aladdin," that belongs to the ages. Statistics compiled by trained investigators working under Vichyssoise estimate that this production put more viewers to sleep than all the tranquillizers sold in the same year. From across the country, television repairmen reported countless instances of picture tubes clogged with a flocculent white substance resembling kapok, which, on analysis proved to be "Aladdin." Subsequently CBS received three tons of mail about the program, half of it containing veiled threats against Mineo, the other half containing unveiled ones. The common stock of the company sponsoring the show plummeted eighteen points the next morning, and I myself only escaped arrest by hiding out in Bismarck, North Dakota. The star of the production was less fortunate. The poor fellow was deported to Australia, his native heath, and to this very day is a homeless vagrant in Queensland, unable to find work even as a sheepherder.

It was all the more remarkable, therefore, that in preparing a new series at CBS called *The Seven Lively Arts,* I should have been appointed to write its initial show, "The Changing Ways of Love." Whether my appeal for the opposite sex influenced the choice—I still wear a badge proclaiming me Chicken Inspector No. 23, bestowed during adolescence in Rhode Island—I cannot say, but in any case, summoned I was. John Crosby, the columnist, served as master of ceremonies, and at the last moment, I was induced to appear with him. The occasion was a landslide for us both. Crosby had been outfitted with a pair of contact lenses which he shrewdly forgot to insert, with the result that he was unable to read the Teleprompter. I wore Hubbell Robinson's reach-me-down tuxedo and thought I looked breathtakingly lovely, but learned from Jack Gould's review in the New York *Times* that I was as photogenic as a pail of lard. Prior to the telecast, my wife injudiciously urged various friends and tradespeople to watch me. The morning after, I received a closing bill from our meat market, regretting that they could no longer extend us credit.

When the critics walk out on a Broadway play halfway through its first night, the perspiration mantling the faces of the actors is technically known as "flop sweat," and at this juncture of my TV career, I was drenched with it. But there appears to be a strange twisted logic in television, whereby an unbroken succession of failures often catapults a man to the top. I was seated at the typewriter one morning last May, my brain enshrouded in cobwebs, when a pair of homunculi representing themselves as producers, whom I shall designate Stiletto and Gouge, phoned me. They had conceived the idea of a travelogue of London to be narrated by Elizabeth Taylor, and needed an eleven-year-old mentality to write it.

"Elizabeth Taylor?" I murmured, racking my memory. "Elizabeth Taylor? The name has a familiar ring, but I can't seem to place it. Who is she?"

In a few maladroit sentences studded with Hollywood subjunctives, Stiletto explained that the lady had recently played an Egyptian in some movie or other. Thinking she possibly planned to narrate the travelogue in Egyptian, I demurred, stating that I had only a minimal grasp of that language. Stiletto interrupted me impatiently. It didn't matter what tongue I wrote in, he said, inasmuch as the viewers would be too dumfounded by her beauty to take notice. I suggested that in this case, I would prefer to write the text in Yiddish, and that it would expedite matters considerably if Miss Taylor were to enroll at Berlitz for lessons in that patois. Gouge assured me that no expense would be spared, and I flew to London at once to begin work.

At our first rendezvous in her Dorchester hotel suite, the dainty Dresden-china star and I found our conversation inhibited by the presence of a scruffy chap named Barton or Merton or something of the sort. His unsolicited advice became so annoying that I finally had to ask him to leave. "All right," he retorted insolently. "But you just wait. Some day I'll be a world-famous actor, and you'll be happy to lick my shoe." Elizabeth and I shared a hearty laugh at his presumptuousness, and Girton or whatever his name was retired sulkily. I twitted her, observing that she seemed rather attracted by his good looks.

"Nonsense," she replied. "Why, you're twice as handsome, and speaking as a woman, I would say that your badge 'Chicken Inspector No. 23' is well deserved." She shot me a languorous glance. "What are you doing for dinner tonight?"

"Eating," I flipped, deftly parrying her query. Elizabeth and I shared another hearty laugh, and then arranged for me to go away and stay away until my writing stint was finished. It was crystal clear that she mistrusted her ability to resist me, whereas I, of course, felt total indifference toward her, being a married man.

Within a month, the bulk of the work was finished, and the producers and I reassembled to "polish" the script, a ritual in which anything that might be construed as amusing is painstakingly removed. Stiletto was exceptionally skilled at this type of surgery, and from youth his deep distrust of any word of more than two syllables stamped him for future leadership. Gouge's talent, contrariwise, was financial; he was in charge of avoiding payment of my fee, and he exhibited positive brilliance at the task. At the slightest mention of money, his face betrayed such suffering that I had to apologize constantly for my boorishness. In due course, the script was hacked and altered beyond recognition, and it was time for the vultures from the advertising agency and the network to descend. Scores of experts flapped in to pontificate on what was wrong with the script, all clad in Italian silk suits and tab collars. Their suggestions were, of course, embodied *in toto,* and the finished product, sparkling and flavorful as a plate of cold gruel, was ready for the oven.

Owing to a sensation of nausea that had suddenly become chronic, I was unable to remain for the shooting. Before I emplaned for New York, however, I yielded to Elizabeth's entreaties and dined with her. Under the influence of cognac that may have been drugged, I promised the creature that if I ever freed myself of my marital ties, she would have first dibs at me. The Merton or Turton person, who had unexpectedly become a world-famous actor in the meanwhile, just as he predicted, was very much in evidence. Although Elizabeth wept floods of tears at my departure, and threatened to throw herself under the wheels of my plane, he showed visible relief. He even smiled toothlessly once or twice, and presented me with a pair of cheap tin cuff-links he had no further use for. I may have misjudged the man.

By an ironic twist of fate that nobody could have foreseen, I missed the spectacular when it was shown. An hour before air time, I chanced to be dozing in a room adjacent to that containing our television set. One of the windows was open, and I haplessly caught a severe cold in my foot. Though I was beside myself with frustration, locomotion was obviously impossible under the circumstances, and I had to send my wife in my stead. She reported that Elizabeth never looked lovelier, and that, for a woman in her fifties, she had retained her looks surprisingly. I asked what she thought of the script, but, like Saudek, she suddenly seemed to have lost the power of speech; I presume the cat had her tongue. Stiletto and Gouge, of course, are today riding the crest of the wave, while I, who created it, who gave unsparingly of myself and asked nothing in return save money, am reduced to panhandling. Ah, well, that's television for you, and the devil take it. It's either a feast or a famine.

Rub-a-Dub-Dub, Scrub
Out the Tub

In RETROSPECT, I suppose it was rather impetuous
of me to call up Gaudeamus-Igitur, my florists, as I did
yesterday, and have a dozen sweetheart roses sent to Lever
Brothers. While they're doubtless accustomed to this kind
of spontaneous homage from admirers, I was so shook up
by their advertisement in my morning paper that I neglected
to enclose an explanatory card. So I'd just like to say this:
working in a medium where one thought that the ultimate
had long ago been reached, they have contrived what is unquestionably the emetic of all time. Seven columns wide and
a full page deep, it presented readers with the photograph
of a personable young chick in her bath, holding aloft a cake
of soap and rapturously phoning a friend. Underneath was the
following turbulent monologue:

"DARLING, I'M HAVING THE MOST EXTRAORDI-
NARY EXPERIENCE . . . *I'm head over heels in* DOVE!
No, darling, *DOVE.* D—like in delicious. I told you, sweet. I'm
in the tub. Taking a bath. A *DOVE* bath—my very first. And
what a positively gorgeous time I'm having! It's just as if I'd
never *really* bathed before! No, dear, it isn't a *soap.* Soap was
never like this, so wickedly *creamy.* That man on television said
that DOVE is one-quarter cleansing cream—that it actually
creams my skin while I bathe—and now I really *believe* him.
Why, DOVE even *smells* creamy. Such a lovely, lush, *expensive* smell! Remember 'The Great Ziegfeld,' dear? How Anna

Held bathed in milk? And Cleopatra—one hundred mares or something *milked* every day for her bath? Well, darling, I'm all over *cream*. Just imagine, cream tip to toe. Arms. Legs. *All* of me! And clean! Just the cleanest girl I've ever been. *Smothered* in suds. Why, honey, DOVE makes suds as quick as bubble bath. Oodles of suds. Oceans of. I don't know what I ever did to *deserve* DOVE! Did I tell you that DOVE is sort of *me*-shaped? That it's curved to fit my hand, so it doesn't keep slithering away in the tub? And you know how soap leaves your skin so *dry?* That nasty stretched feeling? Well, DOVE makes me feel all velvet and silk, all *soft* and *smooth*. Just the most pampered, the most spoiled, the girliest girl in the world. Darling, I'm *purring*. And I won't even have to scrub out the tub when I'm through. DOVE leaves no bathtub ring. It says so right here on the package. Such an *enchanting* package, too—all pale blue and *gold*. Sweet, I can't imagine why I used to save DOVE only for my face. Soap is soap, but a bath with DOVE is *heaven! And just think, darling—tomorrow night I can do it again."*

Fortified with a spoonful of Mothersill's, I have just reread this *extase* a couple of times in an effort to determine who its recipient is, and I believe I've hit on one or two important clues. First, I'm pretty certain it's a male. There is an air of coquetry about the lady's spiel deliberately calculated to set the listener's blood on fire—inflammatory little nuances no woman would ever waste on another. When she speaks of "Dove" as me-shaped and curved to fit her hand, she doesn't mean that at all; she means that she herself is her-shaped and curved to fit *his* hand. Again, take the phrase "the most pampered, the most spoiled, the girliest girl in the world." Is that the sort of clabber two girls commonly exchange? No siree, Bob; you just know it's being ladled out to some poor jasper who's sweating over an audit or a test tube, desperately trying to stave off his creditors. I envision him sitting there at his abacus or microscope or whatever, a vacuous leer on his face and his wattles engorged as visions of trans-telephonic sugarplums dance in his head. Goodbye Bunsen burner, hello Mr. E. Z. Pickens.

The one passage freighted with truly chilling implications, though, is the bather's final boast, or rather threat: *"And just think, darling—tomorrow night I can do it again."* That it foreshadows another Walker-Gordon saturnalia of sloshing around in the dairy fat is inconsequential; what congeals the blood is that she's cooking up an even stickier panegyric, an ordeal by glucose that could easily unhinge her cavalier. I'm just an old-fashioned corner hypothecary, but it strikes me that their subsequent conversation might conceivably run like this:

SHE: Well, my *goodness*—you certainly took long enough to answer. I've been ringing you steadily for a half hour.

HE: What's the matter, darling? Is anything wrong?

SHE: Don't try to squirm out of it. I *told* you last night I was going to take another bath with SMIRK, and you promised to be home so I could phone you my impressions.

HE: Gosh, honey, I'm sorry. I was driving back from the plant with Tex Bratislov and Myrna Schaible and Ernest Mimosa, and right there, at Chafinger's hardware store, the front end of the car broke off and everybody was taken to the hospital.

SHE: It makes no difference. If you really loved me, you could have been home in time.

HE: Well, it won't happen again. Are you still calling me from the tub?

SHE: Yes, and, thanks to SMIRK, the wonder solvent, I guess I'm just about the daintiest, most delectable, yummiest creature there is. You see, a SMIRK bath differs from an ordinary bath in that an ordinary bath contains only hot water, whereas in a SMIRK bath, you have hot water plus SMIRK, the new wonder solvent.

HE: You sure spend a lot of time worrying about your skin.

SHE: I have to, sweetheart. Unlike the average miss, which her pelt is as impervious as the horsehide enveloping a baseball, my personal epidermis cries fie on harsh, scratchy abrasives. That's why SMIRK's effervescent lather, frothier than the spume curling off a tropical simoon, has proved such a boon cleanlinesswise. SMIRK's secret ingredient, as you know, is Y-43, one more product of patient laboratory research. For a long time, scientists have suspected that the skins of chap-prone persons like I were suffering from yeast deficiency. Tests made on one hundred thousand newborn infants conclusively proved that yeast—or Y-43, as pediatricians call it—protects them from unsightly peeling, shedding, etc. Consequently, each individual bar of SMIRK now incorporates the equivalent of eleven jeroboams of foamy, pre-bacterialized yeast, ready to seal your capillaries against destructive grime.

HE: Gee, that's fine. Say, there's a movie down on Iglehart Avenue—

SHE: Speaking of movies, did you see *The Baker's Wife?* That scene where Raimu pours the yeast into the vats and all the dough sort of bulges up in those divine cumulus formations? Well, dearest, I'm *all over yeast.* Can you visualize it? Yeast from my cute tip-tilted nose to my tippy-tiptoe. *Saturated* with yeast. My nose and my eyes and my ears and this receiver are full of yeast, and I'm so light and thistledowny and feathery I could rise up and float out the window. . . . Hello? Hello? Are you listening?

HE: Yeah. I was just loosening my collar.

SHE: Honestly, you're the most *aggravating* man. Every time I start telling you anything important, you're off on Cloud Nine somewhere. What were you thinking about?

HE: Oh, nothing special. I—er—maybe I ought to call up the hospital and see how Myrna Schaible's getting along.

SHE: It seems to me you're pretty concerned about Myrna Schaible all of a sudden. I lie here in a steaming bath all day while you're down at that nice cool factory, and when you get home at night, all you can talk about is Myrna Schaible.

HE: Well, after all, she works at the desk right next to mine.

SHE: Oh, she does, does she? And I suppose she's always undulating up to you in her tight black satin dress, bending over to show you the carloadings for April. Better watch your step, Mister—she sounds like a brazen little package to me. Incidentally, have I told you about the altogether scrumptious package SMIRK comes in? It's flesh-colored so that you can hardly tell where the solvent leaves off and you begin—*so* intriguing. But the most adorable thing about SMIRK, darling, and the reason it's so revolutionary, is that it's *anything*-shaped. It's curved to fit your knees and your tummy, your elbows and your pinkie— What did you say?

HE: I said could you hold it a second, there's someone at the door.

SHE: Well, hurry up. I can't sit here all night while you prattle away . . . I declare, this SMIRK's just too heavenly for words; I feel so utterly *abandoned*. Like the Hollywood starlets who pose for those magazine photos—what do they call it? Yeastcake, that's it. . . . Really, when I think what an absolute knockout I am, I could almost hug myself. I believe I will. . . . M-m-m, you gorgeous thing. Once again. . . . There, that's enough, mustn't be a piggy. Where *is* that impossible man?

HE: Hello? I'm sorry. A friend of mine stopped by. Party I work with.

SHE: What does he want?

HE: Uh—well, it isn't exactly a he . . .

SHE: Don't tell me it's that—that Myrna Schaible of yours.

HE: Say, you must be a mind reader. She just wanted to let me know she was O.K.

SHE: I'll bet she is. And what's more, I'll bet she's bursting out of that tight black dress of hers. Well, I mustn't *keep* you.

HE: No, I've got to show her where the ice is, and the record player.

SHE: She's making herself right at home, isn't she?

HE: Yes, and I don't think she likes the idea of me talking to another woman, so I'd better hang up. Call me back if you ever get off the porcelain, will you? . . . What? . . . *What?* My goodness, darling, what sort of language is *that?*

Goodbye Broadway,
Hello Mr. Square

Wʜᴇɴ I ᴡᴀꜱ ᴏɴᴇ-ᴀɴᴅ-ᴛᴡᴇɴᴛʏ, to paraphrase
A. E. Housman a trifle, I heard a wise man say, "Hey, how's
about we nip down to New York for a week and live it up?
I've got a scheme whereby it won't cost us a red cent!" The
wise man, like myself a senior at Brown and an accomplished
freeloader, was one Conrad Portnoy, business manager on the
university's comic magazine of which I was editor, and the
words were scarcely out of his mouth before the two of us
were racing toward the Providence depot, our cheeks aflame
with anticipation. New York! The Gay White Way! Visions of
Dionysiac revels danced in our heads, bachelor suppers
whereat naked actresses erupted from pies as we reeled
around quaffing jeroboams of champagne. Reared in New
England, Portnoy and I had only the foggiest conception of
Gotham, as we persisted in calling it, but on two points we
were unshakable: the plethora of chorus girls there and their
inability to resist a couple of boulevardiers from Little Rhody.
The gimmick the trip was predicated on was simplicity itself,
and not at all larcenous. Several New York hotels had tendered
our periodical due bills—vouchers, that is to say, in exchange
for ads—entitling us to free lodging. Meals, regrettably, were
excepted, but with a deluge of champagne impending, con-
siderations of food seemed crass in the extreme. The prospect
was dizzying, and it was with difficulty that I restrained Portnoy at New London from telegraphing Flo Ziegfeld that a

pair of big butter-and-egg men were hell-bent for the Main Stem.

Within two days of our arrival, the rosy dreams had evaporated, leaving two haggard, anxiety-ridden tinhorns with shrunken wallets. Not a single dimpled darling had tossed us her garter; despite all our nudging and leering, no bellboy could direct us to a midnight orgy, however paltry. Between tips, subway fares and Spartan meals at a cafeteria run by a Spartan who watched us vigilantly, the pitiful store of cash we shared was fast dwindling, and the smallest indulgence—a milk shake or an extra pack of Fatimas—would have pauperized us. The one thing we could afford to be prodigal with was hotel linen. In a frantic effort to use up our due bills, we switched daily from the Astor to the Vanderbilt to the Martinique, lolling in bridal chambers and suites of Roman magnificence, and such was the superfluity of towels that we had to stay up half the night taking showers, wiping our shoes, and wantonly crumpling the remainder. Ultimately, an unrelieved five-day diet of crullers and coffee exacted its toll: both of us broke down with scurvy. Ingloriously we slunk back to Rhode Island, hitching rides in whatever vehicles we could. The last lap, in a truck laden with poultry, was especially humiliating, since the driver, another Spartan named Steve Magnanimos, insisted on delivering us, plastered with chicken feathers, directly to the campus.

It was small wonder, hence, that Portnoy and I reacted with bitterness the rest of the academic year whenever anybody extolled metropolitan life, but as graduation neared, our memories took on a roseate glow and we became increasingly sentimental about it. New York was the center of the universe, we declared flatly; we grew lyrical enumerating its advantages social, financial, and cultural, its profusion of concerts, theatres, and museums. (We carefully omitted any reference to chorus girls and orgies, feeling that only an adolescent cared about such trivialities.) The upshot of these dithyrambs was that on a sweltering morning in mid-July Portnoy and I once more emerged from Grand Central, this time freighted with all our worldly possessions, and drawing a deep breath, we plunged into the maelstrom.

Our first bivouac was the front parlor of a rooming house on West Twelfth Street operated by a Southern gentlewoman in reduced circumstances. Mrs. Sutphin, who sweetly importuned us to call her Jasmine, derived from Natchez and had an accent clotted with moonlight and magnolias. She wore heavy *maquillage* around her eyes, a thick protective coat of Djer-Kiss face powder, and twin spots of rouge on her cheekbones; and the clash of bracelets as she moved sounded like Mosby's cavalry unsheathing their sabres for a charge. The room was equally dramatic, a dim cavern filled by three walnut armoires, massive twin bedsteads, and a Brobdingnagian pier glass. Between the velvet-draped windows stood a stuffed baby giraffe eleven feet in height, the base of whose neck had been weighted so that it swung freely at the slightest touch. Portnoy, by now a salesman of direct-mail advertising, was anesthetic to the pad, being absent all day, but I was an aspiring cartoonist, and my attempts to be waggish in the dark, faced with a giraffe shaking its head in constant negation, inevitably brought on melancholia. Luckily for me, Mrs. Sutphin saved my equilibrium by marrying a chiropodist who had rejuvenated her feet and who needed the premises for an office.

Over the next few months, my roommate and I tenanted a series of cheerless dovecotes around Greenwich Village made doubly desolate by his inability to cling to a job. Successively clerk in a brokerage house, cashier in a bankrupt tearoom, night watchman for an embalmer, and pool hustler, he finally forsook the hurly-burly of Manhattan for a Cleveland insurance firm. With his departure, my long-smoldering passion for a proper studio burst into flame. After a widespread search, I settled on a cozy *pied-à-terre*, five flights up and boasting its own skylight, a stone's throw from Jefferson Market Court. Having shrouded everything I could reach in monk's cloth, including the gas meter, I painted the bathroom walls black and the woodwork Chinese red, stuck half a dozen wax tapers in candle drippings, and impregnated the whole place with incense. The female callers I hoped to ensnare with this erotic décor reacted in unexpected fashion. Most of them dissolved into shrieks of helpless laughter; the rest assumed an air of arctic dignity and when, flushed with muscatel, I made romantic overtures, savagely fended me off with their parasols. The lacerations to my ego were such that it was months before I again dared essay the role of Don Juan.

New York baked under a blanket of heat that August, and reporters in quest of feature material were frying eggs on the sidewalks as I jubilantly packed my bags for a six-week vacation on Fire Island. I had sublet the studio to two decorous young chaps of good family—I.B.M. statisticians, they glibly assured me—who just wanted a quiet haven where they could listen to Mozart and study the Analects of Confucius. To demand references or surety from such paragons was unthinkable; we exchanged warm handclasps and vowed to attend Carnegie Hall concerts, lectures on flower arrangement, and classes in Dalcroze eurythmics together on my return. Three weeks later, a hysterical telegram from my landlord summoned me back to the mainland. The lessees had flown, and with them my bedding, utensils, curtains and Capehart. Some forerunner of Jackson Pollock had stippled the walls with ketchup and scrawled in lipstick a doggerel verse hymning the charms of Lya de Putti. In the center of the floor, a cherry-nosed vagrant the image of Popeye crouched over a bed of glowing coals, heating a can of Sterno and plucking somberly at a ukulele.

It was a crucial moment, the sort that exercises a profound effect on one's entire future. I felt an overwhelming need to cushion my head on somebody's shoulder and sob aloud, but since my landlord showed no disposition to cuddle, I fell back on the next-best person—a bold-eyed, willowy brunette who had been scanning me as a matrimonial prospect for some time. Scarcely had she sponged away my tears than the silvery peal of wedding bells assailed my ears, and I discovered I was a benedict. Other than her sterling self, my wife's sole contribution to the union was a piece of hard-nosed advice—

viz., that I break my lease and skip. It took two years to pay off the landlord, during which time we honeymooned in a basement flat where I contracted a lifelong case of sciatica.

On the northwest corner of Washington Square, hard by the former Russian Embassy, there stood in those days a gracious five-storied mansion of rose-colored brick. Every once in a while a silver-haired doorman would totter forth supporting some old dragon in caracul or a palsied industrialist, and obsequiously hand them into a 1910 Panhard cabriolet. The only qualifications for residence in this landmark were a six-generation listing in the Social Register, a diploma from Groton or Miss Hewitt's classes, and eleven million dollars. How two parvenus like us ever wheedled a foothold there escapes me, but by strict adherence to a diet of fatback, corn pone and collards, we managed to scrape together the rent each month, if not to achieve social equality with the inmates. Among my fondest memories of the house was a midnight encounter in the Square with e. e. cummings, that most gifted of poets. I was schlepping a half-grown beagle around the park of a subzero evening and getting pretty well teed off with dogdom when I saw cummings headed toward me, plainly immersed in thought. Thinking to safeguard his privacy, I had just started to carom off when he hailed me.

"Look at that!" he said, gesturing theatrically toward three windows aglow in our building. "Isn't it fantastic?"

"What do you mean?" I asked.

"Why, the drama being enacted up there," he exclaimed. "Can't you visualize it—the drunken brute of a husband, the wife spewing out her venom, the ferocity that only George Grosz can portray? I see the man suddenly overcome by homicidal mania—he snatches up a carving knife, the two of them grapple, the knife draws nearer and nearer to her breast, and then, with a convulsive, twisting stab—"

"Hold on there, bub," I interrupted. "If you're really so concerned, I can tell you what's cooking up there. A woman in her stocking feet is about to eat a bagel with cream cheese."

254

"And how would you know that, pray?" he inquired with Olympian scorn.

"Because it's my apartment, wise guy," I retorted.

"That's what I meant," said cummings triumphantly. "Isn't it fantastic?" He turned on his heel and, head cocked at a noble angle, strode off into the shadows.

We might have dwelt on forever in this Henry Jamesian milieu, a pair of musty patricians subsisting on bagels, but for a casual real-estate ad in the Sunday *Times*. Thirty-six hours after I read it, the czarevna and I were standing transfixed on a Pennsylvania hilltop, listening to a foxy-nosed agent rhapsodize about the countryside around us. So abundant was wildlife in the district, he told us emotionally, that rabbits, pheasants, squirrels and even deer leaped straight into the cook pot, sprinkling themselves with salt and pepper. In these lush pastures one could grow his own tobacco, cobble his shoes with tough, fragrant birchbark. He painted a pastoral of my wife bottling raspberry jam and humming contentedly while I snoozed in a hammock amid barns bursting with alfalfa. My glasses misted over at the colored lantern slides flashing before me—the sleigh rides, Halloween parties, sugaring off, sugaring on, bringing in the Yule log. A fortnight later, in a simple ceremony at the county courthouse, two blushing innocents were united for all time, irretrievably and indissolubly, to fourscore and seven acres of the Keystone State.

And so ended my love affair with New York, intoxicating chameleon enchantress I had worshipped this side of idolatry from youth. I knew her every mood, every foible; with the merest effort, I can recapture her unique, indefinable bouquet of monoxide, roast chestnuts and old landladies. Sometimes, in moments of nostalgia, I long to be trampled on again in the subway crush, to be spurned by headwaiters, fleeced by tradesmen and iced by theatre brokers. Ah, well, someday I suppose I will—but not as long as *I* can help it, Charlie.